Become What You Receive

A Systematic Study of the Eucharist

John H. McKenna CM

HillenbrandBooks

Chicago / Mundelein, Illinois

Nihil Obstat
Very Reverend Daniel A. Smilanic, JCD
Vicar for Canonical Services
Archdiocese of Chicago
July 7, 2011

Imprimatur
Reverend Monsignor John F. Canary, STL, DMIN
Vicar General
Archdiocese of Chicago
July 7, 2011

BECOME WHAT YOU RECEIVE: A SYSTEMATIC STUDY OF THE EUCHARIST © 2012 Archdiocese of Chicago: Liturgy Training Publications, 3949 South Racine Avenue, Chicago IL 60609; 1-800-933-1800, fax 1-800-933-7094, e-mail orders@ltp.org. All rights reserved. See our Web site at www.LTP.org.

Hillenbrand Books is an imprint of Liturgy Training Publications (LTP) and the Liturgical Institute at the University of St. Mary of the Lake (USML). The imprint is focused on contemporary and classical theological thought concerning the liturgy of the Catholic Church. Available at bookstores everywhere, through LTP by calling 1-800-933-1800, or visiting www.LTP.org. Further information about Hillenbrand Books publishing program is available from The Liturgical Institute, 1000 E. Maple, Mundelein, IL 60060 (847-837-4542) or on the Web at http://www.usml.edu/liturgicalinstitute/liturgicalinstitute.htm, or e-mail litinst@usml.edu.

Cover Image © Bill and Peggy Wittman.

Printed in USA

Library of Congress Control Number: 2011934987

ISBN 978-1-59525-036-0

HBWR

To my family and friends who help me
believe in the Resurrection and long for its completion.

Contents

Introduction   *vii*

Chapter 1: Symbol and Reality: Some Anthropological
           Considerations   1
    Importance of Symbols   2
    The Symbolic Process   3
    History of Understanding "Symbol"   6
    Nature of Symbol   17
    Approaching Symbols Creatively   23

Chapter 2: Phenomenology of Meal: A Means to Understanding
           the Eucharist   26
    Food and Drink in the Bible   26
    Bread and Wine   29
    Eating and Drinking   30
    Human Meals   31
    Ritual Meals   34

Chapter 3: Meal in the Old Testament (Hebrew Scriptures)   37
    Old Testament (Hebrew Scriptures)   38

Chapter 4: Eucharist: Celebration of Service   58
    Old Testament Background   59
    Identity of the Servant   60
    Traits of a "Corporate Personality"   61
    New Testament Basis   64
    Eucharist: Call to Service   67

Chapter 5: The Eucharist and the Resurrection   74
    The Challenge of Humanism   75
    The Resurrection   76

Link between Eucharist and Resurrection 89
Implications for the Eucharist Today 95
Conclusion 97

Chapter 6: Eucharist and Memorial 99
Historical Background 99
Theological Issues 108
Conclusions 114

Chapter 7: Searching for Our Roots 118
Thomas Talley (1924–2005) 118
Paul F. Bradshaw 135

Chapter 8: Changing Attitudes toward the Eucharist
over the Centuries 144
Creative Origins (first 600 years) 144
Middle Ages (roughly 600–1500) 151
Reaction and Counterreaction: Trent (1545–63) to Pre-Vatican II
(1960) 156
Reformation and Renaissance (especially the sixteenth century) 156
The Baroque Period (especially the seventeenth century) 158
The Liturgical Movement 160

Chapter 9: Eucharistic Presence: An Invitation to Dialogue 164
Symbol and Reality 165
Christ's Resurrection 167
Changing Attitudes toward the Eucharist 169
Eucharistic Presence: A Historical Overview 171
The Ninth Century 173
The Reformation 177
Transubstantiation 181
A Personalist Approach 182
Application to the Eucharist 184
Reactions and Qualifications 188
Conclusion 193

Chapter 10: Eucharist and Sacrifice: An Overview   194
   The "Spiritualization" of Sacrifice   195
   Christian Adaptation   196
   Shifting Trends   199
   Post-Nicene Contributions   201
   Trent and the Reformation   205
   More Recent Developments   208
   The Future   210

Chapter 11: Eucharist and the Holy Spirit   214
   Historical Reflections   214
   Theological Reflections   219
   Pastoral Reflections   228
   Ecumenical Reflections   229

Bibliography   232
Index   247

Introduction

I am concerned primarily with research into the meaning and significance of Eucharist for our lives. In that sense, I have presented in this book a foundation for a eucharistic spirituality that is accessible for an educated laity as well as helpful for professional students of theology. My years as an educator have shaped my outreach to that broader audience and enabled me to address them in an understandable manner. With the publication of the Revised Missal, many of the faithful are reexamining the words of the Mass in order to discover the new depth of meaning in the revised translation. This study will aid in the understanding of the new words of the Mass.

The book's title reflects St. Augustine's strong sense of the link between the Eucharist and the transformation of the people, the Body of Christ.[1] In our time we accept as a given that we are what we eat. Perhaps we can bring new sensitivity to the ancient tradition that as Christians we are called to become the One whom we sacramentally consume.

A good friend of mine, when he heard that I was working on a book about symbols and reality, blurted out that my objective was an oxymoron because the two concepts were mutually exclusive. One of my goals in this book is to show that the terms can be compatible and complementary; in fact, Eucharist is best understood as both symbol and reality.

Besides those educated laity and theology students already mentioned as potential readers, the book's intended audience includes pastors, seminarians, professors, and libraries. I especially hope that, although I write from a Roman Catholic perspective, this book will serve a wider circle of students and teachers who come to the study of the Eucharist from other religious perspectives. My colleagues in the North American Academy of Liturgy (an ecumenical academy of

---

1. An example of this is: "If you receive well you are what you have received." Sermon 227, ed. Solano, (PL 38:1099), II, 314. For the English text see *The Works of Saint Augustine*, ed. John E. Rotelle, trans. Edmund Hill (New Rochelle, N.Y.: New City Press, 1993), III/7, 227.

viii

liturgical scholars of which I was elected president in 1982)—
Protestant and Jewish as well as Roman Catholic—have received my
work approvingly and have consistently pointed out its ecumenical
implications. Most of all, I hope that this book will help readers
explore the richness and beauty of the Eucharist and its transforming
power.

Chapter 1

Symbol and Reality: Some Anthropological[1] Considerations

"We made signs before we could speak," reads the slogan in front of the sign maker's shop in Boynton Beach, Florida. In its own pithy way it expresses a given in human experience. Signs and symbols are part and parcel of our being. If we have deep feelings or experiences, they must be expressed. Otherwise, they atrophy and die.[2] The wife who complains that "You never say you love me anymore" may not be nagging. She may sense that what is not expressed is on its way to not being. The husband who responds, "I may not say it but I show it in many ways," may also be on to something. We don't always need words. We can use other symbols or symbolic actions. But the fact remains: we must express deep realities or risk losing them.[3]

---

1. The term is used here not in the sense of a cultural anthropology, although this has been most helpful at times, but in the sense of a "doctrine of the human person," especially a metaphysical or phenomenological one. This is an attempt to enlarge our understanding of human experience and, in a theological context, to use this enlarged understanding to appreciate better our Christian experience. See Edward Schillebeeckx, *Christ the Sacrament of the Encounter With God* (New York: Sheed & Ward, 1963), xiv–xv. On the relationship between faith and experience, see E. Schillebeeckx, *Interim Report on the Books Jesus & Christ* (New York: Crossroads, 1981), 5–14.

2. *Music in Catholic Worship,* 2nd ed. (Washington, D.C.: Bishops' Committee on the Liturgy, 1983), 9.

3. John Macquarrie, *A Guide to the Sacraments* (New York: Continuum, 1999), 118–19.

IMPORTANCE OF SYMBOLS

We shall see later that any being must express itself in order to know itself, to be. Symbols enable us to do just that. They are basic to our knowing, our loving, our very being. That is why the question (probably rhetorical) which Romano Guardini, the great German thinker and liturgical commentator, posed in an open letter to the Liturgical Congress at Mainz in 1964 was so startling: "Do you really think that modern people are capable of responding to symbols (*symbolfähig*)?"[4]

The subsequent answer, from psychologists, anthropologists, philosophers, theologians, and liturgists — to name a few—has been a resounding "Yes!" Carl Jung would speak of archetypal symbols.[5] Mircea Eliade, the renowned authority on the history of religions, maintains that "today we are well on the way to an understanding of one thing of which the nineteenth century had not even a presentiment that the symbol, the myth and the image are of the very substance of the spiritual life, that they may become disguised, mutilated or degraded, but are never extirpated."[6] "Symbols and myths come from such depths: they are part and parcel of the human being, and it is impossible that they should not be found again in any and every existential situation."[7] Paul Ricoeur remarks that "It is quite noteworthy that before all theology and all speculation, even before any mythical elaboration, we should still encounter symbols."[8] Paul Tillich states: "Man's ultimate concern must be expressed symbolically, because symbolic language alone is able to express the ultimate."[9] Finally, David Power contends that "Without symbols there would be neither affective wholeness nor knowledge of the truth. . . . Through them human experience is brought to expression and so to discovery."[10] "Symbols by nature take hold of experience and give it

4. See *Liturgisches Jahrbuch* 14 (1964): 105–6.

5. See, for example, Carl Jung, *Man and His Symbols* (New York: Dell, 1968).

6. Mircea Eliade, *Images and Symbols: Studies in Religious Symbolism* (Mission, Kans.: Sheed, Andrews, and McMeel, 1961), 11.

7. Ibid., 25.

8. Paul Ricoeur, *Conflict of Interpretations: Essays in Hermeneutics,* ed. Don Ihde (Evanston: Northwestern University Press, 1974), 289.

9. Paul Tillich, *Dynamics of Faith* (New York: Harper & Row, 1957), 41. See also Macquarrie, *A Guide to the Sacraments,* 29–33, on Tillich's approach to symbols.

10. David N. Power, *Unsearchable Riches: the Symbolic Nature of the Liturgy* (New York: Pueblo, 1984), 172.

form and expression in such a way that it becomes accessible to thought."[11]

If a grasp of the interaction among experience, symbols, and thought is important in understanding human existence in general, it is even more so in understanding Christian sacraments. To let the symbols or sacraments speak, we must appreciate how they speak.

THE SYMBOLIC PROCESS

Peter Fink once observed that sacraments speak to us in "three languages" or on three levels.[12] It might be helpful to trace this process. It begins with an experience. It may be some profound human experience like birth, death, falling in love, or feeling your own sinfulness. Maybe the presence of God makes itself felt in the midst of this experience and gives rise to faith in the sense of the most fundamental and immediate belief.[13] There is within us, as mentioned above, a need to express this experience, this awe, this fear, this love, this faith. So we improvise or, more commonly, we turn to already existing symbols to help us express our experience.

The first level or "language" is usually some symbolic action which we accomplish or do. It comes from the world of human dynamics or interchange and has its own language and meaning prior to, and independent of, any word proclaimed over it. We embrace. We share a meal. We wash ourselves. We offer a forgiving glance or gesture to someone. One of Marcel Marceau's famous mimes—without any introductory word or explanation—might be somewhat analogous to this. These actions, in themselves, are able to express us powerfully and move us deeply.

They are also crucial to the experience. A student of mine at St. John's University reporting on his assignment to reflect on the

---

11. Ibid., 69, referring to Susanne K. Langer, *Problems of Art: Ten Philosophical Lectures* (New York: Scribner's, 1957), 130.

12. Peter Fink, "Three Languages of Christian Sacraments," *Worship* 52 (November 1978): 561ff. See also Kevin Irwin, *Models of the Eucharist* (New York: Paulist Press, 2005), 21–25, for a fine treatment of symbols, words, prayers, and rituals although in a slightly different sequence from ours.

13. See Geoffrey Wainwright, *Doxology: The Praise of God in Worship, Doctrine and Life* (New York: Oxford University Press, 1980), 9, and Macquarrie, *A Guide to the Sacraments*, 7–8, 19–22, who uses Moses as an example of such an experience and the need to express it.

meaning of water, with the Brooklyn accent with which I have grown up, exclaimed: "I don't mean any disrespect, Father, but I was at my nephew's baptism this weekend and all I could think of was a Chinese water torture I had seen in a movie once!" It doesn't take a very fertile imagination to picture how the priest had poured the water. "I baptize you in the name of the Father (drip), and of the Son (drip), and of the Holy Spirit (drip)." It was not the rich symbolism of water's death-dealing, life-giving, cleansing force or the theology contained in readings and homily which had touched this young man so deeply. Rather, it was the first level or language of the sacrament—poorly done—which he felt. Peter Fink rightly remarks: "What this does or does not speak, what it speaks well or poorly, will determine the success or failure of the other languages involved as well as of the sacrament itself."[14] We will always have to come back to this first level or language.[15]

We also use words to express ourselves, and these form the second level or language of the sacraments. We sing a song, recite a poem, say a prayer, proclaim a blessing or tell a story about ourselves and our experience. As Amos Wilder puts it: "Before the message there must be the vision, before the sermon the hymn, before the prose the poem."[16] The language of "myth" tells us in a fuller way the same truth as the primitive symbols or first level from which the myth springs and to which it must always return, if it is to be truthful. This second level or language proclaims and gives the deeper meaning of the symbol. It also makes it somewhat less ambiguous. Examples are hymns like "One Bread, One Body" or "Let every tongue proclaim that Jesus Christ is Lord"[17]; blessings or eucharistic prayers proclaimed over bread and wine; a prayer invoking the Holy Spirit upon gifts and people (an epiclesis); the story of Adam and Eve's fall or of

14. Fink, "Three Languages of Christian Sacraments," 568.

15. See Ricoeur, *Conflict of Interpretation*, 289, where he points out that even before any mythical elaboration we would still encounter symbols.

16. Amos Wilder, *Theopoetic: Theology and the Religious Imagination* (Philadelphia: Fortress, 1976), 1. See also Macquarrie, *A Guide to the Sacraments*, 19–22. See also Irwin, *Models of the Eucharist*, 96–121, for a very good development on the power of words.

17. For examples of early Christian hymns, see Lucien Deiss, *Springtime of the Liturgy: Liturgical Texts of the First Four Centuries*, trans. M. J. O'Connell (Collegeville, Minn.: Liturgical Press, 1979), 38ff.

the Exodus event. These tap into common experiences and help us to articulate them.

But are they true? Balthasar Fischer, the great German liturgist from Trier, tells of a father from Seattle teasingly asking his precocious seven-year-old daughter if the stories she was reading were real. Wrinkling her brow, she parried with, "Well, on the outside they're not but on the inside they are!" Although there are many approaches to the term "myth" today, the little girl's description reflects a frequent understanding of religious myths and one which we will employ. There are symbolic expressions—in story form—of a reality or a real experience so profound that it resists cold, logical analysis.[18] When we fall in love, for instance, we turn not to the logician but to the poet, songwriter, or storyteller for ways to express our experience. We are more apt to use imagery like "My heart leapt within me," "The heavens stood still," than a prosaic description of our pulse rate. As David Power puts it: "Where mythic forms are used to describe historical events, the narrative introduces elements of the fabulous."[19] But beneath the imagery lies reality—"on the inside they are real."

This second level or language of the sacraments is only indirectly instructional. It is more evocative or inviting in tone and seeks involvement or consent, an "Amen, so be it."[20] It wants to raise the question, "What does this mean for me (or "us," since the questioning usually takes place in interaction with others with whom we share the experience)?"[21]

The third level in the symbolic process, the third language with which sacraments speak to us, is that of theological reflection. Here we try, in various ways, to explain and illuminate the event or experience which the first two levels proclaim. This language is declarative in tone. It is directly instructional and meant to impart

---

18. See John L. McKenzie, *Myth and Realities: Studies in Biblical Theology* (London: Geoffrey Chapman, 1963), 182–91, on "myth." See also Macquarrie, *A Guide to the Sacraments*, 14–16, on restricting "real" to material, empirically verifiable realities.

19. David N. Power, "Symbolism in Worship: A Survey, III," *The Way* 15 (January 1975): 63. He also points out the difficulty some people have in responding to this genre. See also his *Unsearchable Riches*, 108–30, where he treats myth and narrative, including Christian myth which is much more realistic than classical myths (120).

20. See Fink, "Three Languages of Christian Sacraments," 562.

21. Ibid., 570.

information or clarify what we are saying with the symbolic actions, stories, songs, and so on. It seeks the response, "I understand." Examples would be a theological treatise, a catechism or a commentary during a liturgy. These raise the question, "What does it mean?" or, if we are really lucky, "What might it mean?"[22]

These three levels or languages, the symbolic action, the word, and the theological reflection, are all attempts to express the initial experience and, in expressing it, to deepen it. We shall return to them later when we speak of approaching symbols creatively. At present we need only to underline a few points in their regard. First of all, the second and third languages must always remain rooted in the first language, the symbolic action, if they are to speak truthfully and well of the initial experience.[23] Second, it is possible to misuse these languages. The use of water in a way that led the young man mentioned above to think of "a Chinese water torture" is a case in point. Along this vein, Fink recalls a cartoon in *Critic* depicting a scowling priest, deacon, and subdeacon garbed in black vestments and standing before a smoke-shrouded coffin. The caption read: "I am the resurrection and the life."[24] Third, interaction with others can be a significant factor in our ability to hear what the various languages are saying. It is in the midst of a community struggling to find God in its life as well as in its sharing of symbols, stories, and reflections that what Aidan Kavanagh calls "primary theology" takes place.[25]

HISTORY OF UNDERSTANDING "SYMBOL"

Like all of us, the notion of symbol has a history which has left an imprint on its character and understanding. It is to this history that we now turn ever so briefly.

Not too many years ago, an older priest and I were discussing change. Sensing that he was limiting "real" change to physical or material change, I said as much. Smiling sheepishly, he responded: "I guess

22. Ibid., 562, 570.

23. See Power, *Unsearchable Riches*, 115, referring to Eliade's notion of getting back to the primordial event, "*in illo tempore.*"

24. Fink, "Three Languages of Christian Sacraments," 572.

25. See Aidan Kavanagh, *On Liturgical Theology* (New York: Pueblo, 1984), 74–78. See also Macquarrie, *A Guide to the Sacraments*, 31–32.

I do." Coming from someone with a good background in philosophy, I found the response astounding. Maybe he feared that the subject would turn to change in the Eucharist and was determined to protect the reality of that change at all costs. Or maybe he was simply reflecting the influence that nineteenth-century positivism, a system of philosophy based solely on observable scientific facts and their relations to one another, had on so many of us. There seems to have been, at least for the first half of the twentieth century, a tendency toward an unconscious materialism which equated reality with physical, measurable reality. Water, for instance, was H_2O, a physical substance with many practical, observable uses. Other, symbolic meanings of water belong to the realm of romanticism or fantasy. In this context, the term "symbol" was roughly equivalent to "unreal." The phrase "merely symbolic" was very much at home in such a setting.[26]

This approach is strikingly different from that of ancient peoples. They did not have the tendency to separate matter and spirit, symbol and reality the way we do. Their view of reality was much more unified than ours. For them divine realities or energies flowed to them in the natural symbols they encountered. For the people around the ancient Nile, for example, water was a mystery of life, a wonder. Where water was, there was life. In a sense, therefore, for these people water *is* life. Life, with its deeper realities, reveals itself in water.[27]

This might seem primitive or naive to someone trained to trust only in what is empirically verifiable. But the ancients' way of looking at reality had a wholesomeness and holism that is legitimate and necessary, even for "moderns."[28] In any event, the early Christians basically shared this unified view of persons and things as they tried

26. See J. P. de Jong, *Die Eucharistie Als Symbolwirklichkeit* (Regensberg: Friedrich Pustet, 1969), 15–18, and William R. Crockett, *Eucharist: Symbol of Transformation* (New York: Pueblo, 1989), 80–81. See also Power, *Unsearchable Riches*, 23, and Macquarrie, *A Guide to the Sacraments,* 14–15.

27. See de Jong, 18–19, and Crockett, 81–82.

28. Ibid., 19–22. Cf. Power, *Unsearchable Riches*, 21–24. Citing Northrop Frye's *The Great Code: The Bible and Literature* (New York: Harcourt Brace Jovanovich, 1982), 3–30, Power summarizes three great stages in the use of language and in ways of thinking about reality. The first is the mythological, where there were no clear distinctions between, e.g., truth and fiction, the transcendent and the earthly as these appeared in stories, symbols, and rituals. Second, there is the metonymic stage in which theory distinguished between transcendent and earthly, between the appearance of things and their essential reality. Finally, you have the empirical or descriptive stage closely linked with the advance of the positive sciences. Here there is a tendency to deem the world of mythology unsophisticated and the world of theory or speculative thought unreal.

to express their own experience of God in Jesus Christ. Water, for instance, in the baptismal homilies of people like Tertullian is at once creative, death-dealing, life-giving, cleansing because it contains the Spirit.[29] The same was true for the Eucharist.

We should be careful, therefore, not to impose our view of symbol and like terms on the early Christians, as the encyclical *Mysterium Fidei* seems to do when referring to Theodore of Mopsuestia. Apparently acknowledging that the Second Council of Constantinople (553) condemned him as a heretic, the encyclical quotes Theodore regarding the symbolic character of the Eucharist but notes that *on this point* he is a faithful witness: "The Lord did not say: 'This is the symbol of My body and this is a symbol of My blood,' but: 'This is My body and My blood.' He teaches us not to look to the nature of the thing which lies before us and which is perceived by the senses, for by the prayer of thanksgiving and the words spoken over it, it has been changed into Flesh and Blood."[30] But, as de Jong points out, shortly after in the same sermon when commenting on the epiclesis Theodore speaks of the bread as the symbol of Christ's body.[31] De Jong maintains that Theodore stands firmly in the patristic tradition which regarded the symbol as containing[32] the reality it symbolized.

This accounts for the ability of Ambrose, a strong realist, to pray: "Grant us, Lord, that this sacrifice be pleasing to you since it is the symbol (figura) of our Lord's body and blood."[33] Later in the same work Ambrose explains: "you are given the sacrament in a similitude,

---

Power rightly contends that the challenge lies in holding on to all three while respecting their differences.

29. See de Jong, 20–21.

30. *Mysterium Fidei* 44 (Washington, D.C.: National Catholic Welfare Conference, 1965). See also Johannes Quasten, *Patrology* (Westminster, Md.: Christian Classics, 1986), 3:420–21.

31. See de Jong, 25, and nn. 13, 16, 17, referring to Theodore's *Commentary on the Gospel of St. Matthew* 26:26 (PG 66, 714).

32. A note of caution is in order. The term "contain," while expressive of the strong sense of reality the early Christian writers wished to convey, can also be misleading. It can imply the presence of a static reality, a thing, like water in a bucket, rather than a personal reality, like one person present to another as a person. This latter reality offers and calls for personal interaction and response in a given, often changing, context. See Regis Duffy, *Real Presence: Worship, Sacraments and Commitment* (New York: Harper & Row, 1982), esp. 83–108.

33. de Jong, 25, referring to *De Sacramentis*, IV, V, 2.1. See A. Hänggi and I. Pahl, eds. *Prex Eucharistica*, (Fribourg–Suisse: Editions Universitaires, 1968), 421.

to be sure—but you obtain the grace and power of the reality."[34] Tertullian speaks in similar terms as he explains the institution narrative: "This is my body, that is, this is the symbol (*figura*) of my body."[35] This notion that the symbol contains what it symbolizes seems also to be at the heart of some of Augustine's most powerful preaching: "If you receive well, you are what you have received." "Since you are the body of Christ and His members, it is your mystery that is placed on the Lord's table; it is your mystery that you receive." "Be what you see, and receive what you are."[36]

In the East, Cyril of Jerusalem, in a setting like that of Theodore, also mentions symbol and reality in the same breath: "We did not really die, we were not really buried, we were not really crucified and raised again, but our imitation was but in a figure, while our salvation is in reality."[37] While Cyril may be contrasting symbol and reality, he sees the reality as present in the symbol or figure. He presents the two not in opposition but as complementary: "Since he himself has declared and said of the bread, 'This is my body,' who will thereafter dare to doubt? And since he has strongly affirmed and said, 'This is my blood,' who will ever doubt, saying that it is not his blood? So we partake with all assurance as of the body and blood of Christ. For in the *figure* of bread his body is given to you, and in the *figure* of wine his blood; that, by partaking of the body and blood of Christ, you may become one body and one blood with him."[38]

While witnessing to the notion that a symbol makes present the reality it symbolizes, Cyril may also have sown the seeds of a problem. He (or John, his successor in Jerusalem) compares the

34. See Alasdair I. C. Heron, *Table and Tradition* (Philadelphia: Westminster, 1983) 70, quoting *De Sacramentis* VI, 3, 4, and Crockett, 84.

35. de Jong, 25, referring to *Adversus Marcion*, 4, 40, and Crockett, 84–85.

36. See James J. Megivern, *Concomitance and Communion: A Study in Eucharistic Doctrine and Practice* (New York: Herder, 1963), 68, citing Sermons 227 (PL 38:1999) and 272 (PL 38:1247). De Jong, 28, comments: "The Eucharist cannot be a symbol of the Church as Christ's Body if it were not at the same time a real symbol ('Realsymbol') of Christ himself as the Head of the Church." See also Heron, 70–74, for a discussion of Augustine's view of sacramental symbolism, and Crockett, 85.

37. See Heron, 70, citing *Mystagogical Catecheses* 5.

38. R. C. D. Jasper and G. J. Cuming, (New York: Pueblo, 1987), 84 (italics mine), referring to *Mystagogical Catecheses* 4, 1, and 3. Cf. comments on 83. For numerous other examples of terms like "figure" or "symbol" used by acknowledged "realists" in conjunction with Christ's body and blood in the Eucharist, see J. N. D. Kelly, *Early Christian Doctrines*, 5th ed. (New York: Harper & Row, 1977), 440–49.

symbolic reality of the eucharistic event to the wedding of Cana: "By his own power on a previous occasion he turned the water into wine at Cana in Galilee; so it is surely credible that he has changed wine into blood."[39] While the imagery is forceful and good exegesis will acknowledge the symbolic levels of the Cana account, the fact remains that the change described there was on the physical level—water into wine, wine into blood. The use of physical analogies to explain the eucharistic change will plague the interpretation of the latter, as we shall see, throughout history.[40]

John Chrysostom is a case in point. In his zeal to impress his hearers with the reality of Christ's presence in the Eucharist, he uses images that will make him a favorite of ultrarealists through the centuries. "Not only do we see our Lord, but we can take him in our hands and eat him, chewing his flesh with our teeth so that we can unite ourselves interiorly and perfectly with him."[41] And again, "What our Lord did not suffer on the cross (the breaking of his bones), that he suffers in the eucharistic sacrifice for your sake. He allows himself to be broken so that he can satisfy all."[42] Maybe there were people talking in the back of church.[43] But whatever Chrysostom's intent his overly physical imagery is questionable. It is just as easy to fail through excess as through defect in this area. Moreover, this is untypical of him. Elsewhere, he shows that he understands sacraments less physically and more as symbolic realities. "If you were a non-corporeal being, [Christ] would have given you non-corporeal gifts directly. Since, however, your soul is attached to a body, he offers you the spiritual in a sensible form."[44]

Up to the ninth century, Christian writers generally shared the view that a symbol made present the reality it symbolized, that is, that sacraments were symbolic realities. It is true that there could be differing approaches to these realities. Augustine, for instance, might be more inclined to take a spiritualistic-symbolic approach which

39. See E. Yarnold, *The Awe-inspiring Rites of Initiation: Baptismal Homilies of the Fourth Century* (Slough, England: St. Paul Publications, 1972), 84, citing *Mystagogical Catecheses* 4, 2.

40. See de Jong, 30–1.

41. Ibid., 31, citing Homily 46 on John.

42. Ibid., citing Homily 24 on 1 Cor.

43. Aidan Kavanagh, "The Norm of Baptism: The New Rite of Christian Initiation of Adults," *Worship* 48 (1974): 149–50.

44. de Jong, 32, citing Homily 82 on Matthew.

tends to be more speculative and intellectual. Ambrose, on the other hand, might tend to be more concrete, down to earth, more suited to the ordinary folk.[45] But this was merely a question of emphasis. Both approaches agreed on the reality present in the symbols. This sense of a symbolic reality probably accounts for the remarkable fact that, with all the talking about and preaching on the Eucharist, there is no dispute over Christ's presence there for the first eight centuries.[46]

In the ninth century a shift occurs. Maybe it is the lingering effect of iconoclasm or a more literal, earthy attitude which the barbarian invasion brought with it. In any event, symbol and reality tend to drift apart in the minds of many. This shows up in liturgical books and in writings of the times.[47] Amalar of Metz (d. 853) is one of the key culprits. In the preface of his allegorical interpretation of the Mass, he writes: "Immediately casting aside the restraints of any master whatever . . . I fearlessly wrote down what I felt."[48] What he "felt" was an exaggerated realism or an overly physical approach to the Eucharist and an "inveterate tendency toward allegory."[49] Whereas earlier writers view symbols as rendering present the reality symbolized, Amalar regards them more as dramatic reminders of past events. As David Power notes, the allegorical principle allows one to look to things or words as illustrations of another truth or reality. The sacramental principle allows one to look to symbols for a revelation of the reality present in them as in a distinct mode of being.[50] Unfortunately, Amalar's allegorical approach was to rule the roost throughout the Middle Ages.[51]

Another key figure in this period was Paschasius Radbertus (d. about 860), the author of the first scientific monograph on the Eucharist.[52] Earlier writers had seen the Eucharist primarily as an

---

45. Ibid., 32.
46. Ibid., 33. See also Power, *Unsearchable Riches,* 46–47; Crockett, 88–98; and Megivern, 51–78. Megivern rightly and repeatedly notes that the emphasis throughout this period is not on the reality of Christ's presence in the Eucharist but on the purpose of that presence, namely, the transforming of the community.
47. See Megivern, 79–80.
48. Ibid., 81.
49. Ibid.
50. See Power, *Unsearchable Riches,* 56.
51. See Megivern, 80–81.
52. Ibid., 82.

action and, therefore, mainly in terms of its purpose or end—uniting and transforming the community. Now the tendency is to focus on the contents of the sacrament. In Paschasius's case, the rallying cry comes from an old Ambrosian formula, "No other flesh than that born of Mary."[53] While there may be some question of just how simplistically Paschasius, the abbot of the Benedictine monastery of Corbie in France, took this formula, it is safe to say that he was, at least at times, overly physical in his interpretation.[54] His desire to underline the reality of Christ's presence led him to downplay symbolism to the point that his materialism "shocked the consciences even of his contemporaries, who were no strangers to a grossly realistic notion of the Eucharist."[55] For Paschasius "veritas" or reality seemed to mean physical reality.[56]

This led to an interesting reaction from Ratramnus (d. after 868), another Benedictine from the same monastery. Asked by Emperor Charles the Bald for a reaction to Paschasius's views, Ratramnus found himself in the curious position of having to say that Christ's body is really present *in figura*, that is, in a symbolic manner and not *in veritate*, understood here as not as a physical or material reality. Taken out of context these words would seem to indicate that Ratramnus denied the reality of Christ's presence in the Eucharist and he was in fact condemned by a Synod in Vercelli (1050).[57] Few authors today would accept that judgment, recognizing that, whatever his weaknesses, Ratramnus was closer to the Augustinian view which saw symbol and reality as complementary.[58]

Today most would agree that the issue between Paschasius and Ratramnus was not that one believed Christ to be present in the Eucharist and the other did not. It was not a question of doctrine but rather of interpretation, although as Raymond Brown points out, such differences can be important.[59] The real problem is that the notions of

---

53. Ibid., 82–83, and de Jong, 33.

54. See Heron, 92–93; Megivern, 83; and de Jong, 33.

55. See Megivern, 83.

56. See de Jong, 33.

57. Ibid., 33–34.

58. See Megivern, 85–86; Heron, 93–94; and de Jong, 33–34.

59. See Raymond Brown, "The Importance of How Doctrine is Understood," *Origins* 10/47 (May 7, 1981): 737, 739–43.

symbol and reality were coming apart in the minds of many. This forced them to look elsewhere than to symbol to account for the reality of the Eucharist.[60]

This becomes increasingly evident in the case of Berengar of Tours (d. 1088). Reacting to an overly physical approach to the Eucharist, he taunted his opponents with teaching that we receive "little pieces of Christ's flesh" (*portiuncula carnis Christi*). Embracing what he thought to be Augustine's (and Ratramnus's) position, he rightly returned to viewing sacraments as symbols. The difficulty was that the possibility of a symbol that actually makes present the reality it symbolizes never seems to have crossed his mind. He ends up viewing the sacraments as representations without real content and thus denies the reality of Christ's presence in the Eucharist.

His opponents, apparently unable to appeal to a notion of symbolic reality, found themselves at times pushed into an overly physical corner. An instance of this is the often cited oath demanded of Berengar by the Council of Rome (1059): "I, Berengar . . . believe in my heart and confess with my mouth that the bread and the wine which are placed upon the altar are, after the consecration, not only the symbol (*sacramentum*) but also the real body and blood of our Lord Jesus Christ and physically (*sensualiter*), not only in symbol (*in sacramento*), but in truth (*in veritate*), are passed through the hands of the priest, broken and chewed by the teeth of the faithful."[61] This embarrassingly physical interpretation will be quietly left aside, benignly interpreted or attacked by later writers. Thomas, for instance; will say: "We don't chew Christ with our teeth; Christ isn't eaten in his own bodiliness nor is he chewed with the teeth—what is eaten and broken is the sacramental species. . . . And in this sense is the oath of Berengar to be understood."[62] On the popular level, the growing number of bleeding host stories were seen as bolstering the belief in the reality of Christ's presence. Thomas was equally forceful in

60. See Megivern, 89–91, and de Jong, 34.

61. See H. Denzinger and A. Schönmetzer, eds., *Enchiridion Symbolorum*, 33rd ed. (New York: Herder, 1965), 690. Henceforth DS. See also de Jong, 34–35. For the English text see *The Christian Faith in the Doctrinal Documents of the Catholic Church*, 2nd ed., eds. J. Neuner and J. Dupuis (Westminster, Md.: Christian Classics, 1975).

62. *Summa Theologiae* 111, 71, 7, ad 3. See Megivern, 93; Heron, 96–97; and de Jong, 35.

rejecting this form of reasoning as overly physical and as failing to do justice to the manner of Christ's presence. [63]

The absence of a healthy sense of symbolic reality coupled with a determination to preserve the reality of Christ's presence in the eucharist led to a search for alternate ways of explaining this presence. In this regard, it is interesting to compare the Fourth Lateran Council (1215) with the Council of Constance (1414–18). The Fourth Lateran in speaking of the eucharistic transformation says that the body and blood of Jesus Christ are really (*veraciter*) contained under the species of bread and wine, the bread having been transubstantiated (*transubstantiatis*) into the body and the wine into the blood by the divine power (*potestate divina*). [64] Thomas would have been at home with this because it allowed you to keep substance on the metaphysical level where it belonged rather than putting it on the physical level as the bleeding host stories did. The Council of Constance, on the other hand, when dealing with Wycliffe and Huss says "after the consecration by the priest there is under the veil of bread and wine no material bread and wine, but the very same Christ who suffered on the cross and sits at the right hand of the Father." [65] As John Macquarrie notes, the species have become a veil, the agent of the consecration is the priest and substance has now become identified with physical matter. Thomas would probably have been as uncomfortable with the last as a number of the Reformers were to be. Once again such an overly physical approach seems to ignore the sacramental, even the incarnational, principle that material realities or symbols, without ceasing to be material can become another form of God's ontological presence. [66]

The Reformation period also failed to look to the ancient notion of a symbolic reality for a solution, since this had been lost sight of. So someone like Zwingli (d. 1531) could acknowledge that the Eucharist was a fitting symbol but "merely" a symbol. The

63. See Megivern, 40–45, esp. 43, n. 2. See also Joseph Powers, *Eucharistic Theology* (New York: Herder, 1967), 109–10. In addition to the question of symbolism, this raises the question of Christ's glorified body that is a key to an understanding of Christ's presence in the Eucharist or anywhere else, for that matter. de Jong, 35–36, sees Berengar as a victim of a shift regarding symbol and reality from a Platonic-Augustinian approach to an Aristotelian approach.

64. DS 430 (802).

65. DS 666 (1256).

66. See John Macquarrie, *Christian Unity and Christian Diversity* (Philadelphia: Westminster, 1975), 74–76, and *A Guide to the Sacraments*, 7–8.

Counter Reformation approach was generally to look outside the symbol for a way of establishing the reality of the Eucharist. A result was numerous theories on how the sacraments "caused" and a hardening emphasis on the words of the institution narrative as the "moment of consecration." All this despite the fact that Thomas had combined the Augustinian notion of symbol with the Aristotelian notion of causality ("sacraments cause by signifying").[67] In the seventeenth and eighteenth centuries, the growth of rationalism and the development of science led to the exaltation of scientific experiment, rational argument and the primacy of conceptual clarity. These in turn lessened further the notion of symbol in the minds of many. In the late eighteenth and early nineteenth centuries, however, there was a renewed interest in the realm of symbol. For example, the often painful clash within the Roman Catholic Church between "theologians of renewal" and a neoscholasticism that seemed entrenched as "the" position of the church forced the former back to the biblical, patristic, and liturgical sources. This, together with the contributions of the Catholic members of the Tübingen School, especially J. A. Möhler's *Symbolik* (1832) and the subsequent work of M. J. Scheeben, sowed the seeds to be nurtured still later by the likes of Romano Guardini and Karl Adam and eventually to be reaped in the Second Vatican Council.[68]

In the twentieth century several names can be associated with the rediscovery of the ancient notion of symbolic reality. One of these was Odo Casel (d. 1948), the noted scholar from the Benedictine monastery of Maria Laach. Studying classical antiquity for insights into early Christianity, Casel became convinced that Christian liturgy, parallel to the Greek mystery religions, somehow made the saving event present. Despite difficulties in explaining his position at times, he tenaciously held that in the symbolic action there is a real presence (*Realgegenwart*) of the event. Meanwhile, a Reform theologian, Gerardus van der Leeuw (d. 1950), History of Religions professor at the University of Groningen, was coming to

67. See de Jong, 36; John H. McKenna, *The Eucharistic Epiclesis: A Detailed History From the Partristic to the Modern Era*, 2nd ed. (Chicago: Hillenbrand Books, 2009), 71–90; and S. Happel, "Symbol," in *The New Dictionary of Theology*, ed. J. Komonchak, et al. (Wilmington, Del.: Michael Glazier, 1987), 999. Cf. Power, *Unsearchable Riches*, 180–81.

68. Happel, 1000. See M. Schoof, *A Survey of Catholic Theology* (1800–1970), trans. N. D. Smith (New York: Paulist Press, 1970), 14–156, for an extensive treatment of the interactions of this period.

similar conclusions. Acknowledging that Casel's position was colored by the Platonic Greek writers he studied, van der Leeuw claimed that in the area under discussion there was no essential difference from biblical thought patterns, as long as one realized that symbol and reality were inextricably bound together. Van der Leeuw's sympathy for Casel's position often earned criticism for him in Reform circles as Casel had earned in Roman Catholic circles. Finally, Anscar Vonier, a monk from Buckfast Abbey, came to a conclusion similar to, although developed independently from, Casel. In *A Key to the Doctrine of the Eucharist* (1952) he contended that the key to understanding the Eucharist as sacrament and sacrifice lay in the notion of symbolic reality. [69]

Naturally other views continued to be put forward. For example, an Italian theologian named Selvaggi argued that the protons, neutrons, electrons, and so on, which made up the substance of bread and wine, no longer existed but had been transformed into the body and blood of Christ. His view was countered by Columbo, theologian to Paul VI, who maintained that although the change was ontological it was not on the physical level, as Selvaggi seemed to maintain. [70] In addition, there were nuances in the explanations of Casel, van der Leeuw, and Vonier which still needed to be worked out.

Nevertheless, a revised reading of Thomas Aquinas and a rediscovery of the ancient understanding of the relationship between symbol and reality had led to a rehabilitation of the notion of symbol in current theology. Bernard Lonergan, John Macquarrie, Karl Rahner, Edward Schillebeeckx, and Paul Tillich, to name a few, have made extensive use of this notion in their theology.

---

69. See de Jong, 37–41. See also, Power, *Unsearchable Riches*, 181–84.

70. See de Jong, 41–43. Selvaggi appealed to the body born of Mary which had lived, suffered, and been crucified. He seems to maintain any living, human body must be a physical reality. Once again the whole question of Christ's risen body will have to be raised as well as the tendency to limit ontological to physical, material reality. See *The National Catholic Register*, July 5, 1981, page 5, for another curious, if not amusing, attempt to argue from biology to doctrine. The author argues that, on the basis of parthenogenesis, Mary would have had a female child if the Holy Spirit had not intervened to transmute the chromosome determinant of gender. This "special intervention, which is a corollary of the doctrine of the virginal conception, indicates too clearly God's will for the theory of ordination of women to have any authentic theological or scriptural basis."

NATURE OF SYMBOL

To examine each of these theologians would go beyond the scope of this study. A survey of Karl Rahner's treatment of symbol, however, should offer a basis for further development.[71] Rahner admits that the term "symbol" itself is much more obscure, difficult and ambiguous than is usually thought. It is not surprising, therefore, that there are many different understandings of the term. This fact is rooted in the richness of the Greek words *(eîdos, morphe)* which can mean sign, figure, expression, image, aspect, appearance, and so on.[72] The basic word which concerns us comes from *sym-bállein*, to throw together, compare. For example, if you and I make a pact or covenant, we might cut or break a ring, coin or tablet in two with each of us keeping half as a symbol of the covenant. If someone comes to you with my half and the two (when "thrown together") match, you are to treat that person as you would me—as a partner, friend, one deserving of hospitality. This notion implies a certain identity between the symbol and the one who stands behind it—the symbolizer. As Paul Tillich reminds us, however, despite or precisely because of the importance of this notion we must define our terms.[73] Rahner does. For him symbol in the highest, most primordial or fundamental sense is one reality rendering another present. It expresses or embodies the person or thing so strongly, is so charged with meaning, that it renders the other present. It "allows the other to be there."[74] It is the self-realization of one being in the other. It is extremely close to the one symbolized and it is this closeness, this surplus or superabundance *(Überfluss)* that makes it a symbol in the fundamental, primordial sense. It makes present the reality it symbolizes. This is what Rahner calls a "symbolic reality" *(Realsymbol)*.[75] A consequence of this definition is that a

---

71. Karl Rahner, "The Theology of the Symbol," in *Theological Investigations*, trans. K. Smyth (Baltimore: Helicon, 1966), 4:211–52.

72. Ibid., 222, 224.

73. Tillich, *Dynamics of Faith*, 41: "Man's ultimate concern must be expressed symbolically, because symbolic language alone is able to express the ultimate. This statement demands explanation in several respects. In spite of the manifold research about the meaning and function of symbols which is going on in contemporary philosophy, every writer who uses the term 'symbol' must explain his understanding of it."

74. Rahner, 225.

75. Ibid. See John Macquarrie, *Principles of Christian Theology* (New York: Scribner's, 1966), 123. Macquarrie refers to this as an "intrinsic symbol" and takes exception to Tillich's distinction

symbol in this sense, for example, a ring or sexual intercourse, can lose its closeness to the symbolizer and sink to the level of mere sign or "symbolic representation" because s/he no longer has his or her heart in it.[76]

A "symbolic representation" (signs, signals, codes) is, on the other hand, *not* the self-realization of one being in another. It does not express or embody the person or thing so fully that it allows that other reality to be present in it. The role of bells, for example, is described by Susanne Langer as merely informing: "As for bells, the world is made with their messages. Somebody at the front door, the back door, the side door, the telephone—toast is ready—typewriter line is ended—school begins, work begins, church begins, church is over—time for dinner, time to get up, fire in town!"[77] These merely point to something else, announce some fact or give notification like "Joe's Diner."[78] They are not so close to the person or thing signified. It is this lack of closeness that makes them mere signs or symbolic representations. In addition, they are usually more arbitrary (for instance, red = stop, green = go) but arbitrariness, for Rahner, is not the key norm.[79] Closeness to, or the presence of, the symbolizer is.

Moreover, it is the symbolizer not the recipient who determines whether or not this is a symbolic reality. The margin, therefore, between sign ("symbolic representation") and symbol ("symbolic reality") is fluid. Just as a symbol can become merely a sign, if it loses its

---

between "sign" (as arbitrary pointer) and "symbol" (as participating in what is symbolized) as at variance with good English usage. He notes that we say, "Clouds are a sign of rain," and there is obviously an intrinsic connection between the sign and what it signifies but we could not substitute the word "symbol." See also Ricoeur, 319, who makes a distinction, similar to Rahner, between symbol and sign, "in order to suggest the essential fullness or plenitude of symbols"; "there always remains the trace of a natural relationship between the signifier and the signified." "Such is the fullness of the symbol as opposed to the essential emptiness of the sign." See also Tillich, *Dynamics of Faith,* 42: "Decisive is the fact that signs do not participate in the reality of that to which they point, while symbols do." For a summary of C. S. Peirce's efforts to sort out the notions of "sign," "symbol," and "icon," cf. W. P. Alston, "Sign and Symbol," in *The Encyclopedia of Philosophy* (1967), 7:437–41.

76. Rahner, "The Theology of the Symbol," 215.

77. Langer, *Philosophy in a New Key,* 59.

78. See Nathan Mitchell, "'Symbols Are Actions, Not Objects'– New Directions for an Old Problem," *Living Worship* 13/2 (February 1977): 1–2. He speaks of signs which provide information ("Holiday Inn—5 miles"); signals which supply information designed to provoke appropriate reactions (a traffic signal) and symbols— "actions that disclose relationships."

79. See Rahner, "Theology of Symbol," 225, 240–41. Macquarrie, 123, refers to this as "conventional symbol" and emphasizes the arbitrariness more than Rahner does.

closeness to the symbolizer, so too, an arbitrary or conventional sign, for example, a ring, can become a symbol if it is so charged with, so embodies the other reality as to make it present. Once again the key is whether or not the symbolizer, in a sense, has his or her heart in it.[80]

Consequently, it is not always easy to say where the function of being a sign and indicator so wins the upper hand that a symbol loses its deeper ("surplus," "superabundance" of) meaning and slips to the level of sign. Mistakes in perception can also be made, but they do not rob a genuine symbol of its reality. The one to whom the ring, for instance, is offered may not perceive the depth with which the offerer has entered into it but the reality is there nonetheless. Susanne Langer humorously describes the effects of misperceiving a symbol (in the broader sense): "The word 'water' was never guilty of *denoting* the drink that undid little Willy, in the pathetic laboratory rhyme:

We had a little Willy,
Now Willy is no more,
For what he thought was H_2O
Was H_2SO_4."[81]

What is the ontological foundation for Rahner's understanding of symbol? He contends that being—any being—despite its basic unity is by its very nature multifaceted or plural: "every being as such possesses a plurality as an intrinsic element of its significant unity."[82] Throughout his treatment, Rahner views this plurality positively and not necessarily as a pointer to finiteness and imperfection.[83] Precisely because it is so rich, so many-faceted or plural, each being seeks to express itself. In a sense, it cannot contain itself and still reach fulfillment. All beings, therefore, are by their nature symbolic, because they necessarily express themselves in order to attain their own nature and fulfill themselves. Even simple things like bread and wine reach their fulfillment when they manifest themselves in symbolic form. A bird

---

80. See Rahner, "The Theology of the Symbol," 240, 251–52.

81. Langer, *Philosophy in a New Key*, 65. See also Macquarrie, 9–10, on missing a reality that is present.

82. Rahner, "The Theology of the Symbol," 229.

83. See, for example, "The Theology of the Symbol," 235: "a plurality in a being is not necessarily to be considered as a pointer to finiteness and imperfection . . . [and] may very properly start from the fact that each being bears within itself an intrinsic plurality, without detriment to its unity and perfection . . . precisely as the perfection of its unity."

does the same when it chirps. When I tell you, "I love you," not only do you "discover" me but, through this self-expression, I discover myself. By this self-expression I attain self-realization. I *have* to express myself, even if you do not respond, if I am to reach fulfillment: "each being forms, in its own way, more or less perfectly according to its degree of being, something distinct from itself and yet one with itself, 'for' its own fulfillment."[84] In that sense, being is of itself symbolic.

How then does a being, for example, a bodily person, constitute or perfect himself or herself? By really projecting its visible figure outside itself as its symbol, its appearance, which allows it to be there, which brings it out to existence "in the world," and in doing so, it retains its—"possessing itself in the other."[85] The external manifestation is different from the person and has been created by the person (the symbolizer) as his or her own self-expression and self-realization. The symbol strictly speaking (the "symbolic reality") is, therefore, the self-realization of one being in another. It is the embodiment in concrete form of a many-faceted being.[86] The symbol in this sense does not represent or point to an absent reality. Rather, it shows the reality to be present. The symbol itself has been formed (or transformed) by this reality. The symbol thus renders present what it reveals or symbolizes.[87]

Rahner concludes that no theology can really be complete without also being a theology of the symbol, of the appearance and the expression, of self-presence in that which has been constituted as the other.[88] He then applies this notion of symbolic reality, as does Schillebeeckx[89] and others, to the Trinity, the incarnation, the church and the sacraments: "the Logos is the 'symbol' of the Father, in the

---

84. Ibid., 228. See Power, *Unsearchable Riches*, 199–200.

85. Rahner, "The Theology of Symbol," 231.

86. Ibid., 232–34.

87. For an interesting example of this notion, see Vincent Donovan, *Christianity Rediscovered* (New York: Orbis Books, 1978), 59–60, where the author describes the "spittle of forgiveness" in the Masai tribe of East Africa.

88. Ibid., 135.

89. See, for example, E. Schillebeeckx, *Christ the Sacrament of Encounter With God* and *The Eucharist*, trans. N. D. Smith (New York: Sheed & Ward, 1968). See also Power, *Unsearchable Riches*, 196–200, where he summarizes Schillebeeckx's analysis and applications of symbol as well as that of Rahner. Power notes that Rahner posits a closer unity between symbol and symbolizer than Schillebeeckx does, but both speak of God present communicating and expressing Godself in the symbol.

very sense which we have given the word: the inward symbol which remains distinct from what is symbolized, which is constituted by what is symbolized, where what is symbolized expresses itself and possesses itself."[90] The Incarnate Word is then the absolute symbol of God in this world, the expressive presence of God in the world for us. The Logos, in his humanity, is the revelatory symbol in which the Father expresses himself to the world—revelatory because the symbol renders present what is revealed.[91] The church, in turn, becomes the symbolic reality of the presence of Christ, and the sacraments are symbolic realities of the church.[92] This understanding of symbol underlines the weakness of the question that medieval theologians often got caught up in, namely, "How do the sacraments work on God?"[93]

Having looked at the term "symbol," the distinction between "symbolic reality" (symbol in the strict sense) and "symbolic representation" (sign) and the ontological basis for that distinction in Rahner, it might be good to look briefly at some characteristics of symbols, both in general and in the strict sense. First of all, symbols (or symbolic language) are *two-directional.* As mentioned above, not only do *you* get to know me better through my bodily reactions, words, gestures, and so on; *I* get to know myself better through these expressions of my spirit. The body, for instance, not only expresses attitudes but it also generates such attitudes. That is why we adopt certain bodily positions for prayer. That is why people, as the primary symbolizers, find that in expressing their love they deepen it.

With all their reality however, symbols are *limited.* There is a difference between symbolizer and symbol. In other words, the symbol is not totally identified with, does not totally participate in, the reality which expresses itself in this symbol. Otherwise you have idols like those the Psalmist makes fun of: "They have ears but hear not, eyes but see not." Those who worship idols have failed to "deliteralize" or "break" the symbols, as Tillich would put it. "Those who live in an unbroken mythological world feel safe and certain. They resist, often

90. Rahner, "The Theology of the Symbol," 236.

91. Ibid., 237–39.

92. Ibid., 240–42. See also Rahner, *The Church and the Sacraments* (New York: Herder, 1963).

93. Rahner, "The Theology of the Symbol," 242. For a critique of Rahner's position, see J. J. Buckley, "On Being a Symbol: An Appraisal of Karl Rahner," *Theological Studies* 40 (1979): 453–73, and Paul Molnar, "Can We Know God Directly? Rahner's Solution from Experience," *Theological Studies* 46 (1985): 228–61.

fanatically, any attempt to introduce an element of uncertainty by 'breaking the myth,' namely, by making conscious its symbolic character. . . . Faith, if it takes its symbols literally, becomes idolatrous! It calls something ultimate which is less than ultimate. Faith, conscious of the symbolic character of its symbols, gives God the honor which is due."[94] This may be what the little girl mentioned earlier sensed, when asked if her stories were real: "On the outside they're not, but on the inside they are."

Symbols are also *historical*. Since they are expressions of freedom (in the case of God, people), they can become out of date or empty. This may happen either because of cultural changes or because that freedom chooses to exercise itself in another way. Sacred numbers and the wedding ring given by a person who no longer has his/her "heart in it," might be cases in point. They can lose their "surplus" of meaning or their closeness to the symbolizer. "Like living beings, they grow and they die."[95]

Another characteristic of symbols is that they are *experiential*. They are not just informative. They take hold of a person's mind, will and emotions. A good symbol reaches down through the senses, past reason and into the depths of a person's unconscious psyche to lay hold of the person totally. Advertisers are well aware of this. They count on the ability of symbols to evoke deep feelings in us. As Tillich notes, a symbol opens up levels of reality which otherwise are closed to us. Even more, it "not only opens up dimensions and elements of reality which otherwise would remain unapproachable but also unlocks dimensions and elements of our soul which correspond to the dimensions and elements of reality . . . dimensions of which we cannot become aware except through symbols, as melodies and rhythms in music."[96]

Symbols are thus capable of expressing the deepest aspects of reality in a way that words alone cannot and in a way that has something *universal* about it. "A picture is worth a thousand words," and the picture of my mother looking lovingly at my critically ill father and patting his hand could speak to those who never understood her language.

---

94. Tillich, *Dynamic of Faith*, 51–52.

95. Ibid., 43.

96. Ibid., 42–43.

Part of the richness of symbols is that they are *many-faceted.* They are not limited to one meaning but are, rather, a "bundle of meanings." When an Australasian calls a spade a phallus and likens the act of sowing to the sexual act, it is not because s/he is ignorant of its practical function. The symbolism adds a new value to an object or an activity without denying its other dimensions. Water, for instance, can be life-giving, death-dealing, calming, wisdom-producing, purifying, and so on. To try to limit a symbol rigidly to one meaning is to do worse than mutilate it; it is in a sense to annihilate it.[97]

It is this richness that makes symbols *ambiguous and imprecise.* Some people dislike this. They want a precise meaning. But by allowing your imagination and emotions to work, a good symbol acts as a "cool medium"—it involves you. Ricoeur refers to this as the "mixed texture" of symbols and reminds us that we can never completely capture their reality or exhaust their meaning.[98]

Approaching Symbols Creatively

If symbols are so rich, so promising, how can we approach them creatively? Paul Ricoeur has some evocative suggestions. He proposes a process of "creative interpretation" which involves three intertwining stages.[99] This interpretation would respect the original mystery of symbols, let itself be taught by these symbols, but apply critical reflection to bring out their meaning. The starting point and the point to which we must always return is the original experience or symbol itself.

The first stage is to seek the meaning of the symbol or experience in terms of other symbols and/or experiences. For example, you experience God's saving touch in death or in new life. You draw on all available sources—nature, culture, heritage—to express and deepen this experience. In nature, for example, you discover the death-dealing and life-giving effects of water. In culture you find the purifying power of baths and washings—physically and psychically (ask Lady Macbeth). In heritage, you listen to the hydrants in city streets, the

---

97. See Eliade, *Images and Symbols*, 14, 171–78.

98. See Fink, "Three Languages of Christian Sacraments," 565, and Macquarrie, A *Guide to the Sacraments*, 19.

99. See Ricoeur, *The Conflict of Interpretations,* 300ff. See also "Three Languages of Christian Sacraments," 570–71.

waves lapping against the fishing boats in Maine, the tiny sinks in childcare centers. At this stage, too, you will come in contact with the myths and stories, the prayers and songs with which the community proclaims the meaning of the symbol or experience. The purpose of these is not to give a literal statement of fact but to lure the hearer back to the original experience—to affirm it and embrace it.[100]

The next stage in the process is crucial. You have to understand the symbol in terms of yourself, your own life. Or the community has to understand the symbol in terms of itself, since the process, as we envision it, takes place in community, among people who interact by sharing their life stories and insights.[101] For example, a friend once told me that a difficult couple, disliked by many in the community, called to say that their car had broken down and they would be unable to make the Mass that morning. He mentioned this and "Tony" offered to pick them up. "You know," my friend said, "Tony dislikes them more than I do!" Pause. "I guess that's what Eucharist is all about," he concluded. And I guess so.

Thus, according to Ricoeur, you cannot eliminate the question, "Do I myself believe that? What do I personally make of these symbolic meanings?" Or, "What does this water poured, this bread broken mean for *me (us)*?" Otherwise, you have "a truth without belief, truth at a distance, a reduced truth."[102] "You must understand in order to believe, but you must believe in order to understand."[103] Only then are you really ready to move on to more systematic thought or reflection. It is here that Ricoeur reminds us how personally invested our reflection is, or should be.[104]

In the third stage, the symbol moves to reflective thought. Thought asks, "What does all this mean?" and seeks to explain, to help understand more fully. Thought also asks, "What might it mean?" and seeks to explore for new possibility. "Some see what is and ask, 'Why?' I dream of things yet unseen and ask, 'Why not?'" If, for

---

100. See Ricoeur, *Conflict of Interpretation*, 297, and "Three Languages of Christian Sacraments," 570.

101. See Macquarrie, *A Guide to the Sacraments*, 31–32.

102. Ricoeur, *Conflict of Interpretation*, 297.

103. Ibid., 298. See also Sandra M. Schneiders, *The Revelatory Text: Interpreting the New Testament As Sacred Scripture*, 2nd ed. (Collegeville, Minn.: Liturgical Press, 1999), xxxii–xxxviii.

104. See Fink, "Three Languages of Christian Sacraments," 570. See also Power, *Unsearchable Riches*, 144.

instance, our crucified and risen Lord can feed us in the Eucharist, why do we lack the inventiveness, or the will, to feed others in the world?[105]

The process results, then, in what Ricoeur calls an "imaginative lure" which invites to consent, to choose to live according to the reality experienced. It is here that commitment, vulnerability, and a willingness to let something happen in life enter in. Consent completes the imaginative or meditative process by internalizing and embodying the reality experienced. Without consent that reality remains external to the life of the person. Only *information about* the reality is given.[106]

We have looked at the symbolic process, the history of the notion of symbol, the nature of symbol and a creative approach to symbol. Where does the process finally lead? Where, for instance, will our reflections on Jesus Christ, *the* symbol, take us? Back to the original symbol or experience, which is richer than our ability to understand, which has the power always to say something new. In this sense, Ricoeur notes, our reflection must embrace both the past ("an archeology") and the future ("an eschatology").[107] We return to this reality not as though we already know what it means but open to discovering in a still deeper way the meaning that thought has evolved—and more. Thus our process of reflecting on symbols, especially of Christ and the Eucharist, will lead us through a lifetime of challenge and promise.

---

105. See Ricoeur, *Conflict of Interpretation*, 288, 298–99, and Fink, "Three Languages of Christian Sacraments," 570.

106. See Ricoeur, *Conflict of Interpretation*, 297–98; Fink, "Three Languages of Christian Sacraments," 570–71, and Macquarrie, *A Guide to the Sacraments*, 22.

107. Ricoeur, *Conflict of Interpretation*, 326, 330–34.

Chapter 2

Phenomenology of Meal: A Means to Understanding the Eucharist

In our own culture a child as young as three knows that food and drink are required to celebrate human events. The child knows that a birthday party needs cake and ice cream and soft drinks as much as candles and presents and the song. Food and drink are mysteriously linked to human life and its milestones. Unfortunately, the picture of food and drink is not always a pretty one. "Today about forty million American adults (20 percent) are obese, and more than 55 percent of us are overweight. Every year more than 280,000 people in the U.S. die as a result of being overweight and obesity (which is now the country's second-leading cause of mortality) costs our nation's health care system nearly $240 billion."[1]

FOOD AND DRINK IN THE BIBLE

The Bible reflects the same awareness of the crucial and ethical importance of what we eat and drink. It is interested in food and drink from its beginning in a garden to its ending in a city: both have fruit trees and streams of water. In the garden, as elsewhere in the Scriptures, the warning about eating is portrayed in terms of life and death. The final triumph of God's kingdom and of God's people finds

---

1. Patrick T. McCormick, *A Banqueter's Guide to the All-Night Soup Kitchen of the Kingdom of God* (Collegeville, Minn.: Liturgical Press, 2004), 15–6, citing Eric Schlosser, *Fast Food Nation: The Dark Side of the All-American Meal* (Boston: Houghton Mifflin, 2001), 241–42. See also Nathan Mitchell, "Bread of Crisis, Bread of Justice," *Living Worship* 15/3 (March 1979): 1.

a fitting symbol in the meal of meals: "Happy are they who have been invited to the wedding feast of the Lamb" (Rev. 19:9).[2]

Food and drink in the Bible often reflect God's care. "You spread the table before me in the sight of my foes" (Ps. 23:5). "You produce bread from the earth and wine to gladden our hearts" (Ps. 104:15). Feasts are crucial in Israel's life and history. God demands through Moses, "Let my people go, that they may celebrate a feast to me in the desert" (Ex. 5:1). Festive meals seal covenants (Ex. 24:11b) and kings are enthroned to the tune of a joyful meal (1 Chron. 29:22). At the same time, these feasts, these meals, call the people to live a certain way in keeping with their promises. Meals also point to the future promise, when all will have their share of food and drink. "On this holy mountain the Lord God will provide for all peoples a feast of rich foods and choice wines, juicy, rich food and pure, choice wines. On this mountain he will destroy the veil that veils all peoples, the web that is woven over all nations; he will destroy death forever" (Is. 25:6–7).[3]

Since food and drink and meals are so important, we would do well to follow Paul Ricoeur's suggestions for creative interpretation of symbols by seeing what our human experience of these realities has to tell us. At the same time it might help to let our imagination come into play.[4]

As we have noted, food can speak to us of God's concern that quietly, in the stillness of night, provides unseen growth. God it is who takes the initiative: "You water the mountains from your palace; the earth is replete with the fruit of your works. You raise grass for the cattle, and vegetables for our use, producing bread from the earth and wine to gladden our hearts, so that our faces gleam with oil and bread fortifies our hearts" (Ps. 104:13–15). An early Christian prayer found in the *Didache* reflects a similar emphasis on God's creative initiative: "As this bread that is broken was scattered upon the mountains, and

---

2. See John Burkhart, *Worship: A Searching Examination of the Liturgical Experience* (Philadelphia: Westminster, 1982), 79, 81.

3. Ibid., 80–81, and Mitchell, "Bread of Crisis," 2–3.

4. See John H. McKenna, "Symbol and Reality: Some Anthropological Considerations," *Worship*, 65 (January 1991): 25–26. See also Andrew B. McGowan, *Ascetic Eucharists: Food and Drink in Early Christian Ritual Meals* (New York: Oxford University Press, 1999), 1–7.

gathered together, and became one, so let thy Church be gathered together from the ends of the earth into thy kingdom."[5]

Granted that the experience may vary with differing cultures, food can also speak to us of people. It can speak of the sweat of their brows, the strength of their arms, the swiftness of their minds in producing food. This may be especially true in a hunting or agricultural society but also in a technological setting when you reflect on what goes into packaging, advertising, and selling food products.[6]

Food also speaks to us of life and death. Our words for eating places like "refectory" or "restaurant" remind us of food's ability to restore, and remake. The experience of famine or hunger, whether chronic or occasional, gives people a sense of the fragility of existence at times and provokes anxiety about its cessation. Even children can tell you what bellies swollen from starvation will lead to. Moreover, to nourish us something must die—whether animal or vegetable—its existence must be in a sense sacrificed.[7]

Food, or the absence of it, can also speak to us of love. The archetype of a mother feeding a child comes to mind here. Psychologists are quick to remind us that, if basic needs are not met, it is impossible or extremely difficult to relate intimately. And, conversely, emotionally needy persons sometimes try to compensate by compulsive eating.

Thirst also has powerful connotations, especially when we are talking not simply about ordinary thirst that can be easily quenched. The image of someone lost in the desert searching in vain for water better illustrates the point. Drink is even more urgent than food since thirst puts a person in danger of death much more quickly than

---

5. Gustave Martelet, *The Risen Christ and the Eucharistic World*, trans. R. Hague (New York: Seabury Press, 1976), 32, citing the *Didache (The Doctrine of the Twelve Apostles)*, trans. C. Bigg and A. J. Maclean (London: SPCK, 1922), IX.4, 27–28. See also McCormick, *A Banqueter's Guide*, 28–29.

6. See Martelet, *The Risen Christ*, 32–33. The optional blessing prayers at the presentation of the gifts in the Roman Catholic rite bring out both the divine and the human aspects: "Blessed are you, Lord, God of all creation. Through your goodness we have this bread to offer, which earth has given and human hands have made. It will become for us the bread of life." "Blessed are you, Lord, God of all creation. Through your goodness we have this wine to offer, fruit of the vine and work of human hands. It will become our spiritual drink."

7. See Philippe Rouillard, "From Human Meal to Christian Eucharist," in R. Kevin Seasoltz, ed., *Living Bread, Saving Cup: Readings on the Eucharist* (Collegeville, Minn.: Liturgical Press, 1987), 127–28.

hunger. Speaking metaphorically of a person having a hunger or thirst for power, wealth, justice, knowledge, or happiness epitomizes deep human longings. Such imagery also lies at the root of much religious symbolism. For instance, "O God, you are my God whom I seek; for you my flesh pines and my soul thirsts, like the earth, parched, lifeless and without water" (Ps. 63:2) or "I myself am the bread of life. No one who comes to me shall ever be hungry, no one who believes in me shall ever thirst" (Jn. 6:35).[8]

BREAD AND WINE

Bread and wine in particular form powerful symbols for many cultures.[9] Bread can symbolize the benefits earned by human labor: "By the sweat of your face shall you get bread to eat" (Gen. 3:19). Bread can also symbolize life and death. After an apparent death and a time of gestation or germination, grain emerges a hundred fold. We then crush it, grind and knead it (practically annihilate it) and then bring it together to form one loaf. We also connect many family and social values with the baking and sharing of bread, and this leads to a certain sense of reverence and union.[10] In this context Burkhart remarks: "The crucial term 'lord,' filled as it is with theological, social, and political overtones, is derived from loaf + ward, 'keeper of bread.' A lord is one upon whom you depend for sustenance, life given in a meal."[11]

Wine connotes vigor, vitality, life, earning it such titles as "the water of life," "the nectar of the gods," "the drink of immortality." Especially when it is red, wine is naturally compared to blood, the

---

8. Ibid.

9. See Jan Michael Joncas, "Tasting the Kingdom of God: The Meal Ministry of Jesus and Its Implications for Contemporary Worship and Life," *Worship* 74 (July 2000): 337, "Perhaps the most important conclusion to draw from this consideration of what Greeks and Romans ate and drank is that a meal could consist simply of bread (the staple) and water or wine (the drink); one added relishes to this foundation meal as inclination or finances allowed."

10. See Rouillard, "From Human Meal to Christian Eucharist," 128–29, and Gerardus van der Leeuw, *Sakramentales Denken: Erscheinungsformen Und Wesen Der Ausserchristlichen Und Christlichen Sakramente*, trans. from the Dutch by E. Schwarz (Kassel: J. Stauda, 1959), 115, 118–20. See also Vincent Donovan, *Christianity Rediscovered* (New York: Orbis Books, 1978), 60–61, for an African example of sharing food as an efficacious symbol of forgiveness.

11. Burkhart, *Worship* 79. See also John Macquarrie, *A Guide to the Sacraments* (New York: Continuum, 1999) on the centrality of bread.

source and symbol of life, and is therefore ideally suited to ritual libations. A popular restaurant in Manhattan introduces its wine list with quotes about wine attributed to great names. "Wine is the drink of Gods" (Plato). "Wine rejoices the human heart and joy is the mother of all virtues" (Goethe). "Where there is no wine, there is no love" (Euripides). I am told that there is also an Italian saying: "A meal without wine is like a kiss without love."

Different languages attest to alcohol's ability to stimulate the spirit, to break down barriers, give a sense of peace, and joy (in English *spirits*, in French *spiritueux*, *spiritoso* in Italian, and *geistiges Getränk* in German).[12] Drinking from the same cup, "clinking" or touching glasses, the Jewish wedding ritual of having the couple drink from the same glass and then breaking it as a symbol of their special relationship all reflect a sense of comradeship or union.[13]

EATING AND DRINKING

Human beings have taken these elements (or others like them) and made them into a meal that can speak to us in so many ways. A so-called primitive understanding, with many modern vestiges, saw eating and drinking to relieve hunger and thirst as bringing people into contact with the gods. Van der Leeuw maintains that the prescriptions for the preparation of food and drink which fill the pages of the history of religions stem from a sense, in whatever religion, that eating and drinking put people in contact with powers beyond them, with holy powers. "Don't play with good food" may well reflect this sense.[14]

Among "primitive" people drinking beer or wine was often linked to enhanced joy in living (*Lebensfreude*) and deeper insights into life. Furthermore, numerous cultures saw such drinking not only as strengthening life but also as the means of coming into contact with the gods. It is this contact that links drink with immortality. Drinking together, then, led to community, to joy, to new insights into life (hence the use of ritual "drunkenness" in initiation rites), to a sense of immortality, and to love because it put people in touch with

---

12. Rouillard, "From Human Meal to Christian Eucharist," 129–30.

13. See van der Leeuw, *Sakramentales Denken*, 116–18, and Rouillard, "From Human Meal to Christian Eucharist," 130.

14. See van der Leeuw, *Sakramentales Denken*, 115–16.

gods and godlike powers. The "magic potions" of the sagas and fairy-tales are remnants of the sacramental sense of the mystical powers of any drink. Van der Leeuw argues further that even industrialized societies have such remnants of "pansacramentalism."[15]

Eating too had special meaning for "primitive" people. It expressed and built community. In German sagas, for instance, having eaten even with an enemy meant that you could not kill him. Lawrence of Arabia once narrated how such an understanding saved his life. Eating in such a setting was not just bodily nourishment but "soul stuff"; it had life-giving, unifying power. Moreover, already in primitive societies there was a sense that, although every food means life-giving power, a consecration, a blessing, an exorcism enhances this power. This represents a move from pansacramentalism (which sees any eating as "eating god") to a sacramentalism that narrows down the field of the sacred or underlines certain moments, events, places, or things as especially sacred.[16]

HUMAN MEALS

In our own "modern" societies, even allowing for great cultural diversity, we have taken food and drink and made them into a meal that speaks to us with many voices. Salespersons and business people, for example, often use a meal to "soften up" a client or to seal an agreement (this staple of many an expense account is both functional and relational). Neighbors welcome newcomers and say good-by with a meal.

"Lovers and other strangers" express interest, even love, by eating and drinking together. They also deepen that love through the sharing of meals. This may account for feelings of jealousy one partner often has upon hearing that the other partner is taking someone else out to dinner. Meals express relationship and deepen it. Burkhart cites French sociologist Émile Durkheim: "In a multitude of societies, meals taken in common are believed to create a bond of artificial kinship between those who assist at them. In fact, relatives are people who are naturally made of the same flesh and blood. But food is

---

15. Ibid., 116–18.

16. Ibid., 120–21. See also Mircea Eliade, *Rites and Symbols of Initiation: The Mysteries of Birth and Rebirth*, trans. W. R. Trask (New York: Harper & Row, 1958), v–xv, 13–20.

constantly remaking the substance of the organism. So a common food may produce the same effects as a common origin."[17] Since they are so personal, and can imply kinship or quasi-kinship, meals are also the place for setting limits, for example, what we will eat, how much, and with whom.[18]

In some cultures to invite someone to your home for dinner signals firm friendship and consequent social obligations. Even in cultures with less formal implications for meals, when dating shows signs of becoming serious a family will often invite the girlfriend or boyfriend to dinner. Meals also accompany celebrations of love grown to the point where the couple wishes to marry or love that has aged and mellowed through twenty-five or fifty years of marriage.

Families and nations often express thanks, hope of future prosperity, and appreciation for past and present blessings, with meals or banquets (where hopefully the food and drink are good and the speeches brief). For myself our family's Thanksgiving dinner was a good example of the richness and meaning of meal. The whole family gathered together. We shared; each would bring something to contribute to the meal—wine, a pie, éclairs, etc. Different people played different roles. Some cooked. One uncle cut the turkey and told corny jokes. Someone poured the wine. A number told stories. It was a celebration and a learning experience. We learned manners, respect, listening. The stories gave us a sense of our history, our plans, our achievements. The overall purpose of the day was to thank God for many blessings and, consciously or unconsciously, to ask God to continue those blessings.

Thanksgiving is also a day when we understood that those less fortunate should also be able to celebrate something special. I know an immigrant family who when they first arrived in the United States lived in a garage with little to sustain them. As Thanksgiving approached the mother put aside some tomatoes and rice, so that they

---

17. Burkhart, *Worship* 77, citing Durkheim's *The Elementary Forms of the Religious Life*, trans. J. W. Swain (London: George Allen & Unwin, 1915), 378.

18. Burkhart, *Worship* 78, citing Mary Douglas's study of English middle-class meal customs. See also Blake Leyerle, "Meal Customs in the Greco-Roman World," in Paul F. Bradshaw and Lawrence A. Hoffman, *Passover and Easter: Origin and History to Modern Times* (= vol. 5 of *Two Liturgical Traditions*) (Notre Dame, Ind.: University of Notre Dame Press, 1999), 37, who notes that participants in Graeco-Roman meals though not related by blood often used kinship language (see also 39, 45), and Joncas, "Tasting the Kingdom of God," 338.

could have something special for that day. The evening before Thanksgiving a woman with an infant in her arms appeared and asked for some food. With tears in her eyes the mother shared what she had been saving for a special "treat." The mother really understood much about Thanksgiving.[19] Happily the next day some local sisters arrived with a full Thanksgiving dinner and job offers for her and her husband.

There are many other characteristics of human meals that could help in our understanding of Eucharist. According to some, at least, they can be solitary as well as communal. I also know of a mother who insists that the children eat first and go to bed so that she and her husband can share one another's company in peace. Her sister, on the other hand, wants the whole family to eat together. There are formal and informal meals: with wine, that can add something, or without; everyday and special, peak experiences, when people dress up and go to a "fancy" restaurant; happy ones like weddings and less happy like the meal following a funeral to express support for those grieving. Obviously, the attitudes people bring to a meal are crucial. As Mary Douglas, the social anthropologist, reminds us, "Food is not feed . . . [and] to treat food as feed, thereby rejecting the human dimensions of meals, is to 'make a pig out of oneself.' Those who eat hastily, indifferent to those about them, are said to wolf down their food."[20] Burkhart notes the bond between meals and social solidarity by remarking that the root metaphor for sociability is companionship. And companionship, "from *cum* + *panis*, 'breading together,' is a distinctively human activity, and is the essence of community." While animals may grab a hunk of meat and run off to gnaw it by themselves or crowd together to gobble food from a trough, people come together to eat "companionately."[21]

Attitude is in many ways more important than the food. Have you ever seen a child who has just been rebuked at table trying to swallow the food? Or have you ever experienced the reconciling power of a good meal with people who otherwise are at enmity with

19. What a wonderful example of "eucharistic hospitality." See McCormick, *A Banqueter's Guide*, 48–50, for early Christian examples.

20. Burkhart, *Worship*, 76, citing Mary Douglas's Introduction to Jessica Kuper, ed., *The Anthropologists' Cookbook* (Universe Books, 1977), 7.

21. Burkhart, *Worship*, 76.

one another? The movie *Babbette's Feast* is a classic example of this latter situation.

The film also underscores the importance of preparation in creating a good human experience of meal. And preparation takes time and a patient maturity—something a "gulp and gallop" culture finds difficult. But those who make the time to light a candle or two, arrange some flowers, pour a glass of wine, and engage in conversation are often richly rewarded.

RITUAL MEALS

In addition to reflecting on "ordinary" human meals, it would be helpful to turn our attention to some types of ritual meals. Rouillard describes four categories.

One type involves a ritual in which the people are "eaten by the gods." The underlying idea of these sacrifices is that the divinity has a right to demand a person's life to nourish that divinity just as people have the right to sacrifice the lives of animals to nourish their own lives. Instead of immolating themselves people immolated some victim, for instance, a prisoner, an infant, an animal. The life of the victim was thus sacrificed in place of those offering the sacrifice who, although they ought to offer themselves, understandably shrank from giving their own lives in homage to the gods. This kind of replacement was behind the Phoenicians' sacrifice of their sons to Moloch, Abraham's near sacrifice of Isaac (replaced by an animal), and some tribal customs in times of an epidemic. This also underlies initiation rites that involve some form of ritual death by going into a cave or cabin or hole, then emerging after several days (digestion period) and being replaced by the immolation of some animal.[22]

Another type is a ritual in which the people eat the gods. Almost every religion holds out to its followers a share in the power, energy, life or immortality of the divinity. To obtain this one often has to "eat the god." How? Usually this involves eating an animal or plant that symbolizes the god. In northern Japan the people raised a bear,

---

22. See Rouillard, "From Human Meal to Christian Eucharist," 133–34. See also Eliade, *Rites and Symbols of Initiation*, xii–xv, 18–20, 35–37.

then killed it and ate it to share in the power of the god the bear represented.[23] Once a year in Ireland the king and noblemen ate pork
symbolizing their god Lug. They thus hoped to rule with his power.[24]
Similarly, in Greece the followers of the god Dionysius would eat a
bull, the animal whose appearance Dionysius adopted to escape the
Titans.[25] The Aztecs, prior to the Spanish conquest under Cortez in
1519, would eat sacred bread. The grain that had "died and risen"
symbolized god. The Aztecs formed the bread into a human shape
and distributed it twice a year at their solemn festivals. The priests
would also take it to the sick who were unable to attend the feast.
Van der Leeuw sees gingerbread men and women as vestiges of such
ancient practices.[26]

A third type of ritual meal took the form of sharing a meal
with the gods. The people would divide the immolated victim. Often
they reserved the choice portions, for instance, the blood or fatty portions (considered the seats of life, feeling) for the gods. These parts
went to the gods by being burnt or eaten by the priests while the
people ate the other part. The sharing was a sign of peace and communion among the sharers. It was also a necessary complement to
sealing a pact or alliance, whether the partners were equal or not. The
German sagas and Lawrence of Arabia's experience mentioned above
exemplify this understanding. Some cultures still consider sharing a
meal as an effective reconciliation and refusing to eat with someone as
a symbol of enmity.[27]

Another type of ritual meal is a memorial meal. This recalls
and, in a sense, relives an event in the history of a god or an intervention of a god in favor of the people. The purpose of the memorial meal
is to recall and somehow to enter into the event or the intervention.
This takes place in word (telling the story, giving an instruction) and
in action (partaking of the meal).[28]

23. See van der Leeuw, *Sakramentales Denken*, 122. For a graphic portrayal of such a ritual process see Jean Auel's novel *Clan of the Cave Bear*, 405–17.

24. See Rouillard, "From Human Meal to Christian Eucharist," 135.

25. Ibid.

26. See ibid., and van der Leeuw, *Sakramentales Denken*, 122.

27. See Rouillard, "From Human Meal to Christian Eucharist," 135–36; van der Leeuw, *Sakramentales Denken*, 119–20; and Leyerle, "Meal Customs in the Greco-Roman World," 36.

28. See Rouillard, "From Human Meal to Christian Eucharist," 136.

Obviously the writer's and reader's respective backgrounds (cultural, religious, educational, etc.) color reflections like those in this chapter. But such reflections can enable us to draw on our own experience, "cleanse the Doors of Perception,"[29] and gain new insight into the many-faceted wonder of the symbols with which we celebrate.

---

29. Victor Turner, "Passages, Margins, and Poverty: Religious Symbols of Communitas," *Worship* 46 (Oct. 1972): Part II, 483, in the context of the initiation process's ability to help the initiated persons see things anew.

Chapter 3

Meal in the Old Testament (Hebrew Scriptures)

Trying to understand our Eucharist better leads us to reflect on meals among the ancient Israelites and, in particular, the Passover meal. Reflecting on our heritage is part of Paul Ricoeur's creative approach to symbols, in addition to drawing on our everyday experiences of such realities as water and meals.[1] My purpose here is not to enter into the debate over whether or not the Last Supper was a Passover meal, but simply to seek insight into our Christian sacraments by reflecting on our rich Jewish heritage.[2]

I shall basically limit myself to the biblical data. I am aware that the biblical narrative is a theological document, an expression of faith and not primarily an attempt to present history in a modern sense. As Nahum Sarna puts it: "The overriding aim of the biblical writers was to present a theological, or theocentric, didactic description of events. . . . Animated by the unshakable conviction that divine sovereignty purposefully operates and controls human events, the biblical writers were not consciously composing mere historical records

---

1. See John H. McKenna, "Symbol and Reality: Some Anthropological Considerations," *Worship* 65 (January 1991): 2–27, especially 25–27.

2. For a clear summary of pros and cons, see Jonathan Klawans, "Was Jesus' Last Supper a Seder?" *Bible Review* 17 (October 2001): 24–33, and 47. See also Paul F. Bradshaw, *The Search for the Origins of Christian Worship*, 2nd ed. (New York: Oxford University Press, 2002), 65. "From the point of view of liturgical scholars, the question of whether the Last Supper was a Passover meal does not seem particularly crucial."

but rather documents of faith."[3] Thus narratives often do not fit modern notions of history. But reality in the form of main theological lines does emerge and can offer helpful insights into our Christian Eucharist.[4]

OLD TESTAMENT (HEBREW SCRIPTURES)

In the Old Testament in general two main characteristics of meals appear: community building and a joyful, festive tone.

Common table testifies to and brings about a common life. The Israelites, therefore, linked the sharing of food and drink, with its life-giving power, to the sharing of trust and friendship.[5] That is why the lament in Psalm 41:10 is so poignant: "Even my friend who had my trust and partook of my bread has raised his heel against me." John 13:18 applies the passage to Judas and Jesus.

Any sharing of food should lead to a bond of trust, even kinship. This was especially true of a sacrificial meal and that was why they often sealed a covenant or agreement with such a meal. God was considered present as a witness and, to some extent, a partner to this

---

3. Nahum M. Sarna, *Exploring Exodus: The Origins of Biblical Israel* (New York: Schocken, 1996), xiii. See also, Marc Brettler, "Memory in Ancient Israel," in Michael A. Signer, ed., *Memory and History in Christianity and Judaism* (Notre Dame, Ind.: University of Notre Dame, 2001), 3–13, makes the interesting point that there is a distinction between history and (collective) memory. The former concern is with getting the facts straight. The latter is more concerned with getting a message across—a "remembering that leads to doing."

4. See Blake Leyerle, "Meal Customs in the Greco-Roman World," in Paul F. Bradshaw and Lawrence A. Hoffman, *Passover and Easter: Origin and History to Modern Times* (= vol. 5 of *Two Liturgical Traditions*) (Notre Dame, Ind.: University of Notre Dame Press, 1999), 29, 45–46, who indicates the difficulties in getting a clear picture of meal customs and significance even for first century BC and first century AD but also indicates that we can also learn a great deal about them. See also Lawrence Hoffman, "The Passover Meal in Jewish Tradition," 13, and Jan Michael Joncas, "Tasting the Kingdom of God: The Meal Ministry of Jesus and Its Implications for Contemporary Worship and Life," *Worship* 74 (July 2000): 333–34. For a summary of Judaism in the time of Jesus that makes good use of rabbinic evidence, see E. P. Sanders, *Judaism: Practice and Belief* 63 B.C.E.–66 C.E. (London: SCM Press, 1992), as cited by Klawans, "Was Jesus' Last Supper a Seder?" 47, n. 4.

5. See Stephen A. Reed, "Bread," in David Noel Freedman, et al., eds., *The Anchor Bible Dictionary*, 6 vols. (henceforth ABD) (New York: Doubleday, 1992), 1:779, and Gillian Feeley-Harnik, *The Lord's Table: Eucharist and Passover in Early Christianity* (Philadelphia: University of Pennsylvania,1981), 85–91. See Leyerle, "Meal Customs in the Greco-Roman World," 37, who notes that participants in Graeco-Roman meals though not related by blood often used kinship language (see also 39, 45), and Joncas, "Tasting the Kingdom of God," 338.

agreement. Laban, for instance, speaks to Jacob: "Come, then, we will make a pact, you and I; the Lord shall be a witness between us. . . . May the god of Abraham and the god of Nahor maintain justice between us!" Jacob took the oath by the Awesome One of Isaac. He then offered a sacrifice on the mountain and invited his kinsmen to share in the meal. When they had eaten, they passed the night on the mountain (Gen. 31:44, 53–54; see also Ex. 18:12 where Jethro, Moses' father-in-law, celebrates his own "conversion" with Moses, Aaron and the elders "in the meal before God").

To share a meal with God had a similar idea. God is the Host or King inviting to the banquet. Eat "before the Lord," in his presence, and you share a common life with God (see Deut. 12:7, 12, 18; 14:26; 15:20; 27:7). Thus sharing in such a meal brought union, peace, and harmony with one another and with the divinity.[6]

A joyful, festive tone was also characteristic of the Israelite understanding of meal. They regarded the meal as one of the most fitting, best loved images of messianic times and also to a certain extent as a preparation for the final meal in the last days. "On this mountain the Lord of Hosts will provide for all peoples a feast of rich food and choice juicy wines . . . [and] will destroy death forever" (Is. 25:6–8; see also Matt. 22:1–14). The sacred meal could thus have both covenant and eschatological overtones. The Israelites at times looked on the daily, ordinary meals as a type of, a "rehearsal" for, that final meal they would share with each other in the presence of God. The primary mood then was one of joy and celebration. The Greek term for "mirth," "merriment" became the technical term for meals in general, and specifically for sacrificial meals. The Septuagint uses this term for "meal' in Old Testament texts. So the sense of pleasure and celebration connected with an ordinary meal carried over into the sacred meal.[7]

---

6. See Dennis Smith, "Meal Customs (Sacred Meals)," in ABD 4: 653–55. Paul picks up on this kind of thinking in 1 Cor. 10:14–22. Leyerle, "Meal Customs in the Greco-Roman World," 32, reports: "at meals held in the temple dining rooms, the god was considered to be the host."

7. See Smith, "Meal Customs (Sacred Meals)," 654, and Alan W. Jenks, "Eating and Drinking in the Old Testament," in ABD 2: 252. See also John E. Burkhart, *Worship* (Philadelphia: Westminster Press, 1982), 92. A good example of the joy especially in a sacrificial setting would be David's bringing the ark to Jerusalem in 2 Sm. 6:12b–15, 17–19.

Passover Meal

Early data about the Passover meal is rather sparse. We are not talking about the Passover Seder or order at this point. The precise history
of the seder can only begin at the end of the Second Temple period
(c. 515 BC–70 AD).[8] There is no evidence of the *ceremony* connected
with the eating of the Paschal lamb prior to that. The Mishnah, the
earliest rabbinic law book, was finally redacted only at the beginning
of the third century AD, approximately 150 years after the destruction
of the Temple and the cessation of the paschal sacrifice. It is, however,
safe to say that the earlier Passover meal provided the opportunity to
instruct the younger generation on the origin and history of the
Jewish people. In fact Exodus 13:8, 14 commands that it be done.[9]

Origins

In any event, the Israelite Passover feast seems to have its origin in
two pre-Israelite feasts. The first was *Pesach*, a nomadic springtime
feast which featured the slaying of the firstborn sheep for a cultic meal
to strengthen family ties and to acknowledge once again the entire
clan's need for, and reliance on, the tribal god. The context was breaking camp and moving the flocks to new pastures. This could be dangerous for flock and people. A blood rite was used to ward off evil
spirits and protect all against harm. One theory is that the tribe
believed that the lamb went to god and returned to the flock in the
form of newly born lambs for which the tribe was thankful.[10]

---

8. According to the Timeline of the Rabbinic Conception of History (provided by Prof.
Ruth Langer, Boston College), Sacred History would include Creation, Redemption (Exodus
from Egypt c. 1230), Revelation, the First Temple (built by Solomon, c. 950 BC, destroyed by
Babylonians, 586 BC) the Second Temple (c. 515 BC and destroyed by the Romans in 70 AD).
Webster's Unabridged provides this definition of *Mishnah*: "from instruction, oral law in Hebrew.
The traditional doctrine of the Jews as represented and developed chiefly in the decisions of the
rabbis before AD 200." See also Baruch M. Bokser, *The Origins of the Seder: The Passover Rite and
Early Rabbinic Judaism* (Berkeley: University of California Press, 1984), 145, who describes the
Mishnah as "edited ca. 200 CE, containing the basic teachings of early rabbinic Judaism."

9. Joseph Tabory, "Towards a History of the Paschal Meal," in Bradshaw and Hoffman,
62–63.

10. Baruch M. Bokser, "Unleavened Bread and Passover, Feasts of," in ABD 6: 756, 759–60,
notes that some scholars claim extra biblical rites, especially Ancient Near East holiday rituals,
suggest such nomadic rituals, but he cautions that any details about nomadic patterns remain
conjectures. See also Jakob Petuchowski and Clemens Thoma, "Pesach/Ostern," in *Lexikon der
Judisch-Christlichen Begegnung* (Freiburg im Breisgau: Herder, 1989), 288–89. See also Nahum

While scholars may differ over the prehistory of the Passover festival, there seems to be greater agreement that the feast of Massot or Unleavened Bread was originally an agricultural feast to signal and celebrate the sacred time of the new barley harvest. For seven days the people ate unleavened bread and fruits of the harvest unmixed with, and uncontaminated by, what was left from the old harvest.[11]

"Historicizing"

Both these feasts celebrated new beginnings. The Israelites "historicized" the feasts by linking them to the slaying of the lamb, the applying of blood to the doorposts, God's "passing over" the Israelites' homes, leaving Egypt in such haste that they could not leaven their bread (Ex. 12:1–33). The bread thus became the "bread of affliction" (Deut. 16:3) and of liberation, and the nature feasts became feasts of Israel's God. Gradually the two feasts drew closer together and eventually (we do not know exactly when) formed one feast that was called interchangeably Passover and the feast of Unleavened Bread (see 2 Chron. 30:1, 2, 5 and 21; also Lk. 22:1 "Now the feast of Unleavened Bread, called the Passover was drawing near").[12]

The feast commemorates an Exodus that has become a paradigm of human experience—of bondage, of liberation or freedom from that bondage, and of covenant with the God who saves. As Bokser puts it: "The two festivals became not only powerful symbols of hope and redemption but also central religious experiences in the life of Israel and of people who identified with biblical Israel."[13] The Passover celebrates what Israel had become under God's saving,

---

Sarna, *Exodus: The Traditional Hebrew Text with the New JPS Translation and Commentary* (Philadelphia: Jewish Publication Society, 1991), 57, and Sarna, *Exploring Exodus*, 85, 87–88.

11. Bokser "Feasts of Unleavened Bread," in ABD 6: 756, 760. See also Petuchowski and Thoma, "Pesach/Ostern," 289; Heinz-Martin Döpp, "Pessach," in Julius H. Schoeps, ed., *Neues Lexikon des Judentums* (Gütersloh: Gütersloher Verlag, 2000), 648–49; Sarna, *Exodus*, 57; and Sarna, *Exploring Exodus*, 88–89. William Propp, *Exodus 1–18: A New Translation with Introduction and Commentary* (New York: Doubleday, 1999), 428–29, cautions against making too sharp a distinction between nomadic and agricultural celebrations and the people who celebrated them.

12. See Petuchowski and Thoma, "Pesach/Ostern," 288–89; Döpp, "Pessach," 648; and Sarna, *Exploring Exodus*, 89.

13. Bokser, "Feasts of Unleavened Bread," 756. See Seasoltz, "Human Victimization and Christ as Victim in the Eucharist," *Worship* 76 (March 2002): 99–103, for a Christian perspective on this.

life-giving presence. It also has a quality of refusing to be relegated to the past. This celebration enabled Israel to express and experience itself as a nation in the face of ongoing stress and pressures from unbelievers. It was to set them apart.[14] More importantly, it bound them together (as any good meal or feast can do) making them more capable of facing the present and the future with hope.

Exodus 12–13 gives the fullest biblical account of the two celebrations and the one most reflective of the Bible's theological message. It also gives an idea of how later Jews understood the rites. The narrator seems to have shaped the story with the later use of this experience in mind (Ex. 12:14, 24) and with an eye to how the original experience would later be imitated as a remembrance and memorial.[15] For Philo (20 BC–50 AD) centuries later it "comprised the main and presumably most widely known memorial or celebration for the Exodus. Philo, moreover, describes his image of the pilgrims' experience during such a festival in the capital city, including the respite and release from normal life; the openness to an emotional high, to joy; and to a sense of holiness in honoring god; and even the friendships and positive feelings that would have engendered and would have reinforce the pilgrims' sense of celebrating a national holiday together."[16]

Each Passover was a starting point, a new beginning. The Exodus event ushered in a new way of living dominated by an awareness of God's active presence in history. The calendar reflects this reality by beginning the year with the month of the Exodus.[17] But it was more than a new year. It was a new era for a free new people that God had formed as a social agent in recreating the world.

All traditions bear witness to the link between Passover and new beginnings. The Priestly tradition mentions two Passover feasts. The first is in Egypt as the Israelites prepare to set out for the desert (Ex. 12). The second is in Sinai as they are preparing to cross the desert (Nm. 9:1–14).

---

14. See James A. Michener's novel, *The Source* (New York: Ballantine, 1983), 371–72, for a good fictional portrayal of this attitude and God's part in it.

15. See Bokser, "Feasts of Unleavened Bread," 756.

16. Bokser, "Feasts of Unleavened Bread," 762, referring to *Spec Leg* I, 12.

17. See Sarna, *Exodus*, 54, and *Exploring Exodus*, 81. See also Propp, *Exodus 1–18*, 384.

The Deuteronomic tradition also speaks of two. One the Israelites celebrate after they have crossed the Jordan River on dry ground and are about to lay siege to Jericho (Josh. 4:19–5:12). The other takes place after King Josiah implements his reforms. "Before him there had been no king who turned to the Lord as he did, with his whole heart, his whole soul, and his whole strength, in accord with the entire law of Moses; nor could any after him compare with him" (see 2 Kgs. 23:21–25).

The Chronicler connects Passover closely with three great renewals of the Temple: under Hezekiah (2 Chron. 30), under Josiah (2 Chron. 35:1, 18), and under Ezra (Ezra 6). The Chronicler also views Passover as the great renewal celebration when the Israelite community attempts once again to become what it was meant to be.

A number of sources during the period of approximately two centuries between the composition of the last canonical book of the Hebrew Scriptures and the writings of the New Testament as well as in the rabbinic literature also make the Passover central. They link the feast to the creation of the world, Abraham's circumcision, the sacrifice of Isaac, the entrance of Israel into Egypt, the release of Joseph from prison and, of course, the Exodus event. They also consider this to be the night on which the final, freeing, life-giving event will take place.[18] For many the Passover feast is, in short, *the* celebration of new beginnings.

The Passover meal with its joyful spirit also served, among other things, as a release for the people of Israel. It was a liberating feast. It lifted them above, though not completely out of, the day-to-day struggle to overcome bondage in all its forms. "The book of Exodus is the great seminal text of biblical literature."[19] Its central theme, and that of the Passover celebration, is God's freeing the Jewish people from slavery, and this has influenced ethical and social behavior down to the present. The Torah often invokes the Exodus as the grounds for working on behalf of strangers and the disadvantaged.[20] The memory of God's action in the past freed the Israelites to

---

18. See Lucien Deiss, *It's the Lord's Supper: The Eucharist of Christians*, trans. Edmond Bonin (New York: Paulist Press, 1976), 35; Petuchowski and Thoma, "Pesach/Ostern," 290; and Propp, *Exodus 1–18*, 458–59.

19. Sarna, *Exodus*, xii.

20. Ibid.

dream of change and to struggle for it with hope in the future. "In the end time, in a perfect way never quite experienced in this world, food and drink represent fellowship with other men and women, communion with God through covenant and cult, and the gifts of God to Israel and to all mankind through history and through nature. In the time of God's final victory, the texts affirm, the life force itself will be eternally nourished as the plenty and joy of Eden are restored. The way to the Tree of Life, lost through a primal meal in the Garden, will no longer be barred to a hungering human race."[21]

Stages

Historically there were three stages or forms of the feast. The first one was the "Egyptian Passover" or family celebration. If the family was too small for a whole lamb it was to join the nearest household. Slaughtering the lambs at the same time may have provided an added sense of the larger community. Under Josiah (c. 622–600 BC) the feast became a "Temple Passover" with everything taking place in the Temple. This observance as a national feast and linkage with the feast of Unleavened Bread, a pilgrimage feast, threatened the family dimension of Passover celebration. Those who could not make the pilgrimage, however, celebrated at home without the lamb—a sign of the importance and deep roots of the feast for the people. This arrangement may have heightened still further the role played by the bread in the celebration. Finally, there was the "Late Jewish" Passover that represented a compromise of sorts. At the time of Jesus until the destruction of the Temple in 70 AD the lamb was slaughtered in the Temple but eaten in a family dwelling within the walls of Jerusalem.[22]

---

21. Jenks, "Eating and Drinking in the Old Testament," 254.

22. See Bokser, "Feasts of Unleavened Bread," 756, 758–59, 763, and *The Passover Rite*, xiii: "Already in the Bible, as in Exodus 12, the Passover evening celebration is described as a decentralized celebration organized in the home. Apparently, even when the cult became centralized in Jerusalem, the family meal continued. Thus, the evening celebration provided a prototype for later rabbinic rituals and observances indicating how one could be religiously involved without being in the temple." Lawrence Hoffman, "A Symbol of Salvation in the Passover Seder," in Paul Bradshaw and Lawrence Hoffman, *Passover and Easter: The Symbolic Structuring of Sacred Seasons* (Notre Dame, Ind.: University of Notre Dame Press, 1999) (= vol. 6 of *Two Liturgical Traditions*), 109–31, argues convincingly that even before the destruction of the temple in 70 AD the bread had become a symbol of salvation comparable to the lamb. He understands a "symbol of salvation" as "words and actions understood by ancient worshippers to represent deliverance" (109).

Participants

Another interesting feature of the Passover, as described in the book of Exodus, was the participants. Only those belonging to the chosen people were to share in the feast. Slaves and aliens could partake only on condition of circumcision of the males (Ex. 12:43, 48). There was also a particular concern for widows, orphans, and aliens. In addition, the whole community must take part. Those who did not participate, unless unclean or on a journey, were to be cut off from the community (Ex. 12:47 and Nm. 9:13). So important was this feast that an "alternate" was provided one month later for those unable to share in the original celebration (Nm. 9:5–12).[23]

Elements

There were a number of elements in the ancient Passover meal that merit reflection. In our quest for insights into the Christian Eucharist we shall limit ourselves to the blood and bread symbols and to the notion of memorial. We chose blood because of the New Testament mention of it in the institution narratives of the Eucharist (Matt. 26:28 and 1 Cor. 11:25) and bread because of its key role in the Christian and, as we shall see, Jewish rituals. The same is true of the concept of memorial.

Blood

In our own experience and in our English language the term "blood" still has strong connotations. We have blood donors and blood recipients. We speak of shedding one's blood on the battlefield. "What do you want, blood?" expresses exasperation at high demands being made of us. "Blood brothers and sisters" and "blood is thicker than water" imply strong relationships. "They are out for blood" connotes utmost seriousness and determination whether in a sports event or some other context.

For the ancient Israelites the connotation of "blood" was no less powerful. Because they embodied life, blood and fat were allotted to God who alone had jurisdiction over them. Deuteronomy 12:23

---

23. See Döpp, Pessach, 648. See also Propp, *Exodus 1–18*, 452, and Sarna, *Exodus,* 63. Interestingly, the *Constitution on the Sacred Liturgy,* art.14, speaks of active participation in the liturgy by all the faithful as "their right and duty by reason of their baptism."

makes the identification of blood with life explicit: "But make sure that you do not partake of the blood; for blood is life, and you shall not consume this seat of life with the flesh." Thus one aspect of this blood-life symbolism was God-directed. People poured out the blood or sprinkled it on an altar as an offering to God to whom all life belongs.[24]

The other aspect was people-directed. The basic effect here was atonement, a repairing of the rupture between God and humans. This atonement was in a sense synonymous with the other effects of blood rites, namely, protection, purification, remission of sin, sealing of a covenant. The blood brought life where there had been death of some form. This was not because the blood has power in itself but because God so designated it. "Since the life of a living body is in its blood, I have made you put it on the altar, so that atonement may be made for your own lives, because it is the blood, as the seat of life, that makes atonement"(Lv. 17:11).[25]

The God-directed and the people-directed dimensions are inseparable and intertwined. They ultimately find their explanation in the blood-life symbolism. In the burnt offering and sacrifice meal the blood as life is God's share in the meal. This sharing in the meal also brings about or symbolizes atonement. In the guilt and sin offerings the altar is smeared with blood and thus the life-power, lost by association with sin, is restored. Ritual purification and consecration ceremonies used blood to restore life, for instance, to a leper, and to enhance the life of priests and their vestments. The purpose common to the rites was to change the status of the affected persons and confer on them a new life whether it was to exercise priestly functions or to return the leper, who was reckoned dead (see Nm. 12:10–13), back to life. Purification rites also restored vitality thought to have been lost in sexual intercourse and giving birth. The sprinkling of blood on the

---

24. See Deut. 12:23; Gen. 9:4–5; Lv. 17:11, 14. See S. David Sperling, "Blood," in ABD 1: 761–62. See also Donald Potts, "Blood," in *Eerdmans Dictionary of the Bible* (Grand Rapids, Mich.: Eerdmans, 2000), 193; G. Gerleman, "Blood," in Ernst Jenni and Claus Westermann, eds., *Theological Lexicon of the Old Testament,* trans. Mark Biddle (Peabody, Mass.: Hendrickson Publishers, 1999), 337–39; John Alsup, "Blood," in Paul J. Achtemeier, et al., eds., *The HarperCollins Bible Dictionary,* 2nd ed. (New York: HarperCollins, 1996), 148–49.

25. Sarna, *Exodus,* 55, and *Exploring Exodus,* 93, points out that blood was a natural coloring agent but it also became a visible sign of lifesaving identity for the Israelites. See also Propp, *Exodus 1–18,* 282; Sperling, "Blood," 761; Alsup, 148; Potts, "Blood," 193; Gerleman, 338.

altar and on the people to seal a covenant (Ex. 24:5–8) represented a new blood relationship with God and with one another.[26]

The blood of the original Passover rite could have had a number of meanings. It was a symbol of protection from death. Exactly how this worked or the significance prior to the "Egyptian Passover" is unclear. Was it originally an exchange for the firstborn, or an appeasing of a bloodthirsty demon, or a strengthening of house gods? It certainly seems to have been a sign of a special relationship with God. The Egyptians were struck down but not the Israelites. This protection became a symbol of Israel's selection as God's people and their deliverance from slavery. In short, it was a sign of the covenant with Yahweh.[27]

The use of hyssop to sprinkle the blood (Ex. 12:22), often seen in the Old Testament in conjunction with purification and remission of sin, seems to indicate that the blood was also a means of atonement. The other side of the coin of atonement, blood as a gift for God, God's share, implies that the blood was also an offering to God. In sum, the Passover blood, like any good symbol, had many facets. It was at one and the same time: sign of the covenant, sign of atonement (purification and remission of sin), sign of protection, an offering to God, a memorial, and a means of redemption.[28]

Christianity made abundant use of the blood symbolism. Early Christian writers spoke of the anointing in initiation as a seal and a pledge of God's protection as in Exodus 12:22. 1 Peter 1:19 and Revelation 5:9 speak of the blood of the Paschal lamb as the price of our redemption. Revelation 7:14 talks of Christians washing in the Blood of Christ. The reference to hyssop in John 19:29 seems to be an allusion to the Passover lamb in Exodus 12:22. Blood and water flow from Jesus' side in John 19:34 in a context alluding to the Paschal lamb. Without attempting an exhaustive listing of early Christian examples, we include as a final example these familiar words from Matthew's description of the Last Supper: "Then he took a cup, gave

---

26. Sperling, "Blood," 762. See also Potts, "Blood," 193; Alsup, "Blood," 148; Gerleman, "Blood," 338.

27. Sperling, "Blood," 762. See also Gerleman, "Blood," 338; Alsup, "Blood," 148; Potts, "Blood," 193.

28. Sperling, "Blood," 762. See also Gerleman, "Blood," 338; Alsup, "Blood," 148; and Potts, "Blood," 193.

thanks, and gave it to them. 'All of you must drink from it,' he said, 'for this is my blood, the blood poured out on behalf of many for the forgiveness of sins'" (Matt. 26:27–28). [29]

Bread

Bread in the Bible is another many-faceted symbol. The term "bread" often was used to describe food in general. "To eat bread" meant to have a meal (Mark 3:20). Bread and water made up the whole meal of prisoners and the poor and were considered the basics needed to subsist. The Israelites knew that good land, fertility, rain and hard work were necessary for grain to grow. But they also knew that these essentials were out of their control and therefore they needed God's blessing (see Ps. 127:1–2). The feeding of the Israelites through manna in the desert was a reminder of God's sovereignty and human dependence showing "that not by bread alone does man live, but by every word that comes from the mouth of the Lord" (Deut. 8:3). [30] Gifts of food were offered to God with the hope that God would in turn provide food for God's people. And of course "bread" was used metaphorically to describe spiritual nourishment. [31]

The unleavened bread of the Passover meal is another symbol pregnant with meaning. [32] As noted above, Lawrence Hoffman, a Jewish scholar, makes a convincing case for arguing that by the first century *matsah* had acquired a symbolic value that went far beyond that accorded it in the biblical narrative. "From a historical recollection of the Exodus of the past, it had been transmuted into a symbol

29. See Potts, "Blood," 193; Alsup, "Blood," 148–49.

30. See Jenks, "Eating and Drinking in the Old Testament," 252.

31. See Stephen Reed, "Bread," in ABD 1:779.

32. The Gospels do not indicate that Jesus used unleavened bread but, as Klawans, "Was Jesus' Last Supper a Seder?" 30, notes, Jews often refer to unleavened bread simply as "bread." Our reflections are not limited to unleavened bread but it is obviously very important in a Passover setting. See Propp, *Exodus 1–18*, 433–34, who comments: "I believe that ancient Israelites held comparable [to post-biblical literature] beliefs that purging leaven symbolized moral and ritual purification and regeneration. . . . To purge it [leaven] is to make a fresh start, to experience catharsis." See also Sarna, *Exploring Exodus*, 58, 90–91, and Bokser, *The Passover Rite*, 757, on different interpretations.

of salvation for the future."[33] In fact, he contends that even before the destruction of the Temple in 70 AD the bread had taken on a value comparable to the lamb in the Passover rite. *"Matsah* as a surrogate for the *pesach* recalled the past and pointed to the future."[34] Without belaboring the point, it would be good, therefore, to reflect on the biblical use of bread as a symbol.

In John Cheever's *Falconer*, a harsh novel about prison life, Tiny, one of the inmates, reflects on his apparently wasted life. He muses that the meaning of life can be summed up in a single word, food. He reflects that food "had something to do with his beginnings as a Christian and as a man."[35] The beginning of the Bible bears out Tiny's insight. The beginning of Genesis tells a story about food and life and death. The teller of the tale ponders suffering in this world and gives his resultant theology in story form. The story involves a command. You can eat the food from any of the trees in the garden but not the one in the middle lest you die. There is a punishment: getting bread to eat "by the sweat of your face," and being barred from the tree of life. But the story does not finish there. At the end of the account of primitive history, God promises to make Abram's offspring a great nation and to bless all nations through that offspring (Gen. 12:1–2).

At first glance the story seems to speak only of banishment and estrangement. But like most good stories and symbols, it is richly ambiguous. It speaks of punishment and promise, of banishment and longing for union. And bread often appears when Israel's relationship with the "God of the garden" is about to enter a critical new stage. The crisis is not one of unrelieved calamity but of hopeful change as well.

In the Exodus story the "bread of affliction" (Deut. 16:3) becomes the bread of freedom. And when the people complain in the desert about not having their fill of bread as they had in Egypt, God responds: "I will rain down bread from heaven on you" (Ex. 16:4). Bread becomes then a symbol not of the people's affliction but of God's faithfulness and unrelenting hunger to nourish humanity.

---

33. Hoffman, "A Symbol of Salvation in the Passover Seder," 112.

34. Ibid., 125 (also 112, 117, 123).

35. Nathan Mitchell, "Bread of Crisis, Bread of Justice," *Living Worship* 15/3 (March 1979):1. Much of what follows in this section draws on this article. On the centrality of bread see also John Macquarrie, *A Guide to the Sacraments* (New York: Continuum, 1999), 19–20.

Bread is a classic metaphor for God's faithfulness, even in the face of complaining.

In the Davidic dynasty, when David wisely centralizes both government and worship, bread is placed alongside the ark as a symbol of God's presence among the Israelites. "Then David, girt with a linen apron, came dancing before the Lord with abandon, as he and all the house of Israel were bringing up the ark of the Lord with shouts of joy and the sound of the horn. . . . He then distributed among all the people, to each man and each woman in the entire multitude of Israel, a loaf of bread, a cut of roast meat, and a raisin cake. With this, all the people left for their homes" (2 Sm. 6:14–15, 19). Also the Jewish practice of offering thanks before a meal often involved taking a loaf of bread, giving thanks, and distributing it (Matt. 14:19).[36]

When Jesus, whom John's Gospel portrays as "bread from heaven," appears on the scene, a new crisis, a radical new moment of decision and opportunity manifests itself. It too involves eating and drinking. Jesus often proclaims the reign of God by the way he "welcomes sinners and even eats with them!"[37] Breaking bread, in addition to being a symbol of crisis and change becomes a symbol of forgiveness, which heralds the coming of the kingdom.[38] The parable in deed becomes the parable in word, for instance, in the story of the "prodigal father" who invites both sons to the feast. It is also no coincidence that appearances of Jesus to his disciples often take place in the context of a meal. These meals had come to symbolize new, risen life and the promised future glory.

As Paul was later to remind the Christians in Corinth, bread can also be a symbol of justice—given or denied. Just as the Passover meal was for the whole community of Israel, so too was the Christian Eucharist. Breaking bread and sharing the same loaf was incompatible with neglect of the needy and discrimination against the poor (see 1 Cor. 10 and 11). In urging the Corinthians to see the ethical implications of their eucharistic celebrations Paul exhorts them to become "unleavened bread" themselves: "Get rid of the old yeast to make of

---

36. See Robert A. Stein, "Bread," in *The HarperCollins Bible Dictionary*, 154; Stephen A. Reed, "Bread"; and Thomas B. Dozeman, "Bread of Presence," in *Eerdmans Dictionary of the Bible*, 199.

37. See Joncas, "Tasting the Kingdom of God," 347–50.

38. See Lk. 14:12–24, especially 14:15.

yourselves fresh dough, unleavened loaves, as it were; Christ our Passover has been sacrificed. Let us celebrate the feast not with the old yeast, that of corruption and wickedness, but with the unleavened bread of sincerity and truth" (1 Cor. 5:7–8).

Given the richness of bread as a symbol, it is no wonder that it became such a powerful force in both Jewish and Christian ritual. As Hoffman, speaking of the first century seder with a strong emphasis on the bread, puts it: "the choice of *matsah* rather than some other item on the seder plate was not a haphazard event. It followed from the fact that bread was already a salvational symbol in the common imagination. The use of bread as a symbol in both the Lord's Supper and in the early seder should be seen as two sides of the same coin. Jesus spoke directly to the Jewish context of his listeners. What else could symbolize the body of the new Lamb if not bread?"[39]

Passover as Memorial

Another of the key traits of the ancient Passover celebration is its character as a memorial. Much discussion and debate have revolved around the meaning of this term. We will discuss this notion in more detail in a later chapter. For now we shall simply offer some reflections on this concept in a Jewish setting.

There are a number of possible understandings of remembering, memory, and memorial in ancient times. One is to view memory as a purely intellectual act, if there is such a thing. For instance, Jerusalem recalls, in her affliction, the days of old: "Jerusalem is mindful of the days of her wretched homelessness, when her people fell into enemy hands" (Lam. 1:7), or "Remember not the events of the past, the things of long ago consider not" (Is. 43:18). Tobit remembers Amos' prophecy and weeps. "I was reminded of the oracle pronounced by the prophet Amos against Bethel: 'Your festivals shall be turned into mourning, and all your songs into lamentation'" (Tb. 2:6–7).

---

39. Hoffman, "A Symbol of Salvation in the Passover Seder," 123. He notes that eventually other symbols were emphasized in place of the *matsah* and it lost its pride of place in the celebration of the seder. But it had set the salvation tone for generations. For another angle on the importance of bread, see Andrew B. McGowan, *Ascetic Eucharists: Food and Drink in Early Christian Ritual Meals* (New York: Oxford University Press, 1999), 63: "Despite the use of cereals in some ritual, bread was arguably the prosaic opposite of sacrificial meat: common rather than prized, bloodless not bloody, vegetable not animal, if not raw at least cold."

Another form of remembering is an incentive to behavior. It is intellectual but also motivational. For instance, Israel is to recall God's curses and blessings through Moses and obey: "When all these things which I have set before you, the blessings and the curses, are fulfilled in you, and . . . you ponder them in your heart: then, provided that you and your children return to the Lord, your God, and heed his voice with all your heart and all your soul, just as I now command you, the Lord, your God, will change your lot" (Deut. 30:1–3). Similarly, remembering God's wonders can lead to praise (Ps. 104, 105).

Remembering can also refer to behavior itself. For God, remembering is doing, for instance, punishing. For people, recalling can mean to fear, to pray, to keep the law. Certainly in the admonition "Remember the Sabbath," remembering is not merely an intellectual act, but a matter of observing the law. "Remember your word to your servant since you have given me hope. My comfort in my affliction is that your promise gives me life. . . . I remember your ordinances of old, O Lord, and I am comforted. . . . By night I remember your name, O Lord, and I will keep your law" (Ps. 119:49–55). The psalmist praises God for giving such wonderful ordinances and takes comfort that he has kept them. The Qumran community boasted that the memory of the covenant was always among them.

Remembering could also mean somehow bringing to the present the effects of a past event. The stress here is on the consequences of something already done but realized in a new situation. This presumes the action of God and includes the past deeds of men and women, for instance, their sins or good deeds and the past deeds of God. These would include the covenant and the promises.

Memory could also signify existence. The righteous will be remembered forever. The memory of the wicked shall be erased (by God).

Who was doing the remembering? Certainly Israel was. The people were to remember the saving events not as something distant from them. "Hear, O Israel, the statutes and decrees which I proclaim in your hearing this day, that you may learn them and take care to observe them. The Lord, our God, made a covenant with us at Horeb; not with our fathers did he make this covenant, but with us, all of us who are alive here this day" (Deut. 5:1–3).

Does God remember? A quick look at a biblical concordance, not to mention ancient Jewish prayers, reveals numerous instances where God is the subject of remembering. "God heard their groaning and remembered his covenant with Abraham, Isaac and Jacob" (Ex. 2:24). "And now that I have heard the groaning of the Israelites, whom the Egyptians are treating as slaves, I am mindful of my covenant" (Ex. 6:5).

Hoffman indicates the questions that often arise in this context. What does God remember and why? How can God who is eternal remember at all? His study focuses on postbiblical prayers that, however, reflect the biblical tradition of a God who remembers. He draws his evidence from the ninth-century Seder Rav Amram, the first extant Jewish prayer book that has influenced Jewish liturgy all over the world.[40]

Hoffman concludes his tightly reasoned analysis by contending, among other things, that the word "remember" would be better translated as "to point out" and "that God's 'memory' is actually God's attention being drawn by a variety of pointers, some of them liturgical. . . . Liturgy as memorial is largely an effort to plead for God's attention to be focused on things that save."[41]

In any event, there is widespread agreement that remembering is a mutual reality that involves both God and worshipers. Geoffrey Wainwright responds to those who are uncomfortable with such anthropomorphism: "If it be objected that the notion of God needing to be reminded is too naively anthropomorphic, we can only plead, first, that the Old Testament presents the cult and its memorials as an institution ordained by *God* and, second, that by token of the objection every kind of thanksgiving and intercession would go by the board as well."[42]

Another facet of the ancient Jewish concept of memorial is the sense that somehow the saving mystery is present to later generations or they are to it. The Israelite faith has its roots in a historical

---

40. Lawrence Hoffman, "Does God Remember?" in Michael Signer, ed., *Memory and History in Christianity and Judaism* (Notre Dame, Ind.: University of Notre Dame Press 2001), 41.

41. Ibid., 41–42.

42. Geoffrey Wainwright, *Eucharist and Eschatology* (London: Epworth Press, 1971), 66, as cited by Paul Bradshaw, "Anamnesis in Modern Debate," in *Memory and History in Christianity and Judaism,* 76.

event that is ongoing. There is not simply an identification with a past event. Each generation experiences this once-and-for-all but dynamic event anew in its own setting. "The biblical events have the dynamic characteristic of refusing to be relegated to the past. . . . This reality did not remain static but emerged with new form and content because it identified itself with the changing historical situations of later history."[43] For instance, in recalling the Exodus, the Israelites experienced it, not in the sense that they crossed the Red Sea again but in the sense that they entered the same life-giving reality.

I once invited a rabbi to give a presentation on the meaning of the Passover to modern Jewish people. I was disappointed when he made no mention of the event being somehow present in the celebration. Instead he emphasized that the ritual reminded modern Jews that wherever there is oppression they must oppose it. A few days later, a nationally known rabbi spoke on television on the meaning of the Passover Seder and stressed the experiencing of the ancient event as somehow being present. I was pleased. Only later did I realize that both were right. The Passover is an opportunity and a challenge to involve oneself personally in the saving mystery within one's own historical context. And this will involve sensitivity and opposition to oppression in all its forms. Elie Wiesel, as usual, puts it so well:

> When I was a child, I read these Biblical tales with a wonder mixed with anguish. I imagined Isaac on the altar and I cried. I saw Joseph, prince of Egypt, and I laughed. Why dwell on them again? And why now? It falls to the storyteller to explain. . . . For Jewish history unfolds in the present. . . . Judaism, more than any other tradition, manifests great attachment to its past, jealously keeping it alive. Why? Because we need to. . . . If we have the strength and the will to speak out, it is because every one of our forebears expresses himself through us; if the eyes of the world often seem to be upon us, it is because we evoke a time gone by and a fate that transcends time.[44]

---

43. Brevard Childs, *Memory and Tradition in Israel* (London: SCM Press, 1962), 88.

44. Elie Wiesel, *Messengers of God: Biblical Portraits and Legends* (New York: Random House, 1976), xi–xii.

Passover as Memorial in Word and Symbol

In her study of Greco-Roman meal customs during the first century BC and the first century AD, Blake Leyerle notes that there were two components of the banquet: the supper (*deipnon*) that was primarily the food event, and the symposium or drinking event. The emperor Tiberius (14–37 AD) made the division less sharp by introducing an aperitif of wine.[45]

Once the "impediment" of eating was over, the conversation (philosophical speculation, poetry, mythical stories) could really be enjoyed. Many of the stories were about the gods, so there was no fine distinction between entertainment and liturgy. The primary purpose of eating together was not merely supplying bodily needs but friendship and mutual edification. These gatherings thus had an educational role. They were as much about conversation, teaching, and initiation into the group as they were about drinking and entertainment.[46]

Hoffman sees the first century seder as a form of symposium. This was a banquet leading to "a communion of serious and mirthful entertainment, discourse and actions," in Plutarch's words. The topic of the rabbinic symposium or seder was the Exodus.[47] Hoffman sees the seder as "sacred theatre." The stage was the table and the special foods. The drama began with a rhetorical question or questions that would lead to a free-flowing description of the Exodus. The evening ended with celebrative praise in the form of Hallel psalms. Psalms 113 and 114 seem to have been staples "in the beginning years" (first century AD) but others (115–118) were probably also used.[48]

Sometime in the second century, for reasons unknown, the original order of food, questions, answer, and praise was changed to questions, answer, *hallel* (praise), and only then the food. Without the meal to prompt them, the questions, which were originally quite flexible, became more standardized or stock questions.[49] As we now have

---

45. Leyerle, "Meal Customs in the Greco-Roman World," 36.

46. Ibid., 37–39.

47. Hoffman, "The Passover Meal," 9. See Bokser, *The Passover Rite*, xi, on the relationship between seder and symposium.

48. Hoffman, "The Passover Meal," 13.

49. Ibid., 14.

it, with the meal at the end, the seder looks less like the rabbinic symposium than it originally did. Thus the origin of the seder as a symposium was lost sight of.[50] And the flexibility and spontaneity of the earlier questions and answers settled into much greater fixity.[51]

In any case, the questions could lead to a proclamation or instruction something like this: "My father was a wandering Aramean who went down to Egypt with a small household and lived there as an alien. But there he became a nation great, strong and numerous. When the Egyptians maltreated and oppressed us, imposing hard labor upon us, we cried to the Lord, the God of our fathers, and he heard our cry and saw our affliction, our toil and our oppression. He brought us out of Egypt with his strong hand and outstretched arm, with terrifying power, with signs and wonders; and bringing us into this country, he gave us this land flowing with milk and honey. Therefore, I have now brought you the first fruits of the products of the soil which you, O Lord, have given me. And having set them before the Lord, your God, you shall bow down in his presence. Then you and your family, together with the Levite and the aliens who live among you, shall make merry over all these good things which the Lord, your God, has given you" (Deut. 26:5–11).

The response to the proclamation takes the form of praise and thanks, such as "Praise, you servants of the Lord, praise the name of the Lord. Blessed be the name of the Lord both now and forever" (Ps. 113). Implicit or explicit, there would be a note of petition to God to continue and/or renew God's intervention on Israel's behalf.

The memorial would be in action as well as word and the meal would embody the memorial's three-dimensional character of past, present, and future. The Passover meal recalled the first Exodus and, as we have seen above, other key events in Israel's saving history. Jenks reminds us of the richness of the Passover celebration. "The Passover meal is at the same time an offering or sacrifice of food to God (Ex. 12:2–7); a celebration of God's deliverance of his people from Egyptian bondage (Ex. 12:27, 40–42); a harvest festival celebrating the first fruits of the grain harvest (Lv. 23:1–4), and indeed a celebration of the whole gift of the land of Canaan to Israel (Deut. 16:9–10;

---

50. Ibid., 9.
51. Ibid., 15.

Ex. 13:3–10); the meal also served to confirm familial and community solidarity not only with contemporaries, but with every future generation (Ex. 12:43–49;13:8–10). Participation in the meal was tantamount to participation in the great Exodus event of redemption, for the Passover supper takes on a nearly sacramental significance."[52] "The memorial meal is a way of eating history, of appropriating history to put it at the service of the present."[53]

It was also a challenge to work toward freedom from oppression in all its forms.[54] Elie Wiesel puts it this way:

> If Isaac's averted sacrifice had involved only Abraham and his son, their ordeal would have been limited to their own suffering. But it involves us. All the legends, all the stories . . . involve us. . . . We have but to reread them to realize that they are surprisingly topical. Job is our contemporary.
>
> Somewhere a father and his son are heading toward an altar in flames; somewhere a dreamy boy knows that his father will die under the veiled gaze of God. Somewhere a teller of tales remembers, and overcome by an ancient and nameless sadness, he feels like weeping. He has seen Abraham and he has seen Isaac walk toward death; the angel, busy singing the Almighty's praises, did not come to wrest them from the hushed black night.
>
> In Jewish history, all events are linked. Only today, after the whirlwind of fire and blood that was the Holocaust, do we grasp the full range of implications of the murder of one man by his brother, the deeper meanings of a father's questions and disconcerting silences. Only as we tell them now, in the light of certain experiences of life and death, do we understand them.
>
> And so, faithful to his promise the storyteller does nothing but tell the tale: he transmits what he received, he returns what was entrusted to him. His story does not begin with his own; it is fitted into the memory that is the living tradition of his people. The legends he brings back are the very ones we are living today.[55]

And this kind of memorial, this kind of past and present, longs for, works toward and expects the final, messianic fulfillment yet to come.

---

52. Jenks, "Eating and Drinking in the Old Testament," 254.

53. Phillippe Rouillard, "From Human Meal to Christian Eucharist," in R. Kevin Seasoltz, ed., *Living Bread, Saving Cup: Readings on the Eucharist* (Collegeville, Minn.: Liturgical Press, 1987), 140.

54. See Hoffman, "The Passover Meal," 112, n.10, which cites one author speaking in terms of physical bondage and another author speaking of "the food of inner spiritual liberation" (from bondage of the heart?).

55. Wiesel, *Messengers of God*, xiii–xiv.

Chapter 4

Eucharist: Celebration of Service

In his serious book with a playful title, *A Banqueter's Guide to the All-Night Soup Kitchen of the Kingdom of God*, Patrick McCormick recounts how he grew up without hearing much about the moral obligations of eating and drinking in our Eucharist. "I cannot remember a single childhood sermon making a connection between the bread on our altars and the hunger in the bellies of the poor. . . . We often went home with the ethical implications of the Bread of Life undigested in our hearts."[1] McCormick goes on to say that recent studies have reminded us of such a connection.[2] This is no doubt true, but there remains a lingering concern that a good number of Christians still see their Sunday Eucharist as a religious event totally insulated from their daily life.

The purpose of this chapter is twofold: first, to show the link between Eucharist and service by analyzing the Suffering Servant songs of Isaiah and the New Testament use of this image in regard to Jesus; second, to indicate that the nature of prophetic symbols, the self-understanding of the early Christians, a number of Pauline texts, New Testament cultic and priestly terminology, and the Gospel of John all witness to the tight bond between Eucharist and a call to serve.

The service implication of Eucharist is cryptically expressed in Mark's Gospel. "He likewise took a cup, gave thanks and passed it to them and they all drank from it. He said to them: 'This is my blood, the blood of the covenant, to be poured out on behalf of many'"

---

1. Patrick T. McCormick, *A Banqueter's Guide to the All-Night Soup Kitchen of the Kingdom of God* (Collegeville, Minn.: Liturgical Press, 2004), 3.

2. Ibid., 4 and 34, n. 2.

(Mk. 14:23). "The Son of Man has not come to be served but to serve—to give his life in ransom for many" (Mk. 10:45).

These passages from Mark's Gospel, especially the term "many," have led some scholars to link Jesus in the Last Supper account with the servant theme of Second Isaiah. "Through his suffering, my servant shall justify many, and their guilt he will bear. . . . And he shall take away the sins of many, and win pardon for their offenses" (Is. 53:11b, 12b).

OLD TESTAMENT BACKGROUND

Isaiah portrays a figure that "gives his life as an offering for sin . . . and the will of the Lord shall be accomplished through him" (Is. 53:10). This figure is true to the covenant with Yahweh and embodies it for those who also want to be true to the covenant by joining themselves to that servant.[3]

The whole passage from Isaiah 52:13–53:12 (one of the so-called Songs of the Suffering Servant) provides important background and possible insight into our Eucharist. Verses 4 and 5 link "our sins" with the servant's suffering. "Yet it was our infirmities that he bore, our sufferings that he endured, while we thought of him as stricken, as one smitten by God and afflicted, but he was pierced for our offenses, crushed for our sins." The relatively rare notion of representative suffering is explicit here even though nothing is said about how this takes place. We cannot, therefore, presume that this represents some kind of substitution in the face of an angry God. Rather the emphasis seems to be more on the personal, human relationship with God. The servant's willingness to do God's will brings with it suffering. But, in tones reminiscent of thanksgiving psalms, it will also lead to justifying many, leading them to new life with Yahweh.[4]

---

3. See Richard J. Clifford, *Fair Spoken and Persuading* (New York: Paulist Press, 1984), 152–53, and "Isaiah, Book of (Second Isaiah)," in *The Anchor Bible Dictionary* 3, 6 vols., ed. David Noel Freedman, et al., eds. (henceforth ABD) (New York: Doubleday, 1992), 500. See also Wilhelm Breuning, "Die Eucharistie in Dogma und Kerygma," *Trierer Theologische Zeitschrift* 3 (May/June 1965): 133–35, and C. R. North, "The Servant of the Lord," in *The Interpreter's Dictionary of the Bible* (Nashville: Abingdon 1962), 292.

4. See Clifford, *Fair Spoken and Persuading,* 178–81, and "Book of Isaiah," 500. See also Breuning, "Die Eucharistie," 133–34, and North, "The Servant," 292–93.

Within the context of the other Servant Songs (Is. 42:1–7; 49:1–9; 50:4–9) and the theology of Second Isaiah, we may draw some conclusions: (1) the servant continues the covenant and ultimately in his willingness to suffer personally renews the covenant; (2) in this servant, who reveals the true meaning of the darkness of the exile and provides the opportunity for the covenant coming to life (for all those who join him), is concentrated the remnant of God's people; (3) from this broader context, it seems clear that the significance of the suffering, prophetic martyr lies in his relationship to God, to the covenant, and to the "many."[5]

It is not then a question of three separate relationships. Rather in giving himself to God in loving obedience in the face of suffering and death itself the servant preserves the deepest content of the covenant. He does so, moreover, not just for himself, but for the "many." His suffering involves the highest level of human activity and makes him not just a substitute or a payment to an angry God for others. It makes him a personal focal point, a reconciler, who provides a turning point in people's dealings with God. "Here is my servant whom I uphold, my chosen one with whom I am pleased, upon whom I have put my spirit, he shall bring forth justice to the nations. . . . I formed you, and *set you as a covenant* of the people, a light for the nations, to open the eyes of the blind, to bring out prisoners from confinement, and from the dungeon, those who live in darkness" (Is. 42:1, 6-7, emphasis mine).[6]

IDENTITY OF THE SERVANT

Who is the servant described in the Servant Songs? Scholars have "spilled much ink" on this question.[7] The Servant Songs may reflect an individual like Moses or Jeremiah or Second Isaiah himself. But they seem to be speaking of more than these—a figure that is at

---

5. See Clifford, *Fair Spoken and Persuading*, 143–45, 150–52, 160–63, and "Book of Isaiah," 500. See also North, "The Servant of the Lord," 293–94.

6. See Clifford, *Fair Spoken and Persuading*, 152–53, and "Book of Isaiah," 500. See also Breuning, "Die Eucharistie in Dogma und Kerygma," 133–34.

7. For an overview see Colin Kruse, "The Servant Songs: Interpretive Trends Since C. R. North," *Studia Biblica et Theologica* 8 (1978): 3–27.

once kingly, priestly, but above all prophetic. Or could it be Israel after the exile?[8]

Another possibility would lie in the notion of corporate personality in ancient Israel.[9] According to H. Wheeler Robinson, there are a number of key traits involved in this concept.

TRAITS OF A "CORPORATE PERSONALITY"

First, there is a sense of unity with the past and the future. For the Israelites, their ancestors lived on in them and they will live on in their offspring. This explains, at least partly, the desire to be buried with their ancestors and the importance of having male offspring to continue the family name. "The people are their ancestors, as the patriarchal narratives often illustrate. The conception of history as a unity derives in the last resort through Christianity from the Hebrew prophets and apocalyptists, and they are working with the unity of corporate personality."[10] We may speak of characteristics living on in nations. They speak of persons themselves living on in the nation. We might approximate their outlook sometimes in our desire for the family name to continue.

As Xavier Léon-Dufour puts it: "we must keep in mind the principle of biblical anthropology: human beings are not first and foremost individuals, but members of a people in and through which they exist; they in turn contain in their loins all their descendants. This is what is meant by the expression 'corporate personality.'"[11]

Secondly, the notion of corporate personality entails a great realism. For the Israelites, when one speaks of the nation, tribe or family as a body it is not simply a metaphor. The same "breath" or "soul" really does animate the many members. The Semitic mind also believed in a common consciousness. The unchaste woman in Ezekiel

---

8. Clifford, "Book of Isaiah," 499, notes that almost every important figure in the Bible has been identified as the servant.

9. H. Wheeler Robinson, *Corporate Personality in Ancient Israel* (Philadelphia: Fortress Press, 1964), 1–3. See also Clifford, "Book of Isaiah," 499.

10. See Robinson, *Corporate Personality in Ancient Israel,* 3–5

11. Xavier Léon-Dufour, *Sharing the Eucharistic Bread: The Witness of the New Testament,* trans. M. J. O'Connell (New York: Paulist Press, 1987), 108, referring (343, n. 16) to J. De Fraine, *Adam and the Family of Man,* trans. D. Raible (New York: Alba House, 1965).

16 and 23 and the barren woman in Isaiah 54 really do embody Israel. Gomer's relationship to Hosea is not just a dramatic image. Gomer in both her sin and her anticipated repentance *is* Israel. Similarly, Rachel in Jeremiah 15 weeps because she has died in her children.[12]

Later on, the Maccabean martyrs in their suffering identify themselves with the suffering nation.[13] This notion of a corporate personality "is so realistically conceived that it can be concentrated into a single representative figure. If we ask on what this unity is based, the answer, for the Semites at least, is doubtless that of the common blood tie, whether real or fictitious (as by a blood covenant or some form of adoption), rather than of the cult of a common ancestor—though this itself also expresses the unity."[14]

According to Robinson, Plato's *Republic* reflects this kind of realistic approach to the solidarity between the individual and the state.[15] Paul also makes use of such realism when he describes the indwelling of Christ in the faithful and the Church as the "body of Christ."[16]

Hand in hand with the realism of corporate personality goes a third characteristic, fluidity. For the ancient Israelites it was possible to shift or fluctuate readily from the image of the individual to the society as a whole and vice versa. What Lévy-Bruhl calls the "law of participation" in which, for "primitive" thought, people or things could at the same time be themselves and other than themselves. This "quasi-mystical" identification enabled "the primitive mind to think at the same time of the individual in the collective and the collective in the individual."[17] The sharp antithesis between the individual and the collective was absent for such a mentality. St. Paul provides us with a

---

12. Robinson, *Corporate Personality in Ancient Israel*, 5–6, 12. See also Clifford, *Fair Spoken and Persuading*, 153.

13. Ibid., 12.

14. Ibid., 5–6.

15. Ibid., 6, citing *Republic*, ii. 369, and iv. 435.

16. Ibid., 12. See also Alfred Wikenhauser, Pauline *Mysticism: Christ in the Mystical Teaching of St. Paul*, trans. Joseph Cunningham (New York: Herder, 1960), 72–73, 98.

17. Robinson, *Corporate Personality in Ancient Israel*, 7, citing Lévy–Bruhl, *Les Fonctions Mentales dans les Sociétés Inférieures (1910)*, 100. See also Mircea Eliade, *Images and Symbols: Studies in Religious Symbolism* (Mission, Kans.: Sheed, Andrews & McMeel, 1961), 14, 177–78, and John H. McKenna, "Symbol and Reality: Some Anthropological Considerations," *Worship* 65 (January 1991): 18–24, on the multivalent nature of symbols.

striking example of this kind of thinking: "For just as in Adam all die, so too in Christ shall all be brought to life."[18]

The ability to switch back and forth from the individual to the collectivity and vice versa is not limited to ancient times. We do it in our own way whether it is in regard to a key religious or political figure like a pope or president or hostages or sports figures or heroic people. For instance, when Roman Catholics flock to a stadium to see a visiting pope, it is because they see more than an individual. He embodies the Church as a whole. If some of our military personnel commit massacres or behave abusively, we often feel embarrassment or even shame, as a nation. This trait seems to be part of human nature.

However, in the ancient world it seemed easier to blend the collective with the individual and to move readily from one to the other.[19] In any event, Robinson concludes his preceding remarks on corporate personality with: "In the light of this conception the Servant can be both the prophet himself as a representative of the nation, and the nation whose proper mission is actually being fulfilled only by the prophet and that group of followers who may share his views."[20] Others would agree with the notion of corporate personality applied to the Servant songs but see it pointing to a future fulfillment.[21]

One final note on the notion of corporate personality is necessary. While the destiny of the individual is tied to that of the clan or nation, the society does not swallow up individual responsibility. The prophets Jeremiah and Ezekiel are clear on that. "In those days they shall no longer say, 'The fathers ate unripe grapes and the children's teeth are set on edge,' but through his own fault only shall anyone die: the teeth of him who eats the unripe grapes shall be set on edge."[22] "Only the one who sins shall die. The son shall not be

---

18. 1 Cor. 15:22.

19. Robinson, *Corporate Personality in Ancient Israel*, 8.

20. Ibid., 15; Clifford, *Fair Spoken and Persuading*, 153: "The servant may be an individual but all of Israel is called to obey the word through him"; and "Book of Isaiah," 499: "All Israel becomes a servant when it embraces the divine will and plan as shown by individual servants.... The servant in Second Isaiah is therefore at once a chosen individual and what all Israel is called to be and do."

21. See H. H. Rowley, *The Servant of the Lord and Other Essays on the Old Testament*, 2nd ed. (Oxford: Blackwell, 1965), 53–56, and Kruse, "The Servant Songs," 6–7, 24–25.

22. Jer. 31:29–30, and Ez. 18. See also Robinson, *Corporate Personality in Ancient Israel*, 8–10, 28–31.

charged with the guilt of his father, nor shall the father be charged with the guilt of his son. The virtuous man's virtue shall be his own, as the wicked man's wickedness shall be his."[23] "The individualizing development takes place within the matrix of a social relation to God. On the other hand, it is equally wrong to emphasize the social relation in the earlier period to the point of neglecting the fact of individual religion and morality."[24]

In addition to the examples of "corporate personalities" mentioned above, Abraham, Isaac, and Jacob came to personify contemporary Israelites as did some of the "I" psalms, for instance, Psalm 22. Elie Wiesel says it well:

> Judaism more than any other tradition, manifests great attachment to its past, jealously keeping it alive. Why? Because we need to. Thanks to Abraham whose gaze is our guide, thanks to Jacob whose dream has us spellbound, our survival, prodigious on so many levels, lacks neither mystery nor significance. If we have the strength and the will to speak out, it is because every one of our forebears expresses himself through us; if the eyes of the world often seem to be upon us, it is because we evoke a time gone by and a fate that transcends time.[25]

NEW TESTAMENT BASIS

This being said, is there any basis in the New Testament, apart from the Marcan institution narrative cited above, indicating that Christians interpreted Jesus in terms of the Servant of Isaiah?

To begin with, it is clear that the New Testament in general and the Passion Narratives in particular made use of Old Testament texts, for instance Psalm 22, to interpret the meaning of Jesus and his suffering. The Suffering Servant Songs were also used in this vein in a number of New Testament passages and, to some extent, in the Passion Narratives.[26]

---

23. Ez. 18:20. See also Robinson, *Corporate Personality in Ancient Israel*, 8–10, 28–31.

24. Robinson, *Corporate Personality in Ancient Israel*, 9.

25. Elie Wiesel, *Messengers of God: Biblical Portraits and Legends* (New York: Random, 1976), xii.

26. See Raymond Brown, *The Death of the Messiah: A Commentary on the Passion Narratives in the Four Gospels* (New York: Doubleday, 1994), 2: 1445–67, esp. 1448–51. See also John P. Galvin, "Jesus Christ," in *Systematic Theology I: Roman Catholic Perspectives*, ed. Francis Schüssler Fiorenza and John P. Galvin (Minneapolis: Fortress Press, 1991), 292–97.

Another possible indication that the first Christians saw Jesus in the light of the Suffering Servant is the repeated New Testament use of the phrase *hyper hemon* ("for us"). The Lucan and Pauline versions of the institution narrative speak of Jesus' body "given for you" and his blood "shed for you."[27] Other texts use the phrase "he died for us" (1 Thess. 5:10 and Rom. 5:8) or "he died for all . . . who for their sake died and was raised" (2 Cor. 5:15) or "Christ died for our sins" (1 Cor. 15:3). The references are many-faceted but underlying them all is a sense that Jesus, in giving himself for us in obedience to *Abba*'s will, becomes personally the embodiment of God's saving presence, of God's concern for all people. Jesus *is* the covenant.[28]

A number of modern scholars link Jesus with the servant theme.

[N. T.] Wright does not doubt that Jesus was conscious of a messianic role, shaped by his pondering these passages [Daniel, Zechariah, the Psalms] and others such as Isaiah 40–55. . . . But Wright is not the only scholar to argue that Jesus saw meaning in his death, that he accepted it freely, and that he understood it as part of his ministry. Both Walter Kasper and Edward Schillebeeckx take similar positions. What is interesting is that both scholars find an expression of Jesus' sense of his death as a completion of his life in the story of the Last Supper.[29]

Schillebeeckx goes on to claim that a number of texts speaking of Jesus as servant "appear to have an intrinsic connection with something that happened at the Last Supper shortly before Jesus' death."[30]

In other words, the New Testament presents Jesus as like us in so many ways. One can picture him enjoying the sun set behind the hills surrounding Nazareth. The Gospels portray him as crying over the death of a friend and at the future of his own people. They depict him

---

27. See Lk. 22:19, 20, and 1 Cor. 11:24.

28. See Thomas P. Rausch, *Who Is Jesus?: An Introduction to Christology* (Collegeville, Minn.: Liturgical Press, 2003), 101.

29. Rausch, *Who Is Jesus?* 104, referring to N. T. Wright, *Jesus and the Victory of God* (Minneapolis: Fortress Press, 1996), 601; Walter Kaspar, *Jesus the Christ* (New York: Paulist Press, 1977), 117–18; Schillebeeckx, *Jesus: An Experiment in Christology*, trans. H. Hoskins (New York: Vintage, 1981), 303. Rausch offers a fine treatment of theological perspectives on Jesus' death (99–110).

30. Rausch, *Who Is Jesus?* 104–5, citing Schillebeeckx, *Jesus*, 303. The four texts that Schillebeeckx focuses on are Mark 10:45, Lk. 22:27, Lk. 12:37b, and Jn. 13:1–20.

as enjoying meals with friends and also as burning with anger and aching from loneliness. He could feel betrayed and heartbroken as we do.

The Gospels also reveal him as being unlike us in that he was so free to serve. His relationship with *Abba* whom he loved and wished to obey called him to serve.[31] His relationship with those around him also called him to serve. He was free enough to respond with a love such as the world had never known before him and will never know again apart from him. "To the poor he proclaimed the good news of salvation, / to prisoners, freedom, / and to the sorrowful in heart, joy."[32]

Moreover, the Gospels depict Jesus as finding freedom not in spite of, but precisely because of, his service to those around him. It was here that he found freedom from sin and selfishness. Here, too, he found a final choice: to stop his service short of death *or* take his chances and die in the service of his brothers and sisters and of *Abba*.[33] In choosing to die for his service, Christians believe, he found freedom from death itself. This is the message of the resurrection. This is what we celebrate in the Eucharist.

But did Jesus explicitly link himself, and consequently the Eucharist, with the Servant? There is no clear, unambiguous witness that he did. Nor is that necessary or even important. In the last analysis, it is not important whether or not Jesus himself used the formula "blood of the covenant . . . poured out for the many" which would have linked him to the Servant.

What is important is that he provided the basis for such an interpretation. The correctness of the institution narrative, and of our Eucharist, lies not in the fact that they repeat what Jesus *said*. It lies, rather, in the fact that they express what Jesus *was* (and still is): a "per-

31. See Mary Rose D'Angelo, "Abba and 'Father': Imperial Theology and the Jesus Traditions," *Journal of Biblical Literature* 111/4 (1992): 611–30, and "Theology in Mark and Q: Abba and 'Father' in Context," *The Harvard Theological Review* (April 1992): 149–74, who challenges a number of commonly held assumptions on Jesus and "Abba." See also Gail Ramshaw, *God Beyond Gender: Feminist Christian God-Language* (Minneapolis: Fortress Press, 1995), and Delores Dufner, "With What Language Shall We Pray?" *Worship* 80/2 (March 2006): 140–61.

32. *Roman Missal*, Eucharistic Prayer IV. See also Is. 42:7.

33. See Jerome Murphy-O'Connor, "Eucharist and Community in First Corinthians," *Worship* 51 (January 1977): 61, as cited by Bruce T. Morrill, *Anamnesis as Dangerous Memory: Political and Liturgical Theology in Dialogue* (Collegeville, Minn.: Liturgical Press, 2000), 187.

son for others," a person whose whole life involved the willingness to risk giving himself to and for others even in the face of death itself.

This is what we celebrate in the Eucharist. Jesus was a person who gave himself for others. Jesus was a person who precisely in serving others found freedom from sin and selfishness and even from death itself. Jesus was a person who precisely in serving found happiness and new life for himself and for others. Thus "body" and "blood" bring out different aspects of the same mystery. "Body" reminds us that the whole Christ encounters us bodily in the Eucharist. "Blood" reminds us that Christ our Lord roots the new covenant in the giving of his life for others.

The image of the Suffering Servant thus contributes in an exceptionally high degree to the proper understanding of Jesus and of the Eucharist. In this sense "for us" and "for many" (= "all") form two of the most important phrases in our eucharistic understanding. In this sense, too, the Eucharist is a celebration of service.

EUCHARIST: CALL TO SERVICE

On the other hand, the Eucharist is not just a celebration of what Jesus Christ did but also a call, in and through the Holy Spirit, to make this our own, to involve ourselves in the same kind of attitude toward God and people.[34] This understanding flows from a number of elements.

The first of these is the nature of prophetic symbols. Their dramatization was living, effectual. It set an event in motion. It also called for a response. For instance, Isaiah walking barefoot and naked in public not only attracted attention. He demonstrated what would happen to the Egyptians and all who trusted in them, namely, defeat at the hands of the Assyrians.[35]

Jeremiah with a yoke around his neck called to his people to submit to God's judgment in the form of Nebuchadnezzar and his breaking of a potter's earthen flask represented the destruction of

---

34. See Leon-Dufour, *Sharing the Eucharistic Bread*, 112, and Breuning, "Die Eucharistie in Dogma und Kerygma," 138–41.

35. See Is. 20:2–6. For a fine treatment of symbols in general, and prophetic symbols in particular, see Michael G. Lawler, *Symbol and Sacrament: A Contemporary Sacramental Theology* (New York: Paulist Press, 1987), 5–28.

Jerusalem.[36] Ezekiel's construction of a miniature siege work was similar.[37] Each of these symbols called for a response and, as with our own words and symbols, there is always a response. We may listen and obey. We may, as children do, cover our ears and say, "I can't hear you!" We may despise and reject the prophet. But there is always a response.

The same holds true for the Last Supper and the later Eucharist. The distribution and *acceptance* of food implied, in the Semitic context of Jesus' time, an acceptance of the call. In other words, to share with Jesus in this meal is to acknowledge communion of life with him. Communion in his life, if taken seriously, involves communion in his role as Servant with all the relationships to God, to people, to covenant this implies. Just as bread when eaten disappears only to live on in the eater, Jesus Christ is to disappear only to live on in those who partake with him of this symbolic meal or gesture. "Jesus intends to involve the disciples in his own destiny by assimilating them to himself and even transforming them into himself."[38]

In addition to the nature of prophetic symbols, the self-understanding or nature of the early Christian community also reflects the Eucharist's call to service. A good example of this is the summary texts of the Acts of the Apostles in Acts 2:42–46; 4:32–35; 5:12–15. Exegetically, they are insertions that interrupt the narrative and paint an idyllic picture of the early Christian community. They also represent one of the most ancient New Testament mentions of worship. In their actual context they are meant to give an ideal picture of the community faithful to the teaching of the Lord and docile to the Holy Spirit.[39] As presented in Acts 2:42–46 there are four essential traits of

---

36. See Jer. 28:1–17, and 19:1–15.

37. See Ez. 4:1–3.

38. See Leon-Dufour, *Sharing the Eucharistic Bread,* 112, and also Jacques Guillet, *The Consciousness of Jesus,* trans. E. Bonin (New York: Newman Press, 1972), 180–83. On the realism of this indwelling, see once again Wikenhauser, *Pauline Mysticism,* 72–73, 98. It is crucial to see that we are not only dealing with a cultic act but also a prophetic symbol that possesses the power to transform the lives of believers. In this regard see Morrill, *Anamnesis as Dangerous Memory,* 170, citing David Gregg, *Anamnesis in the Eucharist* (Bramcote Notts, England: Grove Books, 1976), 15.

39. See Stanislas Lyonnet, "La nature du culte dans le nouveau testament," in *La Liturgie Après Vatican II,* Unam Sanctam 66 (Cerf, 1967), 357–59, and "La nature du culte chrétien: Culte eucharistique et promulgation du 'commandement nouveau,'" in *Studia Missionalia* 23 (1974). See also Joseph Fitzmyer, *The Acts of the Apostles, Anchor Bible* 31 (New York: Doubleday, 1998), 97–98, 268–75, 312–15, 327–30.

the community: (1) they are faithful to prayer—morning and evening prayer in the Temple; (2) they are faithful to "the breaking of bread" (the Eucharist) in their homes and characterized by a future-oriented (eschatological) joy; (3) they are faithful to the teaching of the apostles—especially the witness to the resurrection which was accompanied by power; (4) they are faithful to the communal life.[40]

The context of these idealized descriptions of early Christians indicates brotherly and sisterly communion and service to one another not only in the Eucharist but also in their whole life is, in a sense, a condition for the celebration of communion in the liturgy. Acts 4:32–35 and 5:12–15 are a commentary on this. The whole life of the Christians is service to one another. This is an integral part of their covenant, of their life in Christ.[41]

A number of Pauline texts echo the conviction that the Eucharist calls for service, an ethical response.[42] In 1 Corinthians 10:1–22, Paul argues that it is not enough for the Christians to partake in the sacraments. The Israelites of old partook of similar realities. They "were all under the cloud and all passed through the sea; by the cloud and the sea all of them were baptized into Moses. All ate the same spiritual food. All drank the same spiritual drink . . . yet we all know that God was not pleased with most of them, for 'they were struck down in the desert.' "

To share in the sacred meal is to share in Christ or, as the case may be, in demons. Consequently, Christians should respect one another and one another's conscience. Furthermore, Paul contends, the fact that there are factions among the Corinthians, that the poor are embarrassed, and that some go hungry while others get drunk shows a basic misunderstanding of the Eucharist. He reminds them that proclaiming the death of the Lord in a sacrament of eating and

---

40. Lyonnet, "La nature du culte dans le nouveau testament," 359–62, who notes (362) that this last element is missed in the Vulgate translation, "faithful to the communion of the breaking of the bread." Unfortunately, Lyonnet adds, this translation is followed by The Constitution on the Sacred Liturgy, *Mysterium Fidei,* and a number of modern translations. See also Lyonnet, "La nature du culte chrétien," 239–46.

41. See McCormick, *A Banqueter's Guide,* 32–33, and Lyonnet, "La nature du culte dans le nouveau testament," 363–68, and "La nature du culte chrétien," 219–22.

42. See Raymond Collins, *First Corinthians,* Sacra Pagina Series 7 (Collegeville, Minn., 1999), 375–82.

sharing implies giving oneself to, and respecting, others.[43] Interestingly enough, Paul usually applies the Servant theme not to Christ but to the Christians.

Along the same vein, the New Testament use of cultic terminology is revealing. First of all, terms like "liturgy," "cult," "sacrifice," "offering" are used to describe Old Testament worship and pagan rites. Next they describe the passion, death, and Resurrection of Christ. When applied to Christians they refer not to their worship but to their life. Their apostolic ministry or their exercise of charity is their "liturgy" or "spiritual sacrifice."[44] The same is true of priestly terminology.[45] In short, the summary sections in Acts, the use of cultic terminology, and the use of priestly terminology all witness to the inseparable unity between Christian cult or worship and the Christian life of charity and service.[46] The eucharistic sacrifice and the new covenant are primarily to be celebrated not on altars of stone but on tables of flesh, on the hearts of all Christians.[47]

John's Gospel provides a similar thrust. Chapter 6 describes the mysterious presence of Christ in those who nourish themselves with his body and blood. "Those who feed on my flesh and drink my blood have eternal life and I will raise them up on the last day. For my flesh is real food and my blood real drink. Those who feed on my flesh and drink my blood remain in me and I in them" (Jn. 6:54–56). Together with Christ they thus enter the new covenant foretold by Jeremiah and Ezekiel. "But this is the covenant which I will make with the house of Israel. . . . I will place my law within them, and write it upon their hearts; I will be their God and they shall be my people. No longer will they need to teach their friends and kinsmen how to know the Lord. All, from the least to the greatest shall know me" (Jer. 31:33–35). "I will sprinkle clean water upon you to cleanse you from all your impurities, and from all your idols I will cleanse

---

43. 1 Cor. 11:17–34. See Collins, *First Corinthians*, 416–22; McCormick, *A Banqueter's Guide*, 27; and David N. Power, "Eucharistic Justice," *Theological Studies* 67 (Dec. 2006): 858–63.

44. See Lyonnet, "La nature du culte dans le nouveau testament," 368–83, and "La nature du culte chrétien," 214–16.

45. See Lyonnet, "La nature du culte dans le nouveau testament," 379–82, and "La nature du culte chrétien," 216–19.

46. Lyonnet, "La nature du culte dans le nouveau testament," 378–79.

47. Lyonnet, "La nature du culte chrétien," 219–21.

you. I will give you a new heart and place a new spirit within you, taking from your bodies your stony hearts and giving you natural hearts. I will put my spirit within you and make you live my statutes, careful to observe my decrees" (Ez. 36: 25–27). This new covenant gives Christ's disciples a share in his life of love that culminated in his death for others.[48]

If Jesus really lives in his disciples and they in him, how shall people recognize it? John 13 addresses this question by placing the Last Supper within the context of Jesus' servant attitude. Jesus performs a parable in action. Taking on the role of a servant or slave, he washes the feet of his disciples. Then he uses words to explain the symbolic action. "But if I washed your feet—I who am Teacher and Lord, then you must wash each other's feet. What I just did was to give you an example: as I have done, so must you do" (Jn. 13:14–15). Raymond Brown, among others, sees this as more than just an act of humility. It is a symbolic action that prefigures Jesus' death and reveals the depth of his love.[49] As Schillebeeckx puts it: "The Last Supper tradition, therefore, is the oldest starting-point for the Christian interpretation of Jesus' death as a self-giving on Jesus' part that procures salvation."[50]

Then Jesus gives them a new commandment that embodies and anchors the new covenant foretold by Jeremiah and Ezekiel and the Eucharist that celebrates it. "I give you a new commandment: Love one another. Such as my love has been for you, so must your love be for each other. This is how all will know you for my disciples: your love for one another" (Jn. 13:34–35). Ironically, the foot washing and the new commandment are set in a context of the predictions of Judas' betrayal and Peter's denial. In the "worst of times" Jesus calls on his disciples to express their relationship with him in their love for one another.[51]

---

48. See ibid., 378, 382, and "La nature du culte dans le nouveau testament," 222–26. Raymond Brown, *The Gospel According to John (I–XII), Anchor Bible* 29 (New York: Doubleday, 1966), 287–91, suggests that Jn. 6:51–58, may represent another version of the tradition that originally went with Jn. 13.

49. Brown, *The Gospel According to John (XIII–XXI), Anchor Bible* 29A (1970), 565–72, sees the foot washing as a prophetic symbol that, among other things, alludes to Jesus' death which shows Jesus' "consummate" love. See also Power, "Eucharistic Justice," 862–63.

50. Schillebeeckx, Jesus, 306, cited by Rausch, *Who Is Jesus?* 105.

51. Lyonnet, "La nature du culte chrétien," 230–33.

The Eucharist is then not only a celebration of service but also a call to service. Christian liturgy in general and the Eucharist in particular go hand in hand with the "new commandment of love" engraved on the heart, as the prophets had foretold. This kind of love goes beyond the time of the "ceremony" to the whole of one's daily life. That is why the New Testament took Old Testament cultic terminology and applied it to the Christian life of faith and love.[52] Eucharist and the Christian life of charity make no sense without one another any more than the sacrament of baptism without faith or the sacrament of reconciliation without repentance.[53]

Moreover, the call of the Eucharist is a call to serve *all* people. This universality was basic to the Servant of God's context as it was to that of Jesus. "This is my blood . . . poured out for the many" (= "all"). It is a call, for instance, to look beyond the narrow confines of our immediate community to political and economic structures that enable millions of people to go to bed hungry.[54] The response to the call to serve, to share in Christ's service, is really the norm of a good liturgy. This is the acid test. The most important thing is not the beautiful singing, the well-done readings, the good homily, as important as these are. The most important thing is union with Christ and the life of charity, unity, service that flows from it. As Pope Benedict XVI puts it: "Faith, worship, and *ethos* are interwoven as a single reality which takes shape in our encounter with God's *agape*. Here the usual contraposition between worship and ethics simply falls apart. 'Worship' itself, Eucharistic communion, includes the reality both of being loved and of loving others in turn. A Eucharist which does not pass over into the concrete practice of love is intrinsically fragmented."[55]

The correctness of our Eucharist and our lives as Christians, for that matter, lies not in the fact that we repeat what Jesus said. It lies, rather, in the fact that we seek to be what Christ was and still is:

52. Ibid., 249.

53. See Lyonnet, "La nature du culte dans le nouveau testament," 378.

54. See McCormick, A *Banqueter's Guide*, 4–12, 26–34, 48–50, for examples and significance of "eucharistic hospitality." See also Power, "Eucharistic Justice," 863–75.

55. Pope Benedict XVI, *Encyclical Letter, Deus Caritas Est: To the Bishops, Priests and Deacons, Men and Women Religious, and all the Lay Faithful, on Christian Love* (Boston: Pauline Books, 2006), art. 16.

a person for others, a person who chose to die in his service of *Abba* and all peoples, a person who precisely in serving found his freedom and new life. As Paul put it: "Continually we carry about in our bodies the dying of Jesus, so that in our bodies the life of Jesus may also be revealed. While we live we are constantly being delivered to death for Jesus' sake, so that the life of Jesus may be revealed in our mortal flesh. Death is at work in us, but life in you. We have the spirit of faith of which the Scripture says, 'Because I believed, I spoke out.' We believe and so we speak knowing that he who raised up the Lord Jesus will raise us up along with Jesus and place both us and you in his presence" (2 Cor. 4:10–14). In this sense the Eucharist is a celebration of service and a call to service. In this sense we Christians are called, in the beautiful words of Augustine, to *be* what we celebrate and to *become* what we receive. [56]

---

56. See ibid., 73–106, for reflections on being and recognizing the Body of Christ.

Chapter 5

The Eucharist and the Resurrection

This chapter explores certain facets of the Eucharist that are bound up with the reality of the Resurrection and are best understood in light of that event. The links between Resurrection and Eucharist also have implications for the way Christians look at the future.

In the second half of the twentieth century there was a growing realization of just how much the future affects the present. Maybe this accounts for the popularity of such works as McLuhan's *Understanding Media* and Toffler's *Future Shock* as well as the blossoming of numerous theologies of hope.[1] Be that as it may, one basic premise seems to underlie most of these writings: theories about the future, theological or otherwise, are true to the extent that they make sense out of, and help to transform, the present.

The interest in the future, moreover, is characteristic not only of modern people. The early Christians shared the view of many of their Jewish contemporaries that a resurrection of the dead would signal that the "end of the world," "the final future," had begun and that God's decisive intervention had started to break into history. It was precisely because the Christian community experienced and believed that Jesus was personally risen and present to it, that it experienced itself as the community of the future, the eschatological community. The early Christians lived their lives in the light of the Resurrection. Their Eucharist was from earliest times "resurrectional," as we shall shortly see. They linked the Eucharist, not exclusively but nonetheless

---

1. See, for example, Jürgen Moltmann, *Theology of Hope: On the Ground and the Implications of a Christian Eschatology*, trans. J. W. Leitch (New York: Harper & Row, 1967), and more recently, Dermot A. Lane, *Keeping Hope Alive: Stirrings in Christian Theology* (Dublin: Gill & Macmillan, 1996).

emphatically, to the Resurrection and to Sunday, the day of the Resurrection.[2] It is this link with the Resurrection of Jesus Christ which has stamped the Christian tradition with an orientation toward the future and has placed the Christian in a more or less direct confrontation with the humanist.

THE CHALLENGE OF HUMANISM

Paul Tillich once stated that all modern theology is an attempt to unite orthodox and humanist traditions in recent Christian thought.[3] Christian humanism, whether it follows Whitehead, Teilhard de Chardin, or Moltmann, seeks first, to go beyond humanism pure and simple and second, to combine biblical and historical themes of the Judaeo-Christian tradition with humanist concern for humanity and future. To do this, Christian humanism reinterprets Christian tradition in terms of humanist tenets and accusations. This leads to a dialogue of sorts.[4]

Generally both Christian and humanist traditions agree on being traditions of hope, in a quest for the unity of humanity; they disagree on the role belief in God and the afterlife play in this quest for unity. For the humanist, people are on their own. People are responsible for the future, their own and that of all humankind. There is no support or intervention from a Higher Power. Life after death is to be rejected for a number of reasons. For some, there is no cogent evidence in its favor. For others, it violates the modern anthropological concept of man's psychosomatic unity which rejects the notion of a soul continuing to exist apart from bodiliness. For others, belief in the resurrection of the dead leads to an irresponsible otherworldliness which neglects the needs of the present and the hopes for *this world's* future. Such a belief, they contend, fosters a self-centered reward seeking and makes Christians so otherworldly that they are no earthly good.[5]

---

2. See Willi Marxsen, *The Lord's Supper as a Christological Problem*, trans. L. Nieting (Philadelphia: Fortress Press, 1970), 10, 21–23, 26, 32, although here as with the Resurrection, Marxsen's position needs qualifying.

3. Paul Tillich, *Perspectives on 19ᵗʰ and 20ᵗʰ Century Protestant Theology*, ed. C. E. Braaten (New York: Harper, 1967), 4–5, as cited by Donald Gray, "Response to Wolfhart Pannenberg," in Ewert H. Cousins, ed., *Hope and the Future of Man* (Philadelphia: Fortress Press, 1972), 78.

4. Gray, "Response," 78–79.

5. Gray, "Response," 79–80.

For the Christian, on the other hand, people are not on their own. Their efforts are guided and sustained by a caring God. This life is not all there is. The Resurrection is pivotal because it involves hope as well as the transformation of the *whole* of reality, matter as well as spirit. The Christian sees that discouragement, despair, and a lack of solid hope threaten men's and women's commitment to carry the struggle forward, to renew the face of the earth. The Christian sees just as clearly that hope in a resurrection—somewhat like a hoped-for vacation or successful outcome in a sports contest—can be a powerful motive spurring people on to greater efforts to renew this world.

THE RESURRECTION

Many Christians today, however, hasten to add that our belief in Christ's Resurrection as the forerunner and hope of our resurrection is a powerful force only if it is properly understood. They seek to combat the fruits, not of unbelief, but of misbelief. If, for example, one interprets resurrection in a "traditional," *other-worldly* sense, one runs the risk of offering less than the humanists in the realm of personal responsibility for humanity's future. No less a devotee to this world and its honest values than Teilhard was quick to recognize this danger:

> Without denying that some Christians, by their words more than their deeds, do give grounds for the reproach of being, if not the "enemies," at least the "laggards" of the human race, we can safely assert, after what we said above concerning the supernatural value of our work on earth, that their attitude is *due to an incomplete understanding and not at all to some greater perfection of religion.*[6]

Teilhard thus, while admitting the weakness, suggests the cause, not belief but rather "misbelief," that is, the failure to see the implications of our faith:

> One thing is infinitely disappointing. . . . Far too many Christians are insufficiently conscious of the "divine" responsibilities of their lives, and live like other men, giving only half of themselves, never experiencing the spur of

---

6. Pierre Teilhard de Chardin, *The Divine Milieu: An Essay on the Interior Life,* rev. ed. (New York: Harper, 1965), 38.

the intoxication of furthering the Kingdom of God in every domain of mankind. *But do not blame anything but our weakness; our faith imposes on us the right and the duty to throw ourselves into the things of the earth.*[7]

If, on the other hand, one follows certain theologians without qualifying their positions, one runs the risk of watering down the Resurrection to the point where it offers little meaning, little hope to people today.[8] It is not within the scope of this chapter to analyze, explicitly at least, what theologians have been saying about the Resurrection. This has been done elsewhere.[9] Rather, what follows will draw out some of the theological implications in order to shed some light on Christian living and Christian Eucharist.[10] Such an interpretation is essential.[11]

---

7. Teilhard, *The Divine Milieu*, 39. K. Rahner, *Theological Investigations*, trans. K. H. and B. Kruger (Baltimore: Helicon, 1967), 3:58–59, is just as firm in pointing out the danger and its root. See also Schillebeeckx, *God, the Future of Man*, trans. N. D. Smith (New York: Sheed & Ward, 1968), 182–83.

8. See n. 40.

9. See, for example, Stephen T. Davis, et. al., eds. *The Resurrection: An Interdisciplinary Symposium on the Resurrection of Jesus* (New York: Oxford University Press, 1997); Willi Marxsen and C. F. D. Moule, eds., *The Significance of the Message of the Resurrection for Faith in Jesus Christ* (Naperville, Ill.: Allenson, 1968).

10. Much of what follows is based upon a careful study of the following: Rudolf Bultmann, *The History of the Synoptic Tradition*, trans. J. Marsh (New York: Harper & Row, 1963), 284–91, and the same author's "New Testament and Mythology," in H. W. Bartsch, ed., *Kerygma and Myth*, trans. R. H. Fuller (London: SPCK, 1964), 1:1–44; Karl Barth, *Church Dogmatics*, 4 vols., trans. G. W. Bromley (London, 1956), 1:297–357; and "Bultmann—An Attempt to Understand Him," in H. W. Bartsch, ed. *Kerygma and Myth*, trans. R. H. Fuller (London, 1962), 2:83–132; Paul Tillich, *Systematic Theology*, 3 vols. (Chicago: University of Chicago Press, 1957), 2:150–63; (1963) 3:406–23, and *The New Being* (New York: Scribner's, 1955), 15–24, 173–74; Karl Rahner, "Resurrection of Christ," in *Sacramentum Mundi* (New York: Herder & Herder, 1970), 5:323–24, 329–33, and the same author's "Dogmatic Questions on Easter," in *Theological Investigations* 4, trans. K. Smyth (Baltimore: Helicon, 1966), 121–33, as well as "The Resurrection of the Body," in *Theological Investigations* 2, trans. K. H. Kruger (Baltimore: Helicon, 1963), 203–16, and *Foundations of Christian Faith: An Introduction to the Idea of Christianity*, trans. W. V. Dych (New York: Crossroad, 1995), 228–85, 424–30; Wolfhart Pannenberg, *Jesus—God and Man*, trans. L. Wilkens and D. Priebe (Philadelphia: Westminster Press, 1968), 53–114, and "The Revelation of God in Jesus," in J. M. Robinson and J. B. Cobb, Jr., eds., *Theology as History*, (New York: Harper & Row, 1967), 101–33; Willi Marxsen, "The Resurrection of Jesus as a Historical and Theological Problem," in Moule, *The Significance*, 15–50, 121–26; and *The Resurrection of Jesus of Nazareth*, trans. M. Kohl (Philadelphia: Fortress Press, 1970); Xavier Léon-Dufour, *Resurrection and the Message of Easter*, trans. R. N. Wilson (New York: Holt, 1974); and E. Pousset, "Résurrection de Jesus et message pascal" (extended review of Léon-Dufour's book of the same title), NRT 94 (1972): 95–107; E. Pousset, "Croire en la Résurrection," NRT 96 (1974): 147–66, 366–88; and Franz Mussner, *Die Auferstehung Jesu* (Munich: Kösel, 1969).

11. As Léon-Dufour, Resurrection, 228, puts it: "All language is interpretation as the function of an experience and all language is conditioned by a particular environment.

The format for our reflections will have Paul's statement to the Corinthians as a basis: "I passed on to you what I myself received, that Christ died for our sins in accordance with the Scriptures, that he was buried and that, in accordance with the Scriptures, he has been raised on the third day and that he was seen by Cephas, then by the twelve" (I Cor. 15:3–5). Our schema is: . . . *lived, died, was buried, has been raised,* and I will apply this schema to Christ, the disciples and the believer today.

Christ

He lived. To forget the historical dimension of Jesus of Nazareth is to forget who and what has been raised. A failure to see him as really human is a failure to see that the Resurrection affects humanity in its totality and to ignore the often repeated patristic principle: "the whole man would not be saved if he had not taken on the whole man."[12] One ignores this principle at the risk of seeing resurrection as simply a reward for the "old" life rather than its culmination.[13] Despite our inability to write his biography, the starting point of any reflection on the Resurrection is the way Jesus of Nazareth *lived.*[14]

He lived a fully human life, a life of loving service to people within a covenant relationship with his Father. He allowed God and people alike to remain free in response to him. In short, both the words he spoke and the life he lived rang out with the authority of a man who could speak of God as his Father, a man who could heal others, a man who could free others from all sorts of demons.[15] He

---

Interpretation is not a luxury, but a duty which is still incumbent on us today." See also Edward Schillebeeckx, *Interim Report on the Books Jesus & Christ,* trans. J. Bowden (New York: Crossroad, 1981), 10–19, and Dermot Lane, *Christ at the Centre: Selected Issues in Christology* (New York: Paulist Press, 1991), 80–83.

12. Pieter Frans Smulders, *The Fathers on Christology: The Development of Christological Dogma from the Bible to the Great Councils,* trans. L. Roy (De Pere, Wisconsin: St. Norbert Abbey Press, 1968), 15, 41, 67.

13. See Rahner, *Theological Investigations* 4, 127–29.

14. Some attempt to grasp the character and deeds of Jesus, however difficult, is basic to the understanding of his Resurrection. See Bruce Chilton, *Jesus' Prayer and Jesus' Eucharist: His Personal Practice of Spirituality* (Valley Forge, Pa: Trinity Press International, 1997), 3, 6, 9–23, 75–76; J. M. Robinson, *A New Quest of the Historical Jesus* (London, 1959); R. Brown, "After Bultmann, What?" *Catholic Biblical Quarterly* 26 (1964): 1–30; Léon-Dufour, Resurrection, 11ff.; and Pannenberg, *Jesus—God and Man,* chapters 6 and 7, and 53–65.

15. See Pannenberg, *Jesus—God and Man,* 53–65.

invited men and women beyond themselves—to an openness to God in this life, to freedom to love, to the giving of oneself for the neighbor, and to the experience of this self-giving precisely as a movement toward salvation.[16]

He died. The crucifixion and death of Jesus, in light of what has just been said, are not simply historical facts.[17] They represent the culmination, the fulfillment of the life we have just described. In freely accepting death Jesus indicates that he will die as he lived, true to the covenant relationship between the Father and himself[18] and trusting that the relationship endure. He thus makes one final act of trust in someone else's love.[19]

He was buried. The death was no fake. Not only was it real it was also definitive. The identity and the personality of Jesus of Nazareth had been put to rest henceforth to be linked with the tomb, the place of the dead.[20]

He has been raised. The love of God and perfect human love meet and they yield new life. Jesus' loving service and his confidence that his relationship with the Father would endure despite even death have borne fruit. Resurrection then implies, first of all, a relationship with the Father. Jesus in a sense already *stands in the future.*[21]

He has been raised *bodily.* As is often the case, it is easier to say what one does not mean than what one does mean. The apostles had no intention of leaving behind a discourse in biophysics. On the other hand, it is not *simply* a question of Jesus' ideas, example, memory living on—as great as that might be. K. Barth is on target when he observes

---

16. See Marxsen, *The Resurrection*, 147–48.

17. See Bultmann, "New Testament and Mythology," 34ff.

18. On the question of Jesus' consciousness, which we are unable to go into here, see Piet Schoonenberg, *The Christ: The Study of the God-Man Relationship in the Whole of Creation and in Jesus Christ,* trans. D. Couling (New York: Seabury Press, 1971), 123ff., and the references given there, as well as Pannenberg, *Jesus—God and Man,* 325–34.

19. As Pousset, "Croire en la Résurrection," 378, puts it: "The death of this particular being is the most brilliant manifestation of his life." See also Rahner, *On the Theology of Death,* trans. C. H. Henkey and W. J. O'Hara (New York: Herder, 1965), 27–31, 39–44; Pannenberg, *Jesus—God and Man,* 65–66; and Bultmann, *Theology of the New Testament,* trans. K. Grobel (London: SCM Press, 1952), 1: 9–15.

20. Léon-Dufour, *Resurrection,* 11; U. Wilckens, *Die Auferstehung Jesu* (Stuttgart, 1970), 18, 20–22; Mussner, *Die Auferstehung Jesu,* 60–63; and R. H. Fuller, *The Formation of the Resurrection Narratives* (New York: Macmillan, 1971), 15, 54–57, 132–33.

21. See Schillebeeckx, *God the Future,* 172–73, 181–82. See also Pannenberg, *Jesus—God and Man,* 69, 82ff.

that such a view would have Jesus' continuing life totally dependent on others, whereas the Bible proclaims the opposite.[22] To say that Jesus has been raised bodily is to say that his *whole* personality lives on.[23] The totality of that which formed the center of expression and communication with others, of that which enabled him to enter into relationships with the world around him and the people in it, the source of his individuality and uniqueness, has undergone a radical transformation. This in turn involves some form of bodiliness unless one divides man into an ever existent "spirit" and a merely provisional "body."[24]

Does it make any difference whether or not Jesus rose bodily, in the sense just described? One would venture to guess that it would to Jesus. It certainly would to the disciples given their Semitic background. It would have been difficult to envision a resurrection that for them did not involve some sort of bodiliness since for the Semitic mentality of the time, a person was a body-person.[25] This is, in fact, what they proclaim was involved. Moreover, what God has done for Jesus gives *us* some indication of future possibilities for humanity and the whole universe as well. Just as the model one has of the Church affects the way one deals with that reality and vice versa[26] so, too, the

---

22. Barth, *Church Dogmatics*, 4/1: 314.

23. There is general agreement here among theologians. See Tillich, *Systematic Theology*, 3:413; Rahner, "The Resurrection of Christ," *Sacramentum Mundi* (1970): 5:331, and *Theological Investigations*, 2:214–15; Pannenberg, *Jesus—God and Man*, 74–77. Bultmann is unclear in this regard. He has commented that those who attribute to him the claim that Jesus is risen in the kerygma are correct, provided they understand that phrase rightly. See Mussner, *Die Auferstehung Jesu*, 145. See R. Brown, "After Bultmann, What?" 1–30, esp. 2, n. 5. Marxsen, with phrases like, "Jesus' cause lives on," is also unclear about a personal resurrection of Jesus. P. Schoonenberg, *The Christ*, 156, n. 58, may be right in claiming that Marxsen is clearer in his book on the Resurrection of Jesus than he was in his earlier article, but he still remains less than clear on the personal character of Jesus' Resurrection. See R. Brown, *The Virginal Conception and Bodily Resurrection of Jesus* (New York: Paulist Press, 1973), 75, n. 128. The question is not whether people like Bultmann and Marxsen believe Christ's Resurrection to be personal. Rather it is a question, in the course of stressing other facets of the Resurrection which are important and often neglected, of not being clear on it.

24. In addition to Rahner, Tillich, and Pannenberg, as cited in the preceding footnote. See also Léon-Dufour, *Resurrection*, 239–40, 206; Pousset, "Résurrection," 103; and "Croire en la Résurrection," 373–77; A. Feuillet, "Le corps du Seigneur ressuscité et la vie chrétienne, d'après les Epîtres pauliennes," in Barnabas M. Ahern, Édouard Dhanis, and G. Ghiberti, eds., *Resurrexit, Actes du Symposium International sur la Résurrection de Jesus, Rome 1970* (Vatican City: Libreria Editrice Vaticana, 1974), 442.

25. See, for example, Léon-Dufour, *Resurrection*, 18–20, and Pannenberg, *Jesus—God and Man*, 74–82.

26. See Avery Dulles, *Models of the Church* (New York: Image Books, 1987).

model one has of resurrection affects one's understanding of the realities which it involves. It makes a great difference, therefore, whether the future of one's own bodiliness and that of the universe is viewed in terms of destruction or transformation.[27]

Recognizing the importance of bodily resurrection is one thing; describing "what that involves is another. To be sure, it involves some continuity with the earthly or historical body of Jesus. For one who has never seen an oak tree, however, it is hard to imagine what an acorn will eventually look like."[28] Few, if any, of us have seen a "spiritual body." Yet that is how Paul describes the risen body.

One thing that scholars seem to agree on is that there is no question of merely a revivification or resuscitation such as ascribed to Lazarus. With all the stress on the continuity between the historical Jesus and the risen Lord, the witnesses leave no doubt that a radical transformation has taken place.[29] To the image of resurrection, therefore, one must join that of exaltation.[30]

---

27. R. Brown, *The Virginal Conception*, 128–29.

28. Pousset, "Croire en la Résurrection," 382–83. The author uses the analogy somewhat differently. See Gerald O'Collins, *Easter Faith: Believing in the Risen Jesus* (Mahwah, N.J.: Paulist Press, 2003), 5–24, on the use of analogies in regard to the Resurrection.

29. Léon-Dufour, *Resurrection*, 237–39; Tillich, 3:412–14; Pannenberg, Jesus—God and Man, 76ff.; and Rahner, *Theological Investigations* 2, 214–15, just to mention a few. See also Roch A. Kereszty, *Jesus Christ: Fundamentals of Christology*, Revised, Updated edition. (New York: Alba House, 2002), 36–37.

30. Thus it is necessary to see the Jerusalem type of presenting the risen Christ in light of the Galilean type. The Jerusalem type, which eventually prevailed, conceives of the Resurrection more as a rising or awakening from death. This type, with its threefold structure of initiative by Jesus, recognition by the disciples, and giving of a mission, carries with it a number of advantages. By stressing the initiative of the risen Lord this type preserves the believer from the illusion that the appearances in some way stemmed from the disciples; in recognizing the risen One as Jesus of Nazareth it forces the believer to interpret the Resurrection in the light of the historical Jesus; underlining the mission keeps the believer from becoming fixed on the past. One of the disadvantages of this type is that it runs the risk of allowing the Resurrection to appear as some sort of survival after death or a revivification.

The Galilean type takes the Lordship or exaltation of Christ as its basis. It enables us to avoid seeing Jesus simply as someone who has survived death and reducing his presence to physical contacts. It also helps us see the familiar presence of Jesus as something due to his very being as Lord and not simply to extraordinary phenomena. On the difference between exaltation and resurrection see Pheme Perkins, *Resurrection: New Testament Witness and Contemporary Reflection* (Garden City, N.Y.: Doubleday, 1984), 20–21, as cited by Kereszty, *Jesus*, 33; Léon-Dufour, *Resurrection*, 102–4. See also R. Schnackenburg, "Christologie des Neuen Testaments," in J. Feiner and M. Löher, eds., *Mysterium Salutis* (Einsiedeln, 1970), 256–64.

Perhaps we should say, then, that Jesus has been raised "*spiritually*" or "*Spirit-ized*," filled with God's Spirit,[31] a Spirit of love and freedom who enables him to cry out in the fullest sense possible, "Free at last!" This freedom is, however, not a freedom *from* the body; it is rather a freedom *in* the body—in the "Spirit-ized" body of which Paul speaks in 1 Corinthians 15:44.[32] In some way Jesus' body has been transformed into the perfect vehicle of his self-expression and communication. No longer does it impose the limits which it once did. No longer can others use this bodiliness to treat him as a thing, to force him, in a sense, to reveal himself at a time or in a place or in a way not of his own choosing. He is free to give himself with absolute freedom and, therefore, with the greatest degree of personal love. The appearance narratives bear repeated witness to this facet of his new life.

Furthermore, his risen body somehow embraces the whole universe, which has become the center of his self-expression and communication—his body. Teilhard grasped this point as if by intuition: "By virtue of Christ's rising again, nothing any longer kills inevitably but everything is capable of becoming the blessed touch of the divine hands, the blessed influence of the Will of God upon our lives."[33]

Rahner speaks of a sort of pancosmic relationship in which the universe is swept up to its fulfillment in and through the fulfillment of the personal human spirit.[34] More recently, Léon-Dufour has sought to express this same process. "If it is true that Jesus is what he proclaimed, a man with a unique relationship [to God and] to all men, his presence is coextensive with the universe. To use other words, which are not meant to blur the individuality of Jesus nor the continuity of his risen body with his historical body, the body of Jesus is the universe drawn up and transfigured in him."[35] This is what we

---

31. For a qualifying of this statement see my article, "Eucharistic Epiclesis: Myopia or Microcosm," *Theological Studies* 36 (1975): 275ff.

32. See *Systematic Theology*, 3:412; Rahner, *Theological Investigations* 2:214; Léon-Dufour, *Resurrection*, 214.

33. Teilhard de Chardin, *The Divine Milieu*, 55.

34. See Rahner, *Theological Investigations* 2:210–15, and the same author's *On the Theology of Death*, 71–74.

35. See Léon-Dufour, *Resurrection*, 241. The phrase "to God," was left out of the translation. See also G. Martelet, *The Risen Christ and the Eucharist World*, trans. R. Hague (New York: Seabury Press, 1976), 163, 165, 39–47.

have been speaking of, provided that one grants that it is Christ's historic body, distinguishing him from others and transformed by the Resurrection, which plays an active, vital role in the transformation of the universe.[36]

Once one grasps the cosmic scope of Christ's risen or "Spiritized" body, it is easier to see how he can use individual elements of the universe as extensions of his presence. In a way previously unknown, he is to use words, especially those of Scripture, for a personal encounter with others. Natural symbols like water, bread, and wine suddenly become willing instruments in his free, total self-giving.[37] People, too, are invited to enter into this process. They can become more or less willing extensions of his presence in the world. We can thus speak, in realistic terms, of people as members of Christ's Body.[38]

Jesus has then been raised bodily and spiritually. An immediate consequence is that he has also been raised *continuingly*. It hardly seems an accident that Paul, who uses the aorist tense to describe past actions (died, was buried, was seen), employs the perfect tense to describe the Resurrection—an action the effects of which continue in the present ("he has been raised").[39] Because Christ's Resurrection involves the universe and the people in it, what has taken place in him is still taking place in the persons and universe which he has swept up into his new life, his new freedom. There is no need to draw back from proclaiming Christ's Resurrection in order to serve the world well.[40] There is a need to interpret the Resurrection correctly—as an

---

36. See Pousset, "Résurrection," 104–6. The author contends that Léon-Dufour's description (1st ed. [1971], 303) of Christ's body and its relationship to the universe was inverted or at least ambiguous. It is the universe which through the Resurrection somehow becomes Christ's body with Christ's historic body playing an active, vital role in the transformation. This is quite different from saying that Jesus' corpse returns to the universe to which it belongs—a universe, however, that the Resurrection has transformed. Léon-Dufour, Resurrection, xii, has indicated that he has taken these precisions into account in the revised version of his work.

See also Joseph Fitzmyer, "Teilhard's Eucharist: A Reflection," *Theological Studies* 34 (1973): 255–57, who accuses Teilhard of an inversion similar to that for which Pousset criticized Léon-Dufour.

37. See Martelet, *The Risen Christ*, 110, and Léon-Dufour, *Resurrection*, 244–45.

38. See Feuillet, 457–62, and Léon-Dufour, *Resurrection*, 241.

39. See Mussner, *Die Auferstehung Jesu*, 62.

40. One fears that this would be a consequence of overemphasizinig servanthood apart from Christ's resurrection. T. J. Weeden, "Is the Resurrection an Offense to Faith?" *The Christian Century* 89 (Mar. 29, 1972): 357–59, who follows Marxsen, seems to tend in this direction.

ongoing reality. [41] There is an even greater need to live out its implications. And that leads to a consideration of the Resurrection as it pertains to the first disciples and to the believer today.

The Disciples

As with Jesus, one has to begin by seeing these men and women as fully human in their contacts with Jesus. In him they seem to have experienced love as they had never known it. In response to him they began to dream of great things for themselves and for others. True, they did not always understand him. Often they tried to get him to fit their preconceived ideas of what a messiah, a great religious leader should be, but without success. Instead of demanding a decision on the content of his message, he demanded instead a decision *for his person* as the bearer of God's Word. His having come was itself the decisive event through which God was calling his people, thus demanding more of them than simply adherence to a doctrine or a law. It became even more troubling with his crucifixion and death. [42]

Faced with the cross, the disciples had to make their decision to "follow" him anew, and radically so. [43] One should not underestimate the difficulty of this moment. If one sees Christ's risen body in terms of a freedom which radiates in and penetrates all reality, those who are nowhere near the *niveau* of this freedom will be unable to perceive it at first. It is similar to the difficulty someone ignorant of art has distinguishing between a masterpiece painting and a billboard. [44] The disciples thus were at first confused and lacking in faith. Something extraordinary would be required to bring them to a level of faith which involves dying as well as rising. [45]

This is precisely what the disciples claim to have taken place. Something unique happened which *raised* them to a new level of faith.

---

41. See Martelet, *The Risen Christ*, 164, 82–84; and Pousset, "Croire en la Résurrection," 380–81.

42. See R. Bultmann, *Theology of the New Testament*, 1:43; and Pannenberg, *Jesus—God and Man*, 53–66.

43. Bultmann, *Theology of the New Testament*, 1:44.

44. See Pousset, "Croire en la Résurrection," 379; and Rahner, *Theological Investigations* 2, 214.

45. On the historical evidence and its limits see O'Collins, *Easter Faith*, 25–50, and Lane, *Christ at the Centre*, 80–85. See also Pousset, "Croire en la Résurrection," 380.

According to their own testimony the experience revolved around two things: an empty tomb and appearances of Jesus of Nazareth—now, however, radically transformed.

Suffice it to say, first of all, that from a modern point of view there seems no reason to presuppose an empty tomb.[46] God *could* have raised someone from the dead without having to produce an empty tomb. Whether he *did* or not is another question. So is the question of how a first-century Semite could have believed in, much less preached in Jerusalem, the resurrection of someone whose body could be found in a nearby tomb. The point here is simply that today no necessary presupposition (*Vorverständnis*) requires an empty tomb for faith. Secondly, even if historical investigation could prove beyond the shadow of a doubt, which it cannot, that Jesus' tomb was empty, it would still not prove that a resurrection took place. Many other explanations have been and could be offered. All this having been said, we tend to go along with those who see the historical evidence favoring the conclusion that the tomb was empty.[47] The theological significance, however, is of more importance to us here. The proclamation of the empty tomb, taken in its context, seems to say: "His whole personality lives on" and much more.[48]

The other element in the experience which led the disciples to faith is the appearance of Jesus to a number of them.[49] First of all, it is Jesus in *person* who reveals himself.[50] The appearances are a free gift of Jesus, bestowed on selected individuals gifted with faith. They are, therefore, neither purely empirical-sensory (such as a camera or tape recorder could capture) nor purely internal, mystical-ecstatic visions (subjective or objective) such as Paul speaks of in 2 Corinthians 12:1–4. He clearly distinguishes these from the appearances of the risen Lord

---

46. See n. 9, as well as Pannenberg, *Jesus—God and Man*, 99–106; Brown, *The Virginal Conception*, 111–12; Fuller, *Formation*, 52ff., 74ff., 94ff. 132ff.; and Mussner, *Die Auferstehung*, 128–35 .

47. See O'Collins, *Easter Faith*, 66–71; Lane, *Christ at the Centre*, 84–85; and Léon-Dufour, *Resurrection*, 210–12.

48. See O'Collins, *Easter Faith*, 71–84, and Lane, *Christ at the Centre*, 80–85.

49. See n. 46.

50. See among others, Lane, *Christ at the Centre*, 90–94, and M. Kehl, "Eucharistie und Aufenstehung. Zur Deutung der Ostererscheinungen beim Mahl," *Geist und Leben* 43 (1970): 119–21, and 116, n. 65, regarding Marxsen's position.

to him.[51] In addition, the disciples' descriptions of their experience contain certain basic elements: 1) *Initiative.* The initiative is always attributed to Christ. In no way do the disciples think that the appearances originated with them. 2) *Recognition.* They identify the risen one with Jesus of Nazareth. 3) *Mission.* The disciples realize that they are to continue the history of him whom they have recognized—but a history of a radically new kind.[52]

The Resurrection is not an isolated act involving one individual alone. It is a universal event which extends itself from individual to individual, like ripples in a pond, by dint of personal decisions. The process begins with the disciples' experience of the risen Lord—a Lord who comes to them where they are, not just with their bodiliness but also with their lack of understanding and faith.[53] Their experience of the risen Lord is troubling, in a good sense, as their experience of the earthly Jesus had often been, challenging them to make a decision for him, as their experience of the earthly Jesus had often done. This time, however, it is a radically new decision. It will affect their understanding of the Scriptures, of Jesus' earthly life, of death, of history, of their own lives and mission. They begin to live on the basis of a new-found faith, and seem to perceive the Lord's active presence everywhere and at all times. They open themselves to serve God as found in the people and the world around them, even to the risk of death itself, confident that what God has done in Jesus, God can also do in them.[54]

The disciples *testify* that Jesus Christ is risen, both with their written testimony and with their lives. By their witness to the risen Christ, the disciples pose a question: "Are you willing to believe that Jesus has risen from the dead?" This question is part of the historical fact with which the inquirer, especially the believing inquirer, is faced.[55]

---

51. See Kehl, "Eucharistie und Aufenstehung," 43: 114–18, and Kereszty, *Jesus,* 39–40. See also Pannenberg, *Jesus—God and Man,* 88–99, 105–6, although he perhaps goes into too much detail in attempting to describe the five elements involved.

52. See Léon-Dufour, *Resurrection,* 213–14. See also Raymond Brown, *The Gospel According to John (XIII–XXI), Anchor Bible* 29A (Garden City, N.Y.: Doubleday, 1970), 972ff. Henceforth AB 29A.

53. See Pousset, "Croire en la Résurrection," 379.

54. See Lane, *Christ at the Centre,* 95–96; Mussner, *Die Auferstehung Jesu,* 140ff.; Pousset, "Croire en la Résurrection," 367–68; and Bultmann, *Theology of the New Testament,* 1:44ff.

55. See Léon-Dufour, *Resurrection,* 204–7.

Believers Today

Believers today live with a challenge like that of the disciples, whose humanness they also share. They find themselves called to risk making a decision not simply for a set of laws or doctrines but for a person, the decision to enter into a dialogue with a free God, a free Christ who comes to them when, where, and how he chooses.

With the challenge comes hesitation. For to believe means to die freely.[56] Like every man or woman, the believer will have to face thousands of little deaths, frustrations, shattered dreams, betrayals and, finally, the ultimate threat of death itself. Confronted with the decision to place all their hope in one person at these moments, many believers hesitate, tend to cover themselves, and seek alternate securities. They seem, in the words of Francis Thompson, to fear "lest having Him, (they) must have naught beside." It is in this ambivalence that they find themselves continuingly confronted by witnesses to the Resurrection.

Believers today experience both the message of the disciples and the testimony of their lives. They also experience the living presence of Christ and his Spirit in Word, symbols, and community. In this context they are once again called to dream dreams and see visions of what they, and the world around them, could be, to believe in a more unified existence of body and spirit, an existence embracing the whole universe as well as those in it.[57] The risen Christ, they are told, gives them a glimpse of this vision:

> I consider the sufferings of the present to be as nothing compared with the glory to be revealed in us. Indeed, the whole created world eagerly awaits the revelation of the sons of God. Creation was made subject to futility, not of its own accord but by him who once subjected it; yet not without hope, because the world itself will be freed from its slavery to corruption and share in the glorious freedom of the children of God. Yes, we know that all creation groans and is in agony even until now. Not only that, but we ourselves, although we have the Spirit as first fruits, groan inwardly while we await the redemption of our bodies (Rom. 8:18–23; see also Is. 11:1–9).

---

56. Pousset, "Croire en la Résurrection," 380.

57. See O'Collins, *Easter Faith*, 55–65, 88–90, on testimony and experience. See also Lane, *Christ at the Centre*, 95–99, and Pousset, "Croire en la Résurrection," 373–74.

Finally, this risen life is transhistorical. It is rooted in the past, looks to the future, but continuingly takes place in the present.[58] The threefold structure of initiative, recognition, and mission still governs the way the believer enters into and remains in contact with the Lord today. The risen Lord takes the initiative. The believer must measure his or her life against the life of Jesus of Nazareth who gave his life for his friends. In this sense, the believer must return to the past. He or she must also enter into an ongoing process *here and now*, developing the risen life which Christ has already planted within the Christian as a result of baptism. At the same time, the believer must look to the future and work for the final coming of the kingdom.[59]

Are believers today willing to live on the basis of their faith? One should at least be clear about the risk entailed in such a decision.[60] The historical evidence is to a certain extent ambiguous, and would be even if one could produce a photograph of Jesus coming out of the tomb. One cannot prove the Resurrection; one must believe it. To the question one at times hears, "Why didn't more Jews believe in Christ's Resurrection?" one might answer, "For the same reason that many Christians do not." To believe is to risk, to commit oneself.[61] To believe in the Resurrection of Christ is difficult because it involves practical consequences. The believer must be ready to die a thousand times over to serve others. He or she must be ready to let other securities die and trust in Christ alone. To *cling* to anything or anyone else is to that extent either not to believe or to misbelieve.[62] To believe is to unite oneself with Christ on the deepest level of one's being, to make a free, personal decision to join Jesus Christ in his loving service of others even to the point of death, and in all facets of one's life.[63] To believe in the Resurrection is, then, to risk as Christ risked, to have

---

58. Léon-Dufour, *Resurrection*, 222–23. See E. Frank Tupper, *The Theology of Wolfhart Pannenberg* (Philadelphia: Westminster Press, 1973), 285, n. 85, who gives a clear description of Pannenberg's view of the Resurrection, categorizing it as "transhistorical."

59. See Léon-Dufour, *Resurrection*, 234–36. See also Marxsen, *The Resurrection*, 185.

60. See Marxsen, *The Resurrection*, 187–88. Whatever reservations one may have about his overall explanation of the Resurrection, he deserves credit for underscoring the principle that believing is not simply an intellectual assent to doctrines.

61. Marxsen, *The Resurrection*, 187–88.

62. One suspects that such clinging is even more of an obstacle to belief in Christ's Resurrection than some of the theological confusion in this area. See Martelet, *The Risen Christ*, 181.

63. See Pousset, "Croire en la Résurrection," 381–88.

the hope that death—whether of persons, of institutions, of dreams, even of oneself—will give rise to new life in Jesus Christ, not simply in his memory or ideas or example but in *him*, in union with him personally. To believe in this way is to be fully free, human, Christian.

Jesus challenged the disciples to a decision as they lived with him. With his death much of what they believed died with him. Then, confronted by an experience they describe in terms of an empty tomb and appearances, they renewed their decision for him, proclaiming with their lives as well as their lips that he is risen. Believers today find themselves following a similar pattern. They discover in their lives both the challenge to make a personal decision for Christ and a hesitation to embrace its consequences. They also encounter a witness to Christ's Resurrection that involves the proclamation of an empty tomb and appearances, apostolic faith, Word, symbols, and people. In this context they must continually renew their faith in the risen Lord.[64]

Link between Eucharist and Resurrection

At first glance, one would think it sufficient to presume a link between Eucharist and Resurrection. The New Testament quite explicitly links the two. In a passage which biblical scholars generally agree is eucharistic,[65] one reads: "The bread I will give is my own flesh for the life of the world. . . . Those who feed on my flesh and drink my blood have eternal life. And I shall raise them up on the last day. . . . This is the bread that came down from heaven. Unlike your ancestors who ate and died nonetheless, those who feed on this bread shall live forever" (Jn. 6:51, 54, 58).

Moreover, the Eucharist has from earliest times been associated liturgically with Sunday, the "Lord's Day," the day of the Resurrection.[66] The content of the early anaphoras, especially the *anamneses,* also provided a clear link between Eucharist and Resurrection.[67] In addition, patristic writers often underlined the bond between the two.

---

64. See O'Collins, *Easter Faith,* 55–65.

65. See R. Brown, *The Gospel According to John (I–XII), Anchor Bible* 29 (New York: Doubleday, 1966), 284–93, 303.

66. See W. Rordorf, *Sunday,* trans. A. A. K. Graham (Philadelphia: Westminster, 1968), 175ff.; and A. Kavanagh, "Thoughts on the Roman Anaphora," *Worship* 39 (1965): 525.

67. A. Hänggi and I. Pahl, eds., *Prex Eucharistica* (Fribourg: 1968).

St. Ignatius of Antioch, for example, spoke of the Eucharist as "the medicine of immortality, the antidote against death, and everlasting life in Jesus Christ."[68] To Bishop Polycarp of Smyrna he writes: "The Eucharist is the Flesh of our Savior Jesus Christ, which suffered for our sins, and which the Father in His loving-kindness raised from the dead."[69] Irenaeus is no less clear:

> And just as a cutting from the vine in the ground fructifies in its season, or, as a grain of wheat falling into the earth and becoming decomposed rises with manifold increase by the Spirit of God, and becomes the Eucharist, which is the body and blood of Christ, so also our bodies, being nourished by it, and deposited in the earth, and suffering decomposition there, shall rise at their appointed time. . . . For as the bread from the earth, receiving the invocation of God . . . is no longer common bread but a Eucharist composed of two things, both an earthly and a heavenly one, so also our bodies, partaking of the Eucharist, are no longer corruptible, having the hope of eternal resurrection.[70]

Yet for some perhaps the link is not so obvious. The encyclical *Mysterium Fidei* speaks of the Eucharist without the slightest appeal to the Resurrection of Jesus.[71] It may be true that Augustine is a culprit of sorts here. He apparently found himself faced with a dilemma: *either* Christ has a glorified body *localized* in heaven *or* he possesses a divine ubiquity. Since Augustine firmly held that Christ remains forever incarnate, he felt forced to opt for a glorified body localized in heaven. It was Augustine who, with this "spatial" concept of glorification and a "reified" notion of body, would provide the legacy for the West in this area. He could do something, however, that successors like Ratramnus, Berengar, and Calvin apparently could not, namely, rise above the narrow confines of his own system. Basing his position on his Christian heritage he clearly affirmed—perhaps a bit illogically in view of some of his theories—the "real presence" of Christ in the

---

68. Letter to the Ephesians 20:2, as cited by J. Quasten, *Patrology* (Westminster, Md.: Newman Press, 1962), 1: 66. See also Martelet, *The Risen Christ,* 59ff.

69. *Letter to Polycarp of Smyrna,* 7:1, cited by Quasten.

70. *Adversus Haereses* 5, 2, 3, and 4, 18, 5, as cited by Quasten, 304–5. See also A. Hamman, ed., *The Mass: Ancient Liturgies and Patristic Texts,* trans. T. Halton (New York: Alba House, 1967), 171, 184, 222, for further instances.

71. See Martelet, *The Risen Christ,* 119.

Eucharist. Those who followed Augustine, for example, Ratramnus and Berengar, had no anthropology of the body that would allow the Eucharist to be one particular instance of the risen Christ's bodiliness. They therefore changed the point of reference from body to substance, thus moving the question from the anthropological to the metaphysical plane. In so doing, they may well have paved the way for the separation of eucharistic reflection from the mystery of the Resurrection. A number of contemporary, eucharistic "crises" may well stem from the "theological rupture" between Eucharist and Resurrection—a rupture due to the inability to come up with a suitable anthropology of the body.[72]

Be that as it may, a brief examination of the narratives of the risen Lord's appearances to the disciples could serve the double function of underlining once again the bond between Eucharist and Resurrection, and of providing some further insight on the Eucharist in light of the Resurrection. The easiest place to begin is with the Emmaus account in Luke 24. It is easiest because there is general agreement among Scripture scholars that this account, especially verses 30–31, has eucharistic overtones.[73] The pattern is familiar: Jesus takes the initiative, the disciples come to recognize him (in the breaking of the bread), then they go and recount their experience to others (mission?). One purpose of the account, apart from apologetic additions, is to reassure those who have never seen the "earthly Jesus" that there is a way that they, too, can encounter, recognize and enter into union with the risen Lord. In the eucharistic meal, they have the way to an encounter which is "closer than touching and deeper than meeting."[74]

A number of authors also see a parallel between the Emmaus account and the meal by Lake Tiberias in John 21.[75] The account of the meal on the shore, here combined with another account about a

---

72. Martelet, *The Risen Christ*, 122–37.

73. See Kehl, "Eucharistie und Aufenstehung," 43:101–2.

74. A. Shaw, "The Breakfast by the Shore and the Mary Magdalene Encounter as Eucharistic Narratives," *The Journal of Theological Studies*, n.s. 25 (1974): 26. See also Brown, *The Gospel According to John (XIII–XXI), Anchor Bible* 29A, 1100.

75. Léon-Dufour, *Resurrection*, 91–92; R. Brown, *The Gospel According to John (XIII–XXI), Anchor Bible* 29A, 1094; Shaw, "The Breakfast," 13.

catch of fish,[76] forms an epilogue of sorts to show how Jesus provided for the needs of the Church.[77]

Are there eucharistic overtones to this account? One always runs the risk of reading sacramental allusions into every corner of the Gospels. Raymond Brown has proposed a sensible methodology which we shall follow here. Briefly, there must be something in the text and context to indicate that the author/redactor intended a sacramental allusion. In addition, there must be some indication in early Christian art, literature, or liturgy that this passage was so understood.[78]

In John 21:9ff. we read: "When they landed, they saw a charcoal fire there with a fish laid on it and some bread. Jesus came over, took the bread and gave it to them, and did the same with the fish." John records only one other scene on the shore of the lake, namely, the multiplication of the loaves and the discourse on the bread of life, which we have already seen has eucharistic overtones.[79] Here Jesus has bread and fish (at times a eucharistic symbol) ready.[80] He "takes" and "gives" the bread to them just as he "took and gave" in the multiplication of the loaves. It is hard to see how an early Christian audience could miss seeing a link with the Eucharist here. Both early Christian art and literature seem to support this link.[81]

If one can accept this appearance as linked with the Eucharist, and there seems to be good reason to do so,[82] the verse which follows

---

76. See Brown, *The Gospel According to John (XIII–XXI)*, Anchor Bible 29A, 1084–85, 1092; and Shaw, "The Breakfast," 15.

77. Brown, *The Gospel According to John (XIII–XXI)*, Anchor Bible 29A 1063, 1081–82.

78. See Brown, *The Gospel According to John (XIII–XXI)*, Anchor Bible 29A, cxi–cxiv, and the same author's *New Testament Essays* (Milwaukee: Bruce, 1965), 51–76.

79. See n. 63.

80. See Andrew B. McGowan, *Ascetic Eucharists: Food and Drink in Early Christian Ritual Meals* (New York: Oxford University Press, 1999), 127–30, who discusses the Gospels' use of fish in the "feeding stories" and raises the question of whether or not they reflect a eucharistic meal involving fish. After examining examples of fish in the gospels, funerary inscriptions, paintings and sarcophagi, and Christian funerary meals he concludes "the idea of a fish eucharist is not borne out by the evidence. . . . There is simply no persuasive evidence for a fish eucharist" (139–40). See also O. Cullmann and F. J. Leenhardt, *Essays on The Lord's Supper*, trans. J. G. Davies (Richmond, Va.: John Knox Press, 1959), 10; and C. Vogel, "Le repas sacré au poisson chez les chrétiens," *Revue des Sciences Religieuses* 40 (1966): 1–26.

81. See Brown, *The Gospel According to John (XIII–XXI)*, Anchor Bible 29A, 1098–1100; Vogel, "Le repas sacré," esp. 8–10.

82. See Brown, *The Gospel According to John (XIII–XXI)*, Anchor Bible 29A 1100; Vogel, "Le repas sacré," 8–10.

is significant. "This marked the third time that Jesus appeared to the disciples after being raised from the dead" (Jn. 21:14). What were the other two appearances like? Both take place when the disciples are *gathered together inside on a Sunday* (Jn. 20:19–23, 26–29). In view of the parallel appearances in the Synoptics, this seems more than coincidence. In Luke 24:13–43, as we have seen, the disciples recognize Jesus in a meal context. They return to the others and tell "how they had come to know him in the breaking of bread," and as they discuss it Christ appears to them and eats a fish with them. Mark 16:14 tells us, "Finally, *as they were at table*, Jesus was revealed to the Eleven!" To round out the picture, a number of authors see a meal context in the description of the appearances in Acts 1:4 and Acts 10:41.[83]

The fourth Gospel thus mentions three post-Resurrection appearances to the disciples, one with striking similarities to the multiplication of the loaves while the other two are to the disciples gathered on a Sunday. Since the Synoptic parallels are in a meal context, it hardly seems rash to look for eucharistic overtones in the Johannine account. The Johannine answer to the Christian's desire to encounter Jesus here and now seems to be this: The Christian will recognize Christ's presence most perfectly in this life not physically but through faith, the spoken word, and the sacraments, especially the Eucharist. Thus Christ comes to us and implants his gifts, especially the gifts of his Spirit and his life within us.[84] Others also see eucharistic connotations in the post-Resurrection appearances to the women, for example.[85] These seem more tenuous. Moreover, they are unnecessary for our conclusions.

There is certainly good reason to conclude that in presenting many of the post-Resurrection appearances the New Testament writers intend to link them to a meal and probably to the eucharistic meal.[86] M. Kehl suggests that, since we do not know exactly *how* the

---

83. See Kehl, "Eucharistie und Aufenstehung," 43:105–9; Cullmann, *Essays*, 11–12; Brown, *The Gospel According to John (XIII–XXI), Anchor Bible* 29A, 1094.

84. See Brown, *The Gospel According to John (XIII–XXI), Anchor Bible* 29A, 1009, 1100; A. Feuillet, *Etudes Johanniques* (Paris: Desclée, 1962), 156–57; and M. J. Buckley, "Eucharist and the Spirit," *Worship* 37 (1963): 338–41.

85. See Shaw, "The Breakfast," 19ff., and Brown, *The Gospel According to John (XIII–XXI), Anchor Bible* 29A, 1010–11, where the author lists a number of attempts only to disagree with them.

86. See Léon-Dufour, *The Resurrection*, 92–97.

risen Christ "appeared," it is possible that at such meal-assemblies he made his presence felt in the very celebration of the meal without any extraordinary "visions" and "appearances." Kehl is clear that he is not limiting the "appearances" of the risen Lord to the meal setting so described. This would be, he claims, *one* of the signs—perhaps even the most decisive—which the Lord used to reveal his new existence to his disciples. If so, their experience of Jesus' Resurrection in the meal setting is not so different from ours in the Eucharist.[87] Others would claim that it is precisely in the visible nature of Christ's presence that the disciples' experience differs from ours.[88] Be that as it may, the experience of Christ's presence in the appearances and/or in the Eucharist is not simply to show that Jesus lives. It also involves a call to faith and to a mission.[89] Finally, with some qualifications[90] we can subscribe to Cullmann's description of the early Eucharists:

> We can now understand why the Christian Community in the Apostolic Age celebrated its meals "with joy." *The certainty of the Resurrection* was the essential religious motive of the primitive Lord's Supper. The experience of the presence of the Risen One in the midst of the assembly of the faithful was repeated—under a less material form, it is true—each time the community was united for the common meal. This experience was identical with that of Easter, and the first disciples must have considered these cultic meals as the direct continuation of those in which the disciples had participated immediately after the death of the Lord. When they assembled "to break bread," they knew that the Risen One would reveal His presence in a manner less visible but no less real than previously.[91]

Not only was the primitive Eucharist resurrectional; it was also eschatological:

---

87. Kehl, "Eucharistie und Aufenstehung," 105, 111, 120–25.

88. See Martelet, *The Risen Christ,* 118, and Cullmann, *Essays,* 12.

89. Kehl, "Eucharistie und Aufenstehung," 116–18; Léon-Dufour, *Resurrection,* 213–14; and Marxsen, *The Resurrection,* 83–84.

90. For example, Lietzmann's thesis of two distinct, and even different ways of celebrating the Eucharist in the early Church (see Cullmann, *Essays,* 5–7,16) upon which Cullmann draws, is generally regarded as no longer acceptable (see Kehl, "Eucharistie und Aufenstehung," 43: 91–92). Also, one should realize that the *whole* Paschal mystery (passion and death as well as Resurrection) is involved here. Cullmann indicates that this is a later development, attributing to Paul the link between cross and Resurrection in the Eucharist (11–22).

91. Cullmann, *Essays,* 12.

The Lord *appeared* to the disciples after His death, while they were eating; He *appears* now in the cultic meal of the community; He *will appear* soon for the Messianic Banquet. This third motif must have been connected, in the closest fashion, with the other two in the minds of the faithful assembled to make Christ present.[92]

This was another reason for joy and it gave the acclamation *Maranatha* an eschatological as well as a contemporary ring. It gave voice to the twofold longing to have the risen Lord come to this eucharistic assembly *here and now* and also, someday soon, *once, and for all.*[93]

IMPLICATIONS FOR THE EUCHARIST TODAY

To proclaim the *bodily* aspect of the Resurrection in too physical a way (atoms, molecules, blood, bones) is paradoxically to say too much and too little. It is to say more about the risen Lord's bodiliness than even Paul seemed able to say (1 Cor. 15:35–44) and yet to give the impression that a simple resuscitation has taken place. Here we stand on the brink of an ultrarealism that has periodically plagued Christianity with assertions about chewing Christ's bones and sucking his blood,[94] an ultrarealism which Thomas Aquinas attacked forcefully![95] On the other hand, to limit the Resurrection to the realm of ideas or memory or example is to limit the Eucharist as well to that realm. Yet the New Testament proclaims that it is the *person* of Christ whom the disciples once experienced in the appearances and continue to experience in their eucharistic meals.

Moreover, to say that Christ is risen *"spiritually,"* that is, that his whole personality has been so filled with the Spirit that he is free to involve the whole universe in his Resurrection, is to say something about the Eucharist. If the Resurrection has cosmic proportions, the Eucharist also has cosmic proportions. If Jesus has taken on the whole

---

92. Cullmann, *Essays*, 13.

93. See Cullmann, *Essays*, 13–15.

94. See J. P. de Jong, *Die Eucharistie Als Symbolwirklichkeit,* trans. from the Dutch by J. Rommens and T. Handgrätinger (Regensberg: Friedrich Pustet ,1969), 30–36. Of particular interest is the break between eucharistic presence and the risen body of Christ in the thinking of some (see 36).

95. *Summa Theologiae,* III, 77, a. 7: "We do not chew Christ with our teeth; Christ is not eaten in his own bodiliness nor is he chewed with the teeth—what is eaten and broken is the sacramental species."

universe as an extension of himself, of his bodiliness, then we have the roots of what Rahner calls a "Copernican revolution" in sacramental and eucharistic theology.[96] The Eucharist, as well as the other sacraments, can no longer be regarded as havens in which Christians encounter a Christ absent in the rest of their lives. The Eucharist becomes, rather, *one* experience of the risen Lord, a focal point perhaps, which is to sensitize Christians to his presence throughout the universe. Like the appearances to the first disciples, the Eucharist is in no way meant to narrow Christ's presence to one moment but to make the believer conscious, in the Holy Spirit, of his presence always and everywhere.[97] Teilhard once again seems to have had an intuition of this:

> Yes, the human layer of the earth is wholly and continuously under the organizing influx of the incarnate[98] Christ. This we all believe, as one of the most certain points of our faith. . . . The sacramental action of Christ, *precisely because it sanctifies matter,* extends its influence beyond the pure supernatural, over all that makes up the internal and external ambience of the faithful, that is to say that it sets its mark in everything which we call "our providence." If this is the case, then we find ourselves [by simply having followed the "extensions." of the Eucharist] plunged once again precisely into our divine *milieu.* Christ—for whom we are formed, each with his own individuality and his own vocation—Christ reveals himself in each reality around us, and shines like an ultimate determinant, like a centre, one might almost say like a universal element.[99]

In short, what Christ has done in the Eucharist by dint of his Resurrection, he also does in the universe. By thus involving the universe and those within it in his Resurrection, Christ has given to it a *continuing* character in which the Eucharist shares. The presence of the risen Lord was a troubling, agitating force for those encountering him, spurring them on to renewed action as well as renewed hope.

---

96. See K. Rahner, "Secular Life and the Sacraments: A Copernican Revolution," *The Tablet* (March 6,1971): 236–38, and (March 13, 1971): 267–68.

97. See Pousset, "Croire en la Résurrection," 368.

98. We would understand "incarnate" here in the sense that Rahner, *Theological Investigations* 4:130, and E. Schillebeeckx, *Christ the Sacrament of the Encounter with God,* trans. P. Barrett (New York: Sheed & Ward, 1963), 22, speak of the Incarnation, namely, the full process by which Jesus "becomes man," including his death and Resurrection.

99. Teilhard de Chardin, *The Divine Milieu,* 103–4; also 102, 105–7.

The disciples' experience of him as risen fostered in them a *relecture*,[100] a rethinking of their whole lives in the light of their newly found faith. His presence demanded decisions, as it had done before his death. Could one announce that God had vindicated Jesus' way of life by raising him from the dead and not try to live as he did? Could one proclaim that "the life I live now is not my own: Christ is living in me" (Gal. 2:20), and ignore the loving service that characterized this Christ? Could one preach a *bodily* resurrection and say that "the *whole* created world eagerly awaits the revelation of the sons of God" (Rom. 8:19), yet pay no attention to this "created world"?

Once one acknowledges the bond between Eucharist and Resurrection, one finds oneself confronted with similar challenges. If the risen Lord in the appearances provoked a rethinking of the disciples' lives, a radical new commitment for him, one would expect him to require no less when he appears today in the Eucharist. Could one announce that in the Eucharist the risen Lord gives himself in food and drink for *our* nourishment and have no concern for millions who die for want of nourishment? Could one proclaim that Christ's presence in the Eucharist is a microcosm of his presence throughout the *whole,* material universe and be totally insensitive to the use men and women make of that material universe? Could one celebrate the extension of the risen Lord's presence in people, as well as in bread and wine, and be blind to the need many people still have for peace and justice?

If Christians are really "so otherworldly that they are no earthly good," the problem lies not with the Eucharist or with the Resurrection that it celebrates, but with Christians and their varieties of unbelief or misbelief. The answer is not to stop preaching Resurrection but to start living it, not to stop celebrating Eucharist but to take its implications seriously.

Conclusion

Were this done, then the Christian community would become what it was meant to be—the embodiment of Jesus' ongoing Resurrection in this world. For if Jesus is not still in the world agitating, spurring men

---

100. See Pousset, "Croire en la Résurrection," 369–72.

and women on to work for a better world here and now, if he is simply the founder of a religion rather than the creator and initiator of a new universe, then he is not truly risen. Then we *are* on our own. Then the faith, not only of Christians but of all people, humanists included, really is in vain.[101]

The Eucharist, however, proclaims that he is risen; he is present challenging us to transform ourselves and our world. The Eucharist becomes not only a celebration of Christ's service and a call to share in that service, but also the celebration of the future to which this service leads. It can thus provide the basis for *hope-filled* activity as opposed to hopeless inactivity. It proclaims to us that we are moving toward a future goal. It reminds us that this goal will involve accountability, that the Christian call, like that of the Israelite, is one of involvement in God's re-creation of the world through people like ourselves,[102] that here on earth God's work is truly our own.

Through all this, however, the Eucharist proclaims to us that the goal is *our* Lord who will come *again*, whom the Scriptures quote so often as saying, "It is I. Do not be afraid" (Mk. 6:50. See also Lk. 24:36–39 par., Mt. 28:9–10). The Eucharist, then, urges Christians to work for the future *here and now*, to work hopefully, with joyful anticipation and a certain reckless abandon, confident that in Jesus Christ even death will lead to new life. In short, it urges Christians to cry out with their lives as well as their lips:

Marana tha! Come, Lord Jesus!

---

101. See Lane, *Christ at the Centre*, 99–102, and Aidan Kavanagh, "The Theology of Easter: Themes in Cultic Data," *Worship* 42 (1968): 204.

102. See Gray, "Response to Wolfhart Pannenberg," 81–82, who rightly points out the value of Teilhard's insistence that Christians, no less than the rest of humankind, do not just wait for the fulfillment of this world but actively work toward it.

Chapter 6

Eucharist and Memorial

"DO THIS IN MEMORY OF ME. . . . Therefore, as we celebrate / the memorial of his Death and Resurrection, / we offer you, Lord, / the Bread of life and the Chalice of salvation . . ."[1]

Scholars today would disagree on the extent we can reconstruct first-century Jewish and Christian liturgical celebrations. They also disagree on the Jewish prayer form(s) that served as a "model" for the Christian Eucharist. Few, however, if any, would deny that Jesus was firmly rooted in his Jewish tradition that he freely interpreted in light of his own experience of God and Israel. This is certainly true of the Jewish *zakar* or memorial. The purpose of this chapter is twofold: first, to give a brief historical background of the notion of memorial; second, to sketch some underlying theological issues, especially in light of the writings of Edward Kilmartin.

HISTORICAL BACKGROUND

Max Thurian, in his classic study, reminds us that the term *zakar* and its Greek counterpart *anamnesis* have many meanings.[2] Not the least of these meanings is the notion that the "past event became present or rather each person became a contemporary of the past event."[3]

---

1. *The Roman Missal,* Third Typical Edition, Eucharistic Prayer II.

2. Max Thurian, *The Eucharistic Memorial,* trans. J. G. Davies (Richmond: John Knox Press, 1959), I: 5–6, 25.

3. Ibid., I, 19. See also Xavier Léon-Dufour, *Sharing the Eucharistic Bread: The Witness of the New Testament,* trans. M. J. O'Connell (New York: Paulist Press, 1987), 107, 113–16. Léon-Dufour also cautions against using "memorial" for the Eucharist since that word usually refers to an action already completed rather than an action taking place (109–10).

Thurian and others then apply this understanding particularly to the Jewish Passover. Remembering God and reminding God take place in all of Israel's activity but come to the fore especially in ritual activity. The paradigm for this is the Passover memorial.[4]

Passover Context

Of course, as Chauvet points out, there is memory and there is memory. One is a lifeless nostalgia for a past seen in a yellowed photo. The other is an act of communal memory that regenerates those remembering. This kind of memory recalls the suffering, the oppression, but also the fight to liberate. There is still hope that tomorrow will be better. Oppressive regimes fear this kind of memory and try to root it out. It is "dangerous and liberating memory."[5] "In its Passover memorial, Israel receives its past as present, and this gift guarantees a promise of a future."[6] This is why it is so crucial that the exiles not forget Jerusalem. In the midst of their present "death" it reminds them of their past and God's promise for the future. This in turn gives them hope and gets them back on their feet in the present.[7]

The people don't expect to be present at and relive the Exodus literally. "The events remembered, Exodus and covenant serve as a memory and a metaphor that shapes the people's identity and self understanding, but the metaphor takes on new life in face of tragedy and surprise."[8] Such a memorial also reminds them that they have a relation with a God who entered history on behalf of others. They have a responsibility to do the same. Theologically this notion of memorial best expresses the historical and prophetic character of

---

4. Louis-Marie Chauvet, *Symbol and Sacrament: A Sacramental Reinterpretation of Christian Existence,* trans. P. Madigan and M. Beaumont (Collegeville, Minn.: Liturgical Press, 1995), 232.

5. Chauvet, *Symbol and Sacrament,* 233–34, and Léon-Dufour, *Sharing the Eucharistic Bread,* 105–7,112. See also, Hans Küng, *On Being a Christian,* trans. E. Quinn (Garden City, N.Y.: Doubleday, 1976), 121, citing J. B. Metz and Bruce T. Morrill, *Anamnesis as Dangerous Memory: Political and Liturgical Theology in Dialogue* (Collegeville, Minn.: Liturgical Press, 2000), who compares Metz with Alexander Schmemann in a thought-provoking manner. In this context he brings out well Metz's point that remembering should lead Christians to follow Jesus Christ willingly and work toward the future of all (30–35) and he sums up five insights and challenges that Metz provides (70–71).

6. Chauvet, *Symbol and Sacrament,* 234, and Morrill, *Anamnesis as Dangerous Memory,* 174.

7. Ibid., 233.

8. David N. Power, *The Eucharistic Mystery: Revitalizing the Tradition* (New York: Crossroad, 1994), 48–49. See also Léon-Dufour, *Sharing the Eucharistic Bread,* 107, 112.

their cult.[9] The Passover memorial is about covenant. It is a discourse on the relationship between two covenant partners. It involves, first of all, God's remembering and reminding, and then Israel's remembering and reminding, with all that implies on both sides.[10] Psalm 111 reflects well the dynamism at work: God "has caused his wonderful works to be remembered" and God "is ever mindful of his covenant."[11]

David Power, among others, acknowledges the Passover Seder models as helpful for understanding the Christian Eucharist. He offers three cautions, however. First, remember that the Passover Seder in Jesus' day is a historical reconstruction since we have no contemporary documents on it. Second, do not think in terms of a direct transition from seder to Christian memorial rites. Third, realize that neither the Passover Seder nor any table ritual was the only Jewish influence on the Christian eucharistic memorial.[12]

Pre-Nicene Writings

This having been said, one of the keys to understanding the early, Pre-Nicene Eucharist is the believers' concern to be faithful to Jesus' command to celebrate memorial. One Last Supper tradition links the Eucharist to Jesus' death by interpreting that celebration as a "memorial" (*anamnesis*) of that death. Luke 22:19 does this in the context of the bread saying, and 1 Corinthians 11:24–25 does it in the context of both the bread and the cup sayings. The Christians for their memorial joined scripture readings to the blessing of God for creation and redemption. This was their way of participating in Christ's Paschal mystery and its fruits.[13] "However named it has always been part of the Church's grasp of memorial that the mystery remembered becomes a living reality in the lives of those who celebrated it

---

9. Chauvet, *Symbol and Sacrament*, 231.

10. See Patrick McGoldrick, "Memorial," in J. A. Komonchak, et al., eds., *The New Dictionary of Theology* (Wilmington, Del.: Michael Glazier, 1987), 644.

11. See Power, *The Eucharistic Mystery*, 45–46.

12. Ibid., 43. See also Louis Bouyer, *Eucharist: Theology and Spirituality of the Eucharistic Prayer*, trans. C. U. Quinn (Notre Dame, Ind.: University of Notre Dame Press, 1968); more recently, Enrico Mazza, *The Origins of the Eucharistic Prayer*, trans. R. E. Lane (Collegeville, Minn.: Liturgical Press, 1995), and *The Celebration of the Eucharist*, trans. M. J. O'Connell (Collegeville, Minn.: Liturgical Press, 1999).

13. Power, *The Eucharistic Mystery*, 128.

liturgically. For the early writers this was implied in the very idea of symbolic or sacramental representation."[14]

An analysis of homilies of an early unknown Easter Vigil homilist, and of Cyprian, Irenaeus, and Origen reveals, despite their differences, certain common elements in their understanding of the eucharistic memorial: (1) This memorial is a way of participating in Christ's Paschal mystery; (2) an understanding of the passion and the Eucharist go hand in hand; (3) the context of their understanding is one of practical concerns and interests broader than the eucharistic memorial; (4) the practical concerns—such as spirituality, protection in time of martyrdom, and defense of the faith—account for the differences of the four theologies.[15] Efforts to adapt their eucharistic celebrations to their own times and cultures also led naturally to ritual or liturgical diversity.[16]

Later Patristic Writings

Later writers linked the once-for-all sacrifice of Christ with their notion of memorial. John Chrysostom is a good example: "We do not offer a different sacrifice, as the high priest did in the past, but we always offer the same one. Or rather, we celebrate a memorial of a sacrifice."[17] An increased emphasis on propitiation and sacrifice rather than on other images, for instance, victory over death, colored the way Cyril of Jerusalem, Chrysostom, and Theodore of Mopsuestia, among others, saw the historical event as somehow being made present in the Eucharist. Earlier theologians viewed sacramental participation in those events in terms of configuration and fruit. These later writers speak of an event that takes on superterrestrial form and is here and

---

14. Ibid., 304–5. See also Thurian, *The Eucharistic Memorial*, I: 19; Edward J. Kilmartin, *The Eucharist in the West: History and Theology*, ed. Robert J. Daly (Collegeville, Minn.: Liturgical Press, 1998), 202, who also (334) cites C. Giraudo, *Eucaristia per la Chiesa: Prospettive Teologiche Sull' Eucaristia a Partire Dalla "Lex Orandi"* (= *Aloisiana* 22) (Rome: Gregorian University, 1989), to the same effect; Chauvet, *Symbol and Sacrament*, 231–33, among others. William R. Crockett, *Eucharist: Symbol of Transformation* (New York: Pueblo, 1989), 21–28, offers a good treatment of some of the key points. The virtual unanimity *that* the reality is present breaks down when the question of *how* it is present arises, as we shall see later.

15. Power, *The Eucharistic Mystery*, 104–14, especially 113–14.

16. Ibid., 128.

17. Homily on Heb. 17:8, cited by McGoldrick, "Memorial," 645.

now present in the sacramental form.[18] Kilmartin refers to this as "commemorative actual presence." This is how a number of the Greek Fathers explained the presence of the one and unique sacrifice of Christ on the cross and the sacrificial character of the Eucharist.[19]

Kilmartin contends that while Ambrose, for instance, did borrow from the fourth-century Antiochene tradition, he did not see it in the same Platonic context. Ambrose did not speculate on the relationship of the once-for-all historical sacrifice of Christ to the eucharistic sacrifice. Had he done so he might have turned to a notion of an *anamnesis* (a "commemorative actual presence") that enabled the event to be present. Neither he nor Cyprian made use of this notion in their writings, and by the sixth century it had disappeared from the western tradition. This was unfortunate since such a notion could have led to a more balanced theology of the eucharistic sacrifice. Ambrose thus reflected the difficulty that the western mind had in grasping the Greek concept of commemorative sacrifice. His focus was more on the individual, concrete event than on such speculative questions.[20]

On the other hand, Augustine's sense that the Eucharist was the actualization or expression of the Body of Christ, because the Church was in fact the Body of Christ, could have helped immensely in the understanding of the Eucharist as sacrifice and in other areas. "If you receive well, you are what you have received." "Since you are the body of Christ and His members, it is your mystery that is placed on the Lord's table; it is your mystery that you receive. . . . You hear the words: 'The body of Christ,' and you answer, 'Amen.' Be therefore members of Christ that your 'Amen' may be true." "Be what you see, and receive what you are."[21] Christ, in the Spirit, realizes the Eucharist: the "whole Christ," as Augustine put it, Head and members.

Moreover, Augustine interprets the Eucharist as sacrifice in terms of the Church's joining itself to Christ's offering. "Such is the sacrifice of Christians. 'We, the many, are one body in Christ.' This is

18. Power, *The Eucharistic Mystery*, 147–48.

19. Kilmartin, *The Eucharist in the West*, 18.

20. Ibid., 18–23. Could it have been, however, that Cyprian and Ambrose, for instance, had a notion of "symbolic reality" that enabled them to deal with the issue in a way satisfactory to them? See John H. McKenna, "Symbol and Reality: Some Anthropological Considerations," *Worship* 65 (Jan. 1991): 7–12.

21. See James J. Megivern, *Concomitance and Communion: A Study in Eucharistic Doctrine and Practice* (New York: Herder, 1963), 68, citing Augustine, Sermo 227 and 272.

the sacrifice, as the faithful understand, which the church continues to celebrate in the sacrament of the altar, in which it is clear to the church that she herself is offered in the very offering she makes to God."[22] Augustine also rightly linked, as the early eucharistic prayers did, sacrifice with memorial and the church's offering with partaking in communion. "Christians also make the memorial of this sacrifice in the holy offering and partaking of the body and blood of Christ."[23]

Generally, then, during this period "sacrifice" was a descriptive metaphor for the entire thanksgiving-memorial of the Eucharist. The link between Eucharist and sacrifice was primarily through the biblical notion of *anamnesis* or memorial as Augustine understood it. It was neither a merely mental recalling nor a repetition of Christ's once-for-all sacrifice. It was, rather, a sacramental or liturgical celebration of that sacrifice so that the present generation could participate in it.[24]

Unfortunately, the lead of people like Chrysostom and Augustine was not followed. Instead, Gregory the Great would say that Christ in the mystery of the holy sacrifice is offered for us again (*iterum*). This would be used as a "proof text" that Christ's sacrifice is repeated in each Mass in an "unbloody manner." Focusing on the notion that the eucharistic sacrifice was a liturgical repetition of Christ's once-for-all sacrifice in turn obscured the importance of the active participation of the laity. Earlier Latin theology considered their participation essential to the realization of the eucharistic sacrifice, argues Kilmartin. Later theology stressed the ministry of the priest almost to the exclusion of the laity's role.[25]

Ninth-Century Debate

In the ninth-century debate between Paschasius and Ratramnus there is further evidence of the loss of an appreciation of the dynamic character of the eucharistic mystery that some earlier Greek theologians had. There is no sign of the Greek notion of the commemorative actual presence of the once-for-all redeeming work of Christ. In trying

---

22. Augustine, *City of God*, 10:6, as cited by Crockett, *Eucharist*, 72.

23. Augustine, *Against Faustus*, 20:18, as cited by Crockett, *Eucharist*, 72.

24. Crockett, *Eucharist*, 72.

25. Kilmartin, *The Eucharist in the West*, 22.

to deal with the relationship between the eucharistic celebration and the sacrifice of the cross neither is able to draw on such a concept of memorial. Nor, contends Kilmartin, do they have a sense of a "somatic real presence" from the perspective of "prototype image thinking." So the sense of bodily presence originally embedded in the concept of *anamnesis* or memorial becomes isolated.[26] This development also mirrors the loss of the ancient notion of a "symbolic reality," a symbol that enables the reality to be present.[27] The popularity of the allegorical preaching of men like Amalar of Metz, reflecting a sense of memory very different from that of the early church, only underscored the divergence.[28]

Thomas Aquinas

In the thirteenth century Thomas Aquinas, with all his brilliance, was a product of his time. Liturgical reform was not on his agenda. The context of his explanations was the then current eucharistic practice, including the private Mass of the priest. He was mainly interested in giving a good theological explanation of the sacraments, settling disputed questions and bringing all aspects of the sacrament and its celebration into an organic unity.[29] Had he lived beyond the age of forty-nine, he might have developed a "countercultural," more ecclesial understanding of the Eucharist. In his Commentary on the Sentences, he followed those who held that the Eucharist or eucharistic memorial fulfills Christ's promise to be with us until the end of time (Mt. 28:20). In the *Summa* he seems more interested in showing the difference between the ordinary mode of presence and the sacramental.[30] He gives three reasons for Christ's instituting the Eucharist: (1) in departing from his disciples in one way, he wanted to stay with them in another way, sacramentally; (2) salvation comes through faith in Christ's passion which called for its sacramental commemoration;

---

26. Ibid., 83, 87.

27. See McKenna, "Symbol and Reality," 12–14.

28. Ibid., 12, and McGoldrick, "Memorial," 644–45, who also sees the reduced experience of Jewish cult in general and the Passover in particular plus the heavy emphasis on sacrifice as contributing factors in the declining appreciation of memorial.

29. Power, *The Eucharistic Mystery,* 216–17.

30. Ibid., 218–19.

(3) this memory or commemoration at the same time allows believers to make a subjective response.[31]

Operating with an Aristotelian-based "static ontology" Thomas distinguished between the substance of a person that perdures and the accidental actions and relationships of that person's life that do not. Both Catholics and Protestants were to apply this static understanding to the debates over Christ's presence and action in the sacraments. This made it difficult to explain how Christ's passion or paschal mystery could somehow be present in the eucharistic memorial.[32] Edward Kilmartin, in hindsight, argues that if Aquinas had a "relational ontology" that sees being as essentially relational, his approach (and those who followed him) to the question of the presence of Christ's acts in the eucharistic memorial could have been much different. Jesus' choices and actions for others would then be the way he realized himself, part of his self-realization, and therefore part of his being. Wherever the risen Christ is present those temporal choices and actions would be present as well.[33] The fact remains, however, that Thomas and others did not have such a "relational ontology." This fact might also explain why the eucharistic theology of that time was not Trinitarian.

On the other hand, Thomas did remain true to Augustine's interpretation of eucharistic sacrifice as a memorial of Christ's death. The Eucharist is neither a repetition nor a new sacrifice but it can be called a sacrifice because it is the *anamnesis* of Christ's death. "This sacrament . . . commemorates the passion of our Lord, which was the true sacrifice. . . . Because of this it is called 'sacrifice.'"[34] "O Sacred banquet in which Christ is received, the memorial of his passion is renewed, the soul is filled with grace, and a pledge of future glory is given to us, Alleluia."[35]

---

31. Ibid., 218.

32. Kilmartin, *The Eucharist in the West,* 90. Odo Casel and others in the *Mysteriengegenwart* debates in the twentieth century would do the same.

33. See Jerome M. Hall, *We Have the Mind of Christ: The Holy Spirit and Liturgical Memory in the Thought of Edward J. Kilmartin* (Collegeville, Minn.: The Liturgical Press, 2001), 87–90.

34. *Summa Theologiae* 3a, 73, 4, as cited by Crockett, *Eucharist,* 120.

35. Antiphon to the Magnificat for the second Vespers of Corpus Christi, as cited by Crockett, *Eucharist,* 114.

Time of Trent

By the time of the Council of Trent, however, neither Catholics nor Reformers had a notion of memorial that accurately reflected that of the biblical and early liturgical sources.[36] Both sides had lost sight of the original understanding of memorial just as they had lost sight of the original notion of symbol or "symbolic reality."[37] In addition, both had inherited a "fractured" understanding of the eucharistic prayer that isolated the institution narrative from the other elements of that prayer. So they were unable to reconcile the notions of sacrifice of thanksgiving and sacrifice of propitiation. Moreover, their lack of knowledge of liturgical history prevented them from seeing the connection between the entire eucharistic or memorial prayer and sacramental commemoration. Similarly, they no longer grasped the relation of the eucharistic prayer to the rite of communion.[38]

At Trent (Session XXII), for instance, memorial was linked to the institution of ordained priesthood whose function it was to offer the sacrifice of the Mass. The notion of sacrifice clearly dominated that of memorial. Giraudo contends that, as a result, Trent was unable to offer a theological explanation for its solemn definition that the Mass is a sacrifice.[39] Once again, this took place because the early Church understanding of "memorial" and "symbol" had been lost. In addition, both Catholic and Protestant tended to identify sacrifice with immolation, that is, some form of destruction.[40]

In more recent times, biblical, liturgical, theological, and ecumenical studies have led to a renewed appreciation of the ancient Jewish and Christian sense of memorial and symbol. The "sacrament" of

---

36. See Power, *The Eucharistic Mystery*, 259; Kilmartin, *The Eucharist in the West*, 243; McGoldrick, "Memorial," 646; Crockett, *Eucharist*, 124, who adds: "The reformers, therefore, ended up opposing the ideas of 'sacrifice' and 'memorial' rather than understanding the eucharist as a sacrifice precisely because it is the *anamnesis* of Christ's sacrifice on the cross."

37. See McKenna, "Symbol and Reality," 16.

38. See Power, *The Eucharistic Mystery*, 259.

39. See Kilmartin, *The Eucharist in the West*, 332, and McGoldrick, "Memorial," 646. Frank C. Senn, *Christian Liturgy: Catholic and Evangelical* (Minneapolis: Fortress Press, 1997), 261, claims that had Cardinal Cajetan (1468–1534) been given more of a hearing, a helpful dialogue might have ensued.

40. See Robert J. Daly, "Robert Bellarmine and Post-Tridentine Eucharistic Theology," *Theological Studies* 61 (June 2000): 247–48, 257–60.

dogmatic theologians has converged with the "memorial" of biblical and liturgical scholars to provide horizons for dialogue.[41]

THEOLOGICAL ISSUES

Mysteriengegenwart Debate

The debate over the *Mysteriengegenwart* (a difficult term to translate, literally "mystery presence") is longstanding and well known. Odo Casel, a German Benedictine from the Rhineland abbey of Maria Laach, triggered the debate with his claim that Christ and his saving works are the basic mystery (*Urmysterium*). To be saved by Christ's actions, we must somehow come into contact with them. Christ, he claimed, makes himself present in the liturgy together with those saving deeds.[42] The purpose of this presence is to constitute the Church by conforming Christians to Christ's Paschal mystery.[43] Casel offered arguments based on the history of religions, the Scriptures, and early Christian writers.[44] While most of his arguments were challenged, his basic insight that Christ and the mysteries of his life, death and Resurrection are present in the liturgy and that believers, through faith, are configured to Christ's dying and rising, won general acceptance. As Kilmartin, who disagreed with Casel on a number of key points, put it: "The Eucharist renders present the reality of the mystery of the cross in the form of a sacramental memorial meal of the Church. . . . The goal of the Eucharist is the self-offering of the Church with Christ . . . in order that believers be changed into the true body of Christ, and become themselves a holy sacrifice."[45] Nevertheless, the question of how this presence took place remained.[46]

---

41. See McGoldrick, "Memorial," 646; McKenna, "Symbol and Reality,"16–18; and Power, *The Eucharistic Mystery*, 260.

42. Casel, "Mysteriengegenwart," *Jahrbuch fur Liturgiewissenschaft* 8 (1928): 145, as cited by Hall, *We Have the Mind of Christ*, 6–7.

43. Hall, *We Have the Mind of Christ*, 7.

44. Ibid., 11–15.

45. Kilmartin, *The Eucharist in the West*, 199–200, 202.

46. See Hall, *We Have the Mind of Christ*, 35. See n.14.

Edward Kilmartin

It is not possible to go into the debates in any detail here. What we can do is to follow the journey of one scholar, the late Edward Kilmartin, who spent much of his academic life reflecting on the question of *anamnesis* and the mystery presence of Christ's saving deeds.[47] Hopefully that will indicate some of the key theological issues. Kilmartin became convinced that since thirty years of debate over the mystery presence had yielded no satisfactory solution, the question itself was being badly formulated. He suggested a Trinitarian theology of the liturgy as the direction in which to look.[48] His task was to explore the relationship between Christ's works and the liturgical celebration. He saw three avenues as possibly fruitful. First was the relationship between the sacramental symbol and the action or role of the liturgical assembly. Second was the relationship of the different modes of Christ's presence. Third was the dialogic nature of the mystery of salvation celebrated in the liturgy. This last led him to investigate the Trinitarian self-communication and the assembly's response of self-offering. In his teaching and writing he would return repeatedly to the dialogic nature of liturgy, to the active role of the assembly, and to the notion of sacrament as liturgical prayer of the Church in the Holy Spirit.[49]

The Eucharistic Prayer

Kilmartin, with Giraudo and others, became convinced that theology had moved from the first millennium when the law of prayer (*lex orandi*) was generally normative for the law of belief (*lex credendi*) to a reversal of that order in the second millennium. They recommended restoring the original order or at least making the two complementary. This led to a study of the ancient eucharistic prayers and to viewing the institution narrative in relationship to the other elements in those prayers. Giraudo, whose position Kilmartin basically followed, sees

---

47. Our work has been made much easier by Robert Daly's editing Kilmartin's thoughts and publishing them as *The Eucharist in the West*, a monumental work, and by Jerome Hall's fine synthesis in *We Have the Mind of Christ*.

48. Hall, *We Have the Mind of Christ*, xvii–xviii.

49. Ibid., 36, 50.

the Antiochene eucharistic prayer type, associated with Chrysostom and Basil, as a model or example of the theological outlook common to eucharistic prayer types that had a specific reference to the Holy Spirit's role.[50]

An analysis of the ancient eucharistic prayers revealed a "systematic theology" of sorts. When one avoids "fracturing" the eucharistic prayer by taking the institution narrative in isolation, as we have seen above, the *anamnesis*-offering prayer forms a unit with the institution narrative. For instance, "Therefore, O Lord, as we celebrate the memorial / of the saving Passion of your Son, / his wondrous Resurrection / and Ascension into heaven, / and as we look forward to his second coming, / we offer you in thanksgiving / this holy and living sacrifice."[51] This states what the Church is doing, namely, making memorial of Christ's Paschal mystery through the offering of the eucharistic gifts. The epiclesis-intercessions form a second unit linked to the first. For example, "Lord, we pray that in your goodness and mercy your Holy Spirit may descend upon us, and upon these gifts, sanctifying them and showing them to be holy gifts for your holy people, the bread of life and the cup of salvation, the body and blood of your Son Jesus Christ. Grant that all who share this bread and cup may become one body and one spirit, a living sacrifice in Christ to the praise of your name."[52] This tells us why the Church acts, namely, in light of the transformation of the gifts and the consequent transformation of those partaking. The intercessions then broaden the focus from the gathered assembly to the universal Church.[53] The cross and the prophetic sign of the Last Supper are once-for-all. But God through the sacramental memorial re-presents us, the gathered Church, to the saving power of the once-for-all sacrifice.[54]

---

50. See Kilmartin, *The Eucharist in the West*, 327–33.

51. *The Roman Missal*, Third Typical Edition, Eucharistic Prayer III. See David Power, "The *Anamnesis*: Remembering, We Offer," 146–68, in Frank Senn, ed., *New Eucharistic Prayers: An Ecumenical Study of Their Development and Structure* (New York: Paulist Press, 1987).

52. The Presbyterian Great Prayer of Thanksgiving E with parallels in the Roman Catholic Eucharistic Prayer IV, the Methodist Great Thanksgiving 6, and the Anglican Eucharistic Prayer D. See John McKenna, "The Epiclesis Revisited," 169–94, in *New Eucharistic Prayers*.

53. Kilmartin, *The Eucharist in the West*, 333. See also Thurian, *The Eucharistic Memorial*, I: 59, 24–25.

54. Kilmartin, *The Eucharist in the West*, 336, referring to Giraudo's *Eucaristia*.

Kilmartin's analysis of the eucharistic prayers led him to three conclusions. First, all are prayers for the covenant renewal in Jesus Christ. Second, the very remembering of God's action has an epicletic or intercessory character.[55] Third, the institution narrative is the theological center of the eucharistic prayer. The institution narrative grounds the *anamnesis*-offering prayer and at the same time leans toward the epiclesis asking for the sanctification of the gifts and the people. But it is the epiclesis that is the highpoint of the eucharistic prayer. "The highpoint of the prayer itself, then, is not the narrative of institution, but the epiclesis for sanctification of the assembly through its reception of the sacrificial food and drink."[56] This last conclusion reflects two of Kilmartin's key concerns, the role of the Holy Spirit and that of the believing assembly, as we shall see.

His analysis of the eucharistic prayers also led him to conclude that a systematic theology of the liturgy must be Trinitarian, Christological, Pneumatological, and Ecclesial.[57] And this systematic theology became much of his agenda.

Trinitarian Theology

Once again it is not possible to go into detail on Kilmartin's Trinitarian approach. It does, however, show the breadth of his intellect and vision. He took Rahner's understanding of the divine self-communication in Jesus Christ and the continuing of that self-communication in the Church and combined this with other insights. He made use of the personalism of John Cowburn, an Australian Jesuit, who developed the notion of revelation as the communication of God's interpersonal love. He added to that the insights of Ludger Oeing-Hanhoff who contended that the revelation of the Trinity reveals that relationship belongs to the essence of being. If being for others is essential to God and to Jesus Christ, then Jesus' choices and actions were not just accidental and therefore ephemeral but were rather part of who he was and is, part of his "substance." They therefore perdure in the Risen Christ. He applied this to the question of the presence of Christ's actions in

---

55. See John H. McKenna, *The Eucharistic Epiclesis: A Detailed History From the Patristic to the Modern Era*, 2nd. ed. (Chicago: Hillenbrand Books, 2009), 204–6, and E. Schillebeeckx, *Christ the Sacrament* (London: Sheed & Ward, 1963), 87.

56. Kilmartin, *The Eucharist in the West*, 69; see also 67–68.

57. See Hall, *We Have the Mind of Christ*, 72–74.

the liturgical memorial. In Hall's words: "The choices that Jesus made, his history as person-for-others, are, according to a relational ontology, the means by which he realized himself in time and space. Wherever the glorified Christ is personally present, the temporal actions that make up his personal self-realization would . . . be said to be present as well."[58]

Hans Urs von Balthasar provided Kilmartin with a treatment of Christ's faith as a covenant faith that gives Christians access to inner Trinitarian communion. Kilmartin would link this to the role of the Holy Spirit in the faith of Christ.[59] He adapted insights from an Australian theologian, David Coffey, on his way toward an ascending Trinitarian theology. Coffey's "bestowal model" particularly intrigued him. "The Father, begetting the Son, breathes forth and bestows the Spirit on the Son as his love for the Son. The Son, in response, bestows the Spirit on the Father as his love for the Father. . . . Human persons . . . bestow their human love in the Spirit on the Father, as a created participation in Christ's loving bestowal of the Spirit of his love on the Father."[60] Thus the Spirit draws believers to Christ and Christ takes them back to the Father. Kilmartin was trying to complement a processional model of the Trinity, stressing the descending movement of the mission of Christ and the Spirit, with an ascending model that would explain the return of sanctified people to the Trinity. The latter model relates the Holy Spirit's work in the economy of grace to the immanent Trinity.[61]

The Holy Spirit and the Believing Assembly

That leads to another key theme, the role of the Holy Spirit. Kilmartin and many others point to the introduction of the eucharistic epiclesis of sanctification into the Roman eucharistic prayers as a key development. In fact, Giraudo considers it the single most important contribution to eucharistic theology in the Latin church because it highlights the pneumatological dimension of the eucharistic memo-

---

58. Ibid., 90. See also 77, for a fine summary of some of the influences on Kilmartin's thought.

59. Ibid., 77, 93.

60. Ibid., 104–5. See also 100.

61. Ibid., 98–99.

rial. He rightly adds that this would be even clearer if that epiclesis were placed after the institution narrative, as it is in most of the Eastern anaphoras.[62] Moreover, it is the Spirit who sanctifies the gifts, bringing Christ to the communicants and enabling them to respond to Christ and to one another. The sacramental presence (elsewhere "somatic real presence") is ordered to Communion. This is our sacramental response to Christ and his paschal mystery.[63]

In emphasizing the role of the Holy Spirit, Kilmartin also stresses the active role of the believing assembly that he contends was essential in the early church, whether or not it was explicitly recognized as such. He disagrees with Casel, for instance, that Christ's sacrifice is made present to the believers so they can then appropriate it by faith. The notion of memorial or *anamnesis* underscores the fact that we are not simply talking about a subjective recalling by the assembly. "However [this notion of 'objective memorial'] does not adequately express the intimate relation between the activity of the believing community and the mystery presence of Christ and his saving work."[64] The faith of the assembly already plays a role in the realization of the sacrament. Christ is actively present relating his once-for-all self-offering to that of the believing community. But the assembly's role is not that of passive spectators. It is, rather, one of active participants relating themselves to Christ's self-offering. And all of this is the work of the Holy Spirit.[65]

Having questioned the adequacy of other theories, for instance, Casel's mystery presence, various theories about the effects of Christ's passion (*Effektustheorie*), and perennialization of some

---

62. Kilmartin, *The Eucharist in the West*, 336. See also Power, *The Eucharistic Mystery*, 260. On the positioning of the eucharistic epiclesis see McKenna, *The Eucharistic Epiclesis*, 224–27, and "The Epiclesis Revisited," 183, in *New Eucharistic Prayers*.

63. Kilmartin, *The Eucharist in the West*, 330–31. See also McKenna, *The Eucharistic Epiclesis*, 192, 202–3, and "The Epiclesis Revisited," in *New Eucharistic Prayers*, 169–94, especially 182–83.

64. See Hall, *We Have the Mind of Christ*, 110, citing Kilmartin, *The Eucharist in the West*, 303–4.

65. Kilmartin, *The Eucharist in the West*, 148. See also McKenna, *The Eucharistic Epiclesis*, 192–99, and "Eucharistic Epiclesis: Myopia or Microcosm?" *Theological Studies* 36 (June 1975): 267–74; Hall, *We Have the Mind of Christ*, 119–20, speaking of the modes of Christ's presence: "The interrelation of these modes of presence makes clear that Christian sanctification necessarily involves the interpersonal cooperation of worshipers, through which the Spirit makes Christ present."

element of Christ's temporal acts,[66] to explain how Christ's saving actions can be present to the assembly, Kilmartin continued to pursue his own synthesis. He examined a number of studies on the nature and function of human memory. All of these see the Holy Spirit playing a vital role in moving people to a "memory of the heart" that responds to God's call to conform to the image in which we were made.[67] He thus links the Holy Spirit, memory, the faith of Christ, and the assembly's faith to form a memorial. This memorial enables the saving actions of Christ to be present to the believing assembly or, rather, as Thurian, Giraudo, Kilmartin, Hans Bernard Meyer, and others stress, the assembly to be present to the saving events in Christ.[68] "The dynamic of memory, Kilmartin believed, indicates that the Holy Spirit's action does not bring the perennialized essence of Christ's temporal actions from the past into the present of the liturgy . . . [but] the Holy Spirit takes the assembly back to the cross in order to grace the assembly with communion with the Trinity achieved by Christ in the Holy Spirit."[69] While the saving works of Christ themselves remain in the past, the Holy Spirit brings the believing assembly, in memory, to them. The deeds are present in the sacrificial attitudes of Christ that the believers make their own in the liturgy.[70] In other words, the Holy Spirit brings the assembly, in its remembering, into contact with Christ and his saving mysteries.

Conclusions

Although Kilmartin died before he could finish his synthesis, his journey offers a microcosm of key theological issues connected with the notion of memorial. Attentiveness to the *lex orandi* leads to

---

66. See Hall, *We Have the Mind of Christ*, 1–37. J. B. Metz, for example, offers two bases to explain how an event of the past can be present here and now. First, the acting subject is the eternal Logos and so the saving deeds of Jesus become in a sense "eternal." In addition, these acts are present in the glorified humanity of Christ. The saving deeds can now be present through a "symbolic reality," a being in which another being enters and reveals itself. See also Kilmartin, *The Eucharist in the West*, 321, and McKenna, "Symbol and Reality," 18–22.

67. Kilmartin, *The Eucharist in the West*, 304–7.

68. They all make the point that rather than the events being present to us, we somehow are made present to, or contemporaneous with them.

69. Hall, *We Have the Mind of Christ*, 124. See also 144. The term "back," however, could be problematic; "into contact with" might be better.

70. Ibid., 148.

attentiveness to the eucharistic prayer in its entirety. This, together with our stories, our songs, our "breaking of the bread," calls us to the wonder and mystery of inner Trinitarian life, a life of accepting and bestowing the Spirit of love. This same Spirit leads the believing assembly, through their remembering, to thankfulness, the "memory of the heart." This in turn leads us to Christ who, in his dying and rising for us, in his self-offering, will lead us to the Father. The Holy Spirit also enables the praying assembly to respond with the gift it has received, Jesus Christ, and with its own self-offering.[71]

As Chauvet puts it: "The *anamnesis* is thus the fundamental place of the Church's offering."[72] The *anamnesis* makes explicit what is at stake in the institution narrative. The phrase "we offer you" is a key to understanding what is going on. At the very moment that the Church is receiving the sacramental body and blood of Christ it offers them. There is a long tradition in early eucharistic prayers that "calling to mind" leads to the Church's offering precisely what the Church has been given. It receives the sacramental body of Christ by offering it in thanksgiving. And that offering spills out beyond the ritual into love of brothers and sisters or ethical practices.[73] In other words, the Church's memorial of Christ's self-giving calls that same Church to be what it celebrates in its own self-giving. "As Augustine put it, this is what is expressed 'in the sacrament, well known to the faithful where it is made clear to the Church that, itself is offered in what it offers.'"[74] This is memorial and symbol in its strongest sense: "This sacrifice is the symbol of what we are" (Augustine, Sermon 227). The ritual memory of Christ's dying and rising must be verified in the believers' bodies.[75] This is to re-member in the fullest sense of that word.

---

71. See Robert J. Daly, "Sacrifice Unveiled or Sacrifice Revisited: Trinitarian and Liturgical Perspectives," *Theological Studies* 64 (March 2003): 24–42, who continues Kilmartin's trajectory: "In plain terms, sacrifice is not something the Father does to the Son; and thus, since all authentic sacrifice begins here, authentic sacrifice can never be something that someone does to someone else. At its core, sacrifice is *self*-offering/*self*-gift—in the Father, and in the Son, and in us" (28) through the Holy Spirit.

72. Chauvet, *Symbol and Sacrament*, 276.

73. Ibid., 275–78. The importance of the ethical dimension is another frequently occurring theme in treatments of the notion of memorial, as it is throughout other elements of the Eucharist.

74. Ibid., 277.

75. See ibid., 260–61.

The eucharistic prayer is thus a covenant memorial of God's saving acts that culminate in the Christ event, especially in the life, death, and resurrection of Jesus. It also contains the assembly's commitment to the covenant relationship, a petition for God's help to be faithful to that covenant, and a petition for the salvation of the world.[76]

Such a memorial has a power to reveal and transform, especially when the community is open to a prophetic mode of narrative and ritual which is able to reinterpret the foundational event in light of present times and vice versa. That does not always lead to a view of history that is neat and orderly. Sometimes the setting for remembering the presence of Christ in his dying and rising is one of anguish and heartbreak. But memory, remembering and making memorial, when living, has the power to move believers to action in the present and hope for the future when the fullness of God's reign will prevail in justice and love.[77]

To sum up: Why such emphasis on our coming into contact with the saving actions of Jesus Christ? Because we are saved only through them. Therefore we must somehow come into contact with them. That we come into contact with those saving mysteries, that in the ritual celebration we are somehow made present to them, is generally agreed upon by theologians of the major denominations or churches. That is also why there is so much discussion on how this takes place.

With all the difficulty arriving at a consensus on just how Christ's actions are present to the assembly or vice versa, the notion of memorial or *anamnesis* has been helpful ecumenically.[78] In particular, it has benefited dialogue on the Eucharist and sacrifice. The Anglican/Roman Catholic International Commission (ARCIC) in

---

76. See Kilmartin, *The Eucharist in the West,* 331, referring to Giraudo, *Eucaristia.*

77. See Power, *The Eucharistic,* 308–16; McGoldrick, "Memorial," 649; Léon-Dufour, *Sharing the Eucharistic Bread,* 111; and Morrill, *Anamnesis as Dangerous Memory,* 146–63, who shows the biblical link between remembering and action (146–63). Morrill also underlines the importance of the eschatological dimension of the Eucharist's *anamnesis,* so often lost sight of (40–50, 92–125, 175–86, and 194–205).

78. Even some critics of the application of memorial to the Eucharist often argue not against the notion of actualizing or presence to the saving actions. Rather they question whether this was the "mindset" in the Jewish Scriptures. See Paul Bradshaw, "*Anamnesis* in Modern Debate," in Michael Signer, ed., *Memory and History in Christianity and Judaism* (Notre Dame, Ind.: University of Notre Dame Press, 2001), 73–84, esp. 80–82.

its Eucharistic Doctrine Statement (1971), the Roman Catholic/ Evangelical Lutheran Commission in its Document on the Eucharist (1979), the Faith and Order Commission of the World Council of Churches in its Lima document (1982), the Lutheran-Catholic Dialogue in Germany (1983)[79] and numerous studies have made use of the biblical notion of memorial to advance discussion beyond the extremes of "mere symbol" on the one hand and exaggerated realism or an overly physical approach on the other.[80]

79. The final report of this group is a good example. See Karl Lehmann and Edmund Schlink, eds., *Das Opfer Jesu Christi und Seiner Gegenwart in Der Kirche: Klärungen zum Opfercharackter des Herrenmahles* (Freiburg im Breisgau: Herder, 1983) (= vol. 3 of *Dialog Der Kirchen*), 215–38.

80. McGoldrick, "Memorial," 649. See also Power, *The Eucharistic,* 255, 260–62, referring to *The Condemnations of the Reformation Era: Do They Still Divide?*, ed. Karl Lehmann and Wolfhart Pannenberg, trans. M. Kohl (Minneapolis: Fortress Press, 1990), and indicating points of agreement among the churches, especially making use of the biblical sense of memorial.

Chapter 7

Searching for Our Roots

Recent decades have seen an increased interest in searching for our roots as computerized records make it easier to trace our ancestry. Toward the end of the last century and the beginning of this one, an analogous search by a number of scholars for the roots of our eucharistic prayers and our eucharistic origins has been a veritable odyssey. For the sake of brevity I have chosen two significant representatives of that odyssey, the late Thomas J. Talley and, more recently, Paul F. Bradshaw.

THOMAS TALLEY (1924–2005)

Talley, for many years a professor at General Theological Seminary of the Episcopal Church, liked to cite Gregory Dix, who in 1949 remarked, "Our understanding of our forms of worship underwent a radical transformation some forty years ago when it finally occurred to someone that Jesus was a Jew."[1] The stage had been set by earlier studies of Jewish worship.[2] It was, however, Jean-Paul Audet's essay on the broad literary genre of *berakah* rather than on particular *berakoth* that

---

1. Thomas J. Talley, "The Eucharistic Prayer of the Ancient Church according to Recent Research: Results and Reflections," *Studia Liturgica* 11 (1976): 138–58. This was originally presented to the Congress of Societas Liturgica held at Trier, Germany in August 1975. It first appeared, in a slightly expanded form, as "From Berakah to Eucharistia: A Reopening Question," *Worship* 50 (March 1976): 115–36. See also John H. McKenna, "From 'Berakah' to 'Eucharistia' to T. Talley and Beyond," *Proceedings of the North American Academy of Liturgy* (Valparaiso, Ind.: Valparaiso University, 1995), 87–100, and Paul F. Bradshaw, *The Search for the Origins of Christian Worship: Sources and Methods for the Study of Early Liturgy*, 2nd ed. (New York: Oxford University Press, 2002), 131–33.

2. See Talley, "The Eucharistic Prayer," nn. 2, 3, 8.

provided a turning point.[3] The reaction to his position provides a backdrop to Talley's thought.

Background

Audet acknowledged the dictionary description of "Eucharist" in terms of receiving a gift, being moved to gratitude, and giving back a gift in return with words of thanks and praise. But "Eucharist" belongs to a wider family of words, "to bless, praise." Thus "the Christian *eucharistia,* as a literary genre, is the natural offspring of the older Jewish *eucharistia* form known as the *berakah* (plural = *berakoth*)."[4] In its simpler form, the *berakah* consists of an opening blessing or praise and the motive, for example, Genesis 24:27 (Abraham's servant upon finding Rebecca for Isaac); Luke 10:21 (see Matt. 11:25) (for hiding these things from the learned and clever and revealing them to mere children); John 11:41-43 (prior to raising Lazarus). The motive is the wonder deeds or works of God (*mirabilia Dei*). The mood is, above all, admiration and joy; gratitude remains subordinated to the fundamental feeling of admiration and is, therefore, secondary.

In its more developed form *berakah* might involve (1) an invitatory blessing which is an initial doxology or blessing, an enthusiastic call to enter into the act of blessing God, for instance, "Let us bless the Lord . . ." (2) a statement of the motive which is more detailed, based on the wonder of all that God has done as experienced here and now by the community. It is a memorial of what has been done in the past and an expectation of the future destiny prepared for Israel. It is also a "kerygmatic annunciation to the assembly that this same *mirabile* is present and active here-and-now, accomplishing its purpose still within the life of . . . the worshipping people. By reason of its immediacy and its grandeur, the proclamation of it as fact is more than just

---

3. Jean-Paul Audet, "Literary Forms and Contents of a Normal 'eucharistia' in the First Century," *Studia Evangelica: Papers Presented to the International Congress on the Four Gospels* in 1957, Texte und Untersuchungen zur Geschichte der Altchristliches Literatur 73, ed. K. Aland, et al. (Berlin, 1959), 643–62. The essay also appeared in English in *The Gospels Reconsidered* (Oxford, 1960), 16–35. See Bradshaw, *The Search,* 127–28, and McKenna, "From 'Berakah,'" 87–89.

4. Aidan Kavanagh, "Thoughts on the Roman Anaphora (1)," *Worship* 39 (Nov. 1965): 518. In this article (515–29), Kavanagh has given a good summary of Audet's key points plus insights to be drawn from them. See McKenna, "From 'Berakah,'" 88–89.

joyful and full of admiration: it is *ecstatic*."[5] Often there is a statement
of response on the people's part which might include an appeal for
intervention here and now. (3) a concluding blessing or doxology.

An educated guess or assumption that Jesus used a festal,
possibly Passover, form of *berakah* at the Last Supper followed.[6] The
reconstruction might envision some invitatory blessing, a statement
of motives employing the elasticity of the festal form to interpret or
insert here-and-now events, perhaps a prayer for eschatological fulfillment, and a concluding blessing. The eucharistic prayer found in the
Apostolic Tradition attributed to Hippolytus did in fact contain similar
elements with its invitatory, its narration of the wonders worked in
and through Jesus, including the institution of the Eucharist, a
response in the form of an *anamnesis,* a prayer for the Holy Spirit to
unite the Church and sanctify the communicants, and a concluding
blessing or doxology.[7]

Applications such as these led to a number of conclusions in
relation to the spirit and form of a eucharistic prayer. The psychologi-
cal attitude is one of joyful admiration, not merely gratitude. This
prayer type places emphasis on the Resurrection since it has traditionally been linked with Easter and with Sunday rather than with the
night of Christ's betrayal or of his death (although this is not absent
since we celebrate the Paschal Mystery in its entirety). The Church
not only celebrates but also "confesses" or proclaims his death and
Resurrection until he comes. She does so in an atmosphere that is
"ecstatic," wondering, exultant, and eucharistic in that sense.[8]

Such applications then affected the theological understanding
of the eucharistic prayer as a joyous, wondering proclamation. They
also impacted the structure of "modern" eucharistic prayers. Following
research on the *berakah* genre, the recommended structure became:

---

5. Ibid., 520.

6. See Bryan D. Spinks, "Beware the Liturgical Horses! An English Interjection on
Anaphoral Evolution," *Worship* 59 (May 1985): 211, 213–14, referring to Talley and Louis Ligier,
"The Origins of the Eucharistic Prayer: From the Last Supper to the Eucharist," *Studia Liturgica*
9 (1973): 176–85. Spinks himself questions the assumption. See Bradshaw, *The Search*, 133–34,
and McKenna, "From 'Berakah,'" 92–93.

7. See R. C. D. Jasper and G. J. Cuming, *Prayers of the Eucharist: Early and Reformed*, 3rd. ed.
(New York: Pueblo, 1987), 34–35, for the text. As we shall see below, a number of questions have
arisen about the date, author, and place of origin of the *Apostolic Tradition.*

8. See Kavanagh, "Thoughts on the Roman Anaphora (2)," *Worship* 40 (Jan. 1966): 2.

1. Invitation to praise or opening doxology
2. Narration of God's wonders (preface, *Sanctus*, institution narrative)
3. Statement of the Church's response to the wonders narrated, the "good news"
4. Petition for blessings on the Church and communicants (a form of epiclesis or invocation of the Holy Spirit)
5. Closing doxology [9]

Applying this pattern to the Roman Canon, for example, immediately raised issues. Extrinsic factors, such as genuflections, repeated signs of the cross, bows, kissing of the altar and, to some extent, the elevation tended to obscure primary traits and break the flow of the narration. Intrinsically, certain prefaces revealed themselves to be either doctrinal discourses (Trinity), supplications (Apostles), or an empty shell without any wonders (former weekday preface). [10] The position of certain petitions (for instance, the five-fold *Te igitur—Quam oblationem* group) that follows the *Sanctus* and the repeated ending (*per Christum Dominum Nostrum. Amen*) before the institution narrative, broke the movement of proclaiming God's wonders leading to the assembly's response in the *anamnesis* and anticipated that response and a petition for acceptance. [11] "The only proper methodology for solving this problem will be to keep in mind the primary structure-sequence of biblical *berakoth* and of the classic Christian *eucharistia* developing from them—as can be seen in the outline of an anaphora found in Hippolytus' *Apostolic Tradition*, in the full anaphora given in the *Apostolic Constitutions*, and in other early sources." [12]

The vast majority of eucharistic prayers introduced since then in the various churches have in fact followed that pattern, with some glaring exceptions, for example, the Roman eucharistic prayers. [13]

---

9. Ibid., 5.

10. Ibid., 9.

11. Ibid., 3–5.

12. Ibid., 3.

13. See John H. McKenna, "The Epiclesis Revisited: A Look at Modern Eucharistic Prayers," *Ephemerides Liturgicae* 99 (1985): 314–36. The charts on 329–34 show, among other things, the content and positioning of the epiclesis in ancient and modern eucharistic prayers may be particularly helpful in the present context. A version of this study also appeared as "The Epiclesis Revisited," in Frank Senn, ed., *New Eucharistic Prayers: An Ecumenical Study of Their Development and Structure* (New York: Paulist Press, 1987), 169–94, with the charts on 187–94.

There are a number of advantages of such a pattern or structure. The narrating of God's wonderful works is not broken and it is clearer that the institution of the Eucharist is one of these. The response character of the *anamnesis* and following prayers is more evident. The shorter, clearer structure makes the eucharistic prayers pastorally and catechetically more effective. They are easier to explain to people. Finally, the public, communal nature is underlined. A danger of the notion of personal gratitude is that it could lead to an individualistic approach (God and myself), whereas, in fact, the root words used to describe the Eucharist had the sense of a public act, a proclamation before witnesses of the qualities and deeds of God, an acknowledgment.[14] Of course, there were also other theories, such as Louis Bouyer's heavily criticized claim that the Roman Canon really reflects the earliest form of the eucharistic prayer better than that of Hippolytus.[15]

Studia Liturgica (1976)

This then was the backdrop for Thomas Talley's writings on eucharistic prayers.[16] In 1975 he addressed the Congress of the Societas Liturgica on the topic in Trier, Germany.[17] Talley noted that Audet's starting point was the "established regulations for the form of the *berakah* set forth in the third century AD by the Amoraim" (139). In addition, Audet had examined the literary genre of *berakah*, not the actual prayer form, and had treated *eulogein, exomologeomai,* and *eucharistein* as equivalent to *barak* (139). He pointed out that Ledogar rightly questioned equating *berakah* with *eucharistein* (140). *Berakah*

---

14. See Robert Ledogar, *Acknowledgement: Praise Verbs in the Early Greek Anaphoras* (Rome: Herder, 1968), 161–67.

15. See Louis Bouyer, *Eucharistie, Théologie et Spiritualité de la Prière Eucharistique,* 2nd ed. (Paris: Desclée, 1966); and the sharp critique of this position by B. Botte in *QLP* 48 (1967): 173, and Jos. Jungmann, *Zeitschrift Fur Katholische Theologie* 89 (1967): 460–66. Ligier, Talley, and Mazza, however, followed him. See Bradshaw, *Eucharistic Origins,* 30–31. Bouyer's study appeared in English as *Eucharist: Theology and Spirituality of the Eucharistic Prayer,* trans. C. U. Quinn (Notre Dame, Ind.: University of Notre Dame Press, 1968). See also Bradshaw, *Eucharistic Origins,* 128–29.

16. See David J. Kennedy, *Eucharistic Sacramentality in an Ecumenical Context: The Anglican Epiclesis* (Burlington, Vt.: Ashgate, 2008), 222–26.

17. See n. 1. The page numbers cited here are from Talley, "The Eucharistic Prayer of the Ancient Church," *Studia Liturgica* 11 (1976). See Paul F. Bradshaw, ed., *Essays on Early Eastern Eucharistic Prayers* (Collegeville, Minn.: Liturgical Press, 1997), for treatments of the individual eucharistic prayers mentioned below.

and *eucharistia* are not the same (156). Talley agreed with Louis Ligier that *Birkat Ha-Mazon*, the grace after meals, was the basis of Christian eucharistic prayers (155). If so, we could better appreciate the precision of the Markan and Matthean institution narratives which used both "blessed" and "gave thanks" (146). The original pattern then was praise for creation, thanks for redemption, and supplication (155)—not blessing, *anamnesis*, and doxology, as Audet suggested (145). The early Christians developed the thanksgiving section of the pattern, providing motives for thanking God and they came to adapt the threefold pattern into a twofold pattern of thanks and supplication, for instance, *Didache*, Hippolytus' *Apostolic Tradition*, and Epiphanius of Salamis (151).

Talley summarized his position: "if we consider seriously the precision of the Didachist's revision of the Jewish grace in such wise as to remove all use of the benediction formularies which were critical for the meal *berakoth*, and to give unprecedented priority and prominence to eucharistic forms, and if we further consider this in the light of the sacrificial nuance of such eucharistic language as has been revealed by the studies of Cazelles and Laporte—we should find ourselves much less immersed with what has seemed the wide difference between *Didache*'s two uses of Eucharist, as meal and as sacrifice. Indeed, in spite of all the problems of dating, authenticity and the rest, it should not be considered impossible that *Didache* 10 either is or wishes to seem to be a careful adaptation of *Birkat Ha-Mazon* to the requirements of the Supper of the Lord become a Christian *zebach todah*, a eucharistic sacrifice. Something of the same alteration of the Jewish grace's pattern of benediction-thanksgiving-supplication can be seen in Hippolytus and in Epiphanius" (150–51).

Talley went on to say that Addai and Mari and the Third Anaphora of St. Peter (commonly known as *Sharar* after the first word of the manuscript) reasserted the original pattern but with prominence being given to thanksgiving which characterized the tradition since Paul's version of the institution narrative (156). This threefold pattern can still be seen in the classic eucharistic prayers like James and Basil—where the opening praise of the Creator, culminating in the *Sanctus*, is clearly distinguishable from the thanksgiving for redemption which leads to the institution narrative and anamnesis and thence to the supplication for the spirit-community (156).

Equating *berakah* and *eucharistia* obscures that pattern and the possible reasons for changing it. Thus, we should pay attention to the differences between Jewish and Christian usages as well as the similarities because the differences had meaning and consequences helpful in understanding our eucharistic tradition (156-57). Talley looked forward to studies that would help in this direction.

In my brief response to Talley at the time,[18] I commented that he had shown us once again, if we still needed a reminder, the complexity of the relationship between Jewish and Christian liturgical forms. He rightly relied on a number of Jewish liturgiologists and upon available texts rather than ideal reconstructions. He repeatedly stressed the need to distinguish *eucharistein* from *eulogein* and *berakah*. I noted his suggestion that the stress on thanksgiving rather than blessing might be *Didache*'s way of adapting the *Birkat Ha-Mazon* to the requirements of the Lord's Supper, now viewed by the Christians as eucharistic sacrifice. I also noted that his leaning toward an institution narrative in a primitive source of Addai and Mari was in the face of growing sentiment—on the basis of Macomber's text of Addai and Mari—for the absence of such a narrative. I pointed out that theories are only as good as the data they rest upon and that in the area under consideration the gaps are great. The desire to find solutions to liturgical problems, however, sometimes dulls our awareness of these gaps.[19] Talley had shown an awareness of the complexity of the matter at hand. At the same time, he had not run away from the function of a liturgiologist to reflect seriously on the data available.

Worship (1984)

Talley returned to the topic of eucharistic prayers in an article published in *Worship* in 1984.[20] It represented a lengthy review of what he considered to be two significant studies in this area. Rather than comment at length on the article, I limit myself to some points that may help set a context for further discussion. The first work is Joseph Heinemann's *Prayer In The Talmud: Forms And Patterns*, Studia

---

18. See Talley, "The Eucharistic Prayer of the Ancient Church," *Studia Liturgica* 11 (1976): 207–8.

19. See Spinks, *Beware*, 211–14, for similar but more detailed reservations.

20. Talley, "The Literary Structure of Eucharistic Prayer," *Worship* 58 (Sept. 1984): 404–20.

Judaica: Forschungen zur Wissenschaft des Judentums 9 (Berlin, 1977). Talley notes that Heinemann "argues persuasively that the *berakah* which would become so central a prayer form in the Amoraic period [c. 200–500 AD] had been, in its biblical background not a prayer addressed to God at all, but a praise of God stated in the third person" (406). New Testament examples of such "biblical *berakoth*" are Luke 1:68, Ephesians 1:3, and 1 Peter 1:3. Heinemann also sees the opening blessing of the meal grace as universalistic, praising God as Creator of all. The thanksgiving is more "historical-particularistic," thanking God for intervening in the history of humankind, as is the future oriented supplication (408). As Jewish theology saw God's intervention as the "critical turning point," Talley stated that Christian theology would see the critical turning point as redemption in Christ and its future consummation as the goal of all history (408). After describing briefly Heinemann's findings, he concluded that they indicate the critique of Audet's position was far more profound than the difference between *berakah* and *eucharistia*. "If we are talking about prayer structures, then the difference between the benediction form and the thanksgiving form goes far beyond the semantic differences of the two words 'benediction' and 'thanksgiving'" (406–7). He commended Heinemann for helping us appreciate even more the tripartite structure of Jewish prayer (419) and once again raised the question, "Why did early Christian prayer ignore *brk* (blessing) forms and why do forms of *ydh* (thanksgiving, acknowledgment) loom so large?" (408).[21]

This led Talley to the study of Cesare Giraudo, *La Struttura Letteraria Della Preghiera Eucaristica: Saggio Sulla Genesi Letteraria Di Una Forma—Toda Veterotestamentaria, Beraka Guidaica, Anafora Cristiana, Analecta Biblica* 92 (Rome: Biblical Institute, 1981). After examining the sections on the Old Testament *tôdâ*, the Jewish *berakah*, and the Christian anaphoras, Talley rejoiced that another voice has joined the chorus against identifying *berakah* and *eucharistia*. In passing, he notes that William Macomber is more convinced than ever that the absence of the institution narrative in Addai and Mari resulted from a seventh century reform and that the *Sharar*, which

---

21. See also Bradshaw, *The Search*, 44–45, 59.

contains the institution narrative, at that point is the truer text
(414–15).[22]

Talley criticized Giraudo for rejecting out of hand the important studies of Laporte and Cazelles "which examined the sacrificial
context of the use of eucharistic language" and for minimizing the
connection between the *tôdâ*, that Giraudo alludes to, and the *zebach
todah*, "the sacrifice of thanksgiving" so often mentioned in the Old
Testament. He states that Giraudo's work fails to break new ground in
the area of the anaphoras themselves. "The great value of Giraudo's
work, nonetheless, lies in the biblical roots he has demonstrated for
such a bipartite structure as we see in the *Apostolic Tradition* and even
earlier, perhaps, in the Strasbourg Papyrus" (419).

In 1985 Bryan Spinks addressed the issue of "anaphoral
evolution."[23] He referred to Talley's work in outlining the main data of
"the emerging 'common understanding,' including the identification
of the Last Supper meal prayers with those of the Passover, especially
the *Birkat Ha-Mazon*" (211). In summarizing some of Talley's main
points, he acknowledged Talley's work as seminal but commented that
such studies tend to be concerned almost exclusively with the literary
structure of the prayers. He cautioned that they suggest a smooth evolution from *berakoth* to eucharistic prayer and that some are taking
what "*might have been the case . . . as what was the case*" (212–13).
Spinks then raised a number of specific objections. First, Jesus was an
innovator. How can we be certain that he recited the usual *Birkat Ha-
Mazon* at the Last Supper? Maybe, as Heinemann suggested, Jesus'
prayers were a repudiation of the official *berakoth* prayers. "The simple
equation: the prayers of Jesus at the Last Supper = *berakoth* of the
Passover liturgy, may be less certain than liturgists have suggested"
(213–14).[24] Furthermore, whether the similarities between *Didache*
and *Birkat Ha-Mazon* represent a radical transformation or conserva-
tive Jewish-Christians clinging to the past is mere speculation (214).

---

22. See William Macomber, "The Ancient Form of the Anaphora of the Apostles," in *East of
Byzantium: Syria and Armenia in the Formative Period*, Dunbarton Oaks Symposium 1980
(Washington, D.C., 1982), 73–88.

23. See Spinks, *Beware*, 211–14.

24. Bradshaw, *The Search*, 65, states more recently: "From the point of view of liturgical
scholars, the question of whether the Last Supper was a Passover meal does not seem particularly
crucial."

Second, until well into the third century the presiders were free to compose their own anaphoras. The models they used may have varied widely and, therefore, the anaphoras themselves may have varied widely in composition, theme, and structure (215).

Spinks also questioned the "absolute priority" Talley gave to *eucharistein*. Other words, for example, *doxazein,* were used instead of *brk* (215–17). He also questioned whether or not the creation theme was everywhere abandoned in Christian anaphoras. Rather than Addai and Mari, for instance, reintroducing the creation theme in a Jewish-Christian environment, as Talley had suggested, that theme may have been in a variety of anaphoras all along (217). Finally, Spinks underlined the gaps in the evidence. Between 80 and 250 AD it is impossible to estimate how many anaphoras were around. We have only "a few pieces of a vast jigsaw; the rest is lost. To guess what the full picture might have been on the basis of these few pieces is indeed hazardous" (218). For example, to use the text of Hippolytus as a basis of comparison ignores the fact that we do not know how representative of the period it is (218).

La Maison Dieu

In an article to honor Balthasar Fischer's 80th birthday in 1992, Talley once again returned to the topic of eucharistic prayers.[25] He acknowledged that discerning the Jewish tradition that influenced the Christian prayer forms is more difficult than was assumed a few decades before. The lack of Jewish prayer texts from the first century of our era is due to rabbinic opposition to committing to writing a prayer tradition that was deliberately oral (16). He also admitted that seventeen years after his original essay, with help from his critics, some of his positions needed emending. For example, he went beyond the evidence in assuming that Jesus prayed a version of the *Birkat Ha-Mazon* at the Last Supper. The relevance of that Jewish prayer, however, to *Didache* 10 did not depend on its use by Jesus (19–20).

Talley also remarked that his earlier explanation of the Christian preference for thanksgiving language over blessing formulas was that it reflected the sacrificial nuance in *eucharistein* which Cazelles and

25. Thomas J. Talley, "Structures des anaphores anciennes et modernes," *La Maison Dieu* 191 (1992): 15–43.

Laporte observed. Now, influenced by Heinemann, he sees a more fundamental reason for the revision of the Jewish grace as it appears in the *Didache*. It is "a distinction between ordinary food provided for all and God's gift to those who have received the revelation that led the Didachist, I believe, to transfer the reference to food and drink from an opening benediction of the creator to an extension of the thanksgiving for the revelation through Jesus. Indeed the distinction is overt in *Didache* 10:

> You, almighty Master, created all things for the sake of your Name; and gave food and drink to mankind for their enjoyment, [that they might give you thanks;] but to us you have granted spiritual food and drink and eternal life through your child Jesus. Above all we give you thanks because you are mighty; glory to you forevermore. Amen.

"By its structural revision of the Jewish grace . . . *Didache* 10 asserts the cultic uniqueness of the bread and wine of the eucharist" (20-21). Talley added that in 1975 he should have taken Ligier more seriously when Ligier made this point.[26] It is an indication that *Didache* 10 has to do with Eucharist, not agape (21).

Given the presumption that most early eucharistic prayer was extemporaneous, while conforming to some extent to an oral tradition, and that freedom to compose such prayers continued for centuries,[27] Talley finds the similarities between the *Didache* and the anaphora of the *Apostolic Tradition* all the more remarkable. Both have a pattern of thanksgiving for salvation in Christ and supplication for the community (24). The *Apostolic Tradition* is obviously more developed, containing as it does a more detailed thanksgiving for Christ's saving work and climaxing in the institution narrative and *anamnesis* and a supplication for the community that explicitly invokes the Holy Spirit (25). Talley was careful not to suggest that the *Apostolic Tradition* was influenced by the *Didache* or was even familiar with it. The same is true of the Syro-Byzantine tradition. Although its anaphoras follow the distinctive structure of the *Apostolic Tradition*—a Christological thanksgiving climaxed in institution narrative and *anamnesis*

---

26. See Louis Ligier, "The Origins of the Eucharistic Prayer: From the Last Supper to the Eucharist," *Studia Liturgica* 9 (1973): 177. See also Bradshaw, *The Search*, 129–31.

27. See Allan Bouley, *From Freedom to Formula: The Evolution of the Eucharistic Prayer from Oral Improvisation to Written Texts* (Washington, D.C.: The Catholic University of America Press, 1981).

and a supplication with a reference to the Spirit—it does not follow that they were influenced by it or by the *Didache* (26–27).

Talley then turned to the so-called Alexandrian family, with its intercessions prior to the *Sanctus*. He focuses especially on the Strasbourg papyrus and sees a growing consensus that it represents a complete anaphora (27–31). He regarded this, at least potentially, as one of the most important insights in recent history into the development of eucharistic prayers. "If the Strasbourg papyrus is a complete anaphora, much of the peculiarity of the longer St. Mark becomes intelligible as an extension of a very early prayer to bring it into closer agreement with anaphoral developments elsewhere. The very unusual 'Alexandrian family' would be revealed to be a hybrid formed by the addition of the *sanctus,* institution narrative, *anamnesis,* and *epiclesis* to a very primitive indigenous prayer whose structure was not at all unusual" (28). Later in this context he stated: "Generalizations are perilous, but while praise and thanksgiving are often so closely related as to be indistinguishable, once a prayer has turned to supplication it seems unlikely to return to praise or thanksgiving" (31). This poses a problem with the position, in this "family," of the *Sanctus* which appears to be a hymn of praise but which leads not into Christological thanksgiving but into a petition that God will fill this sacrifice with blessing (31–32). Talley cited Spinks in this regard: "In the anaphoral texts which have survived, although textually the sanctus is a hymn of praise, contextually it occurs within the intercessions and is used as a spring-board to further intercession, namely an *epiclesis.*"[28] Talley concluded his examination of the "Alexandrian family" with a quote from Enrico Mazza: "In summary, of the eight texts in question, only one—the Dêr Balizeh fragment—shows a first, consecratory epiclesis which is followed, after the *anamnesis,* by a second epiclesis of unknown content. This is certainly very little on which to base the theology of the two epicleses, one consecratory and the other sanctificatory."[29]

This turned Talley's attention to modern anaphoral structures. He first dealt with the so-called split *epiclesis* (with one section before

---

28. Bryan D. Spinks, *The Sanctus in the Eucharistic Prayer* (New York: Cambridge University Press, 1991), 91, as cited by Talley, "Structures des anaphores anciennes et modernes," 32.

29. Enrico Mazza, *The Eucharistic Prayers of the Roman Rite,* trans. M. J. O'Connell (New York: Pueblo, 1986), 92.

the institution narrative and another after) found primarily in the modern Roman eucharistic prayers.[30] He pointed out that despite misgivings and recognizing that tradition offers no support for a distinction of "consecratory" and "sanctificatory" *epicleses*, Mazza speaks of an Alexandrian anaphoral structure which he claims "probably provides the sole conscious liturgical basis for the theological decision made," that is, to have a "split *epiclesis*" in the Roman eucharistic prayers (35).[31]

Talley maintained, and I agree, that the *epiclesis* for the consecration of the gifts prior to the institution narrative stems from a theological decision rather than a liturgical one. Such positioning reflects the medieval "moment of consecration" debate and ignores evidence that in the ancient church the eucharistic prayer as a whole was seen as "consecratory" with two high points, the institution narrative and the *epiclesis* (35).[32] Talley acknowledged that the new prayers of the Roman Missal represent a vast advance on the *Canon Missae* but argued that the "theological preoccupation" that demanded a consecratory *epiclesis* before the institution narrative is a departure from structural tradition. Consequently, for example, the narrative and *anamnesis* are shifted from the thanksgiving proclamation to a supplication mode (37–38).

Another structural change that has been widely adopted, to heighten participation by the people, is the "popular acclamation" between the institution narrative and the *anamnesis*. "The placement of a single such acclamation after the narrative, especially when it is sung, sunders the intimate bond between narrative and *anamnesis*, a bond that may be [the French reads "without doubt"] as old as the inclusion of the narrative itself" (38–39). Talley noted that this acclamation has rightly been placed after the *anamnesis* in the Roman Masses with Children and voiced the hope that this positioning will be considered with regard to other prayers (39).

Next he turned his gaze to a more marked departure from tradition that appears in the Roman Eucharistic Prayer IV. "The

---

30. See n.13.

31. Ibid., 212–13.

32. See John H. McKenna, *The Eucharistic Epiclesis: A Detailed History from the Patristic to the Modern Era*, 2nd ed. (Chicago: Hillenbrand Books, 2009), esp. 70–92, 173–89. See also, Pierre-Marie Gy, *La Liturgie dans L'Histoire* (Paris: Cerf, 1990), 195, 211.

traditional language of the *anamnesis* has never been so bold as to say
'... *offerimus tibi ejus Corpus and Sanguinem, sacrificium tibi acceptabile
et toti mundo salutare*.'" Talley argued that this notion of eucharistic
sacrifice may have been widely held in the fifteenth century, as evidenced in Gabriel Biel's commentary on the Roman canon, but that it
was resisted by Thomas Aquinas (39). Talley appreciated the softening
of the language in the *Revision of the Roman Missal* that reads:

> we offer you the sacrifice of his Body and Blood,
> an offering pleasing to you,
> which brings salvation to all the world.[33]

He also acknowledged the note on the revised text that indicates that
the revision was in keeping with the long established tradition of
using a "more 'sacramental' mode of expression" in eucharistic
prayers (40).

Finally, Talley had high praise for a Roman Catholic eucharistic
prayer developed in conjunction with the Swiss Synod of 1972 and
approved for use in numerous countries, now including the United
States. The prayer is titled: *Eucharistic Prayer for Masses for Various
Needs and Occasions*. Characteristic of the prayer are a number of vari-
able parts, an epiclesis prior to the institution narrative which, while
clearly "consecratory," is a supplication for the community as well, an
anamnesis and oblation which are distinct, and a supplicatory mode in
the oblation itself which leads into an invocation of the Spirit upon
the people:

> Holy Father, look upon this offering: it is Christ who gives himself, body
> and blood, and by his sacrifice opens for us the road that leads to you.
> God, Father of mercies, grant us the Spirit of love, the Spirit of your
> Son.[34]

Thus, "Once established, the supplicatory mode is sustained, coloring
even the oblation that leads, through the prayer for the Spirit, into the
intercession and doxology" (43, see 41–42).

---

33. It is interesting to note that, contrary to Talley, *The Roman Missal* Third Typical Edition
(2000) reverts to an explicit mention of sacrifice "... we offer you his Body and Blood, / the
sacrifice acceptable to you / which brings salvation to the whole world." (Eucharistic Prayer IV.)

34. Quoted from Mazza, *The Eucharistic Prayers of the Roman Rite*, 214.

Anglican Consultation (1994)

Talley once again addressed the issue of eucharistic prayers, this time as part of an Anglican Consultation.[35] His intent here seemed aimed more at providing pastoral direction than historical exploration. He sketched the history of eucharistic prayers dealing first with those whose transition from thanksgiving to supplication takes place after the institution narrative and *anamnesis*. He acknowledged that there were alternative structures in which the fulcrum, as he so aptly put it, or transition to supplication appears earlier, for instance, soon after the *Sanctus*. He concluded: "These alternative structures, then, proved to be only temporary exceptions to a growing oriental consensus in which the Antiochene form today reigns almost supreme" (9).

In the West, he suggested sometime in the fourth century the Church of Rome abandoned the Greek tradition in favor of the *Canon Missae* or Roman Canon with its fulcrum following the *Sanctus* and breaking the flow of the narration of the wonderful works of God (9–10). (We have discussed this structure above in conjunction with the *Te igitur—Quam oblationem* grouping). He noted the general medieval view that only the words of Christ are necessary to complete the sacrament, the view that led to Luther's statement: "From here on almost everything smacks and savours of sacrifice" (11). After tracing variations in the eucharistic prayer during the Reformation period and leading up to our own day, Talley turned his attention to new eucharistic prayers.

In this context, he focused on several issues. First, he again dealt with the "split *epiclesis*" which some claim as necessary to maintain the specifically Roman character of the prayers but which has been roundly criticized inside and outside the Roman Catholic Church. He referred to the "totally untraditional distinction between consecratory and sanctificatory 'epicleses'" and characterized the result, when compared to classical structures of East or West, as "institutionalized vacillation" (13–14). Here Talley was echoing critiques by many of his colleagues. In 1969, Aidan Kavanagh had expressed fears that a split *epiclesis* would again raise the "tired old controversy" over the agent

---

35. Thomas J. Talley, "Eucharistic Prayers, Past, Present and Future," in D. R. Holeton, ed., *Revising the Eucharist: Groundwork for the Anglican Communion*, Alcuin/GROW Liturgical Study 27 (Nottingham, England: Grove, 1994), 6–19.

and moment of consecration.[36] Kavanagh argued that such an *epiclesis* interrupts the flow in narrating the divine mercies and sets the institution narrative off from this flow. In addition, it underlines the "formula of consecration" even more than before. He thinks that the choice for a split *epiclesis* is due less to Roman views on "real presence" and "consecration" than to a liturgical bias on the part of C. Vagaggini. He contends that Vagaggini had an *a priori* bias toward dividing the *epiclesis* into a prayer for consecrating the offerings and a prayer for fruitful communion, despite the fact that there is little data to support such a position.[37] I have also repeatedly argued against a split *epiclesis*. With Talley I do think its tenacious and rigid application to Roman eucharistic prayers has its roots in theology and is a vestige of the "moment of consecration" problem. A split *epiclesis* ignores the far stronger ancient tradition, interrupts the flow of the narrative, fails to emphasize the basic helplessness or *praying* attitude of the assembly, and also fails to underline the unity of "consecration" and communion which was one of the great strengths of the early *epicleses*.[38]

Talley again turned to the *anamnesis* of the Roman Catholic Eucharistic Prayer IV, "a formulation utterly novel to the tradition, and one that has received withering criticism from Roman Catholic liturgists" (14, 15–17). In his critique, especially of the phrase "we offer you his body and blood," he was not alone.[39] In 1975 Geoffrey Wainwright was to state: "I have never come across a starker statement than this in the whole of liturgical history."[40] He went on to say that it forces Protestants to ask Catholics once again what they really mean when they say, "We offer Christ." "Believers might offer *themselves*, in Christ, to God. But a Protestant finds it very difficult indeed to think that *we* might 'offer Christ.'"[41] Wainwright went on to suggest that Catholics might actually mean something different by "offer" than the obvious and strict meaning of that word. He offered examples from the hymns of John and Charles Wesley and concluded,

36. Aidan Kavanagh, "Thoughts on the New Eucharistic Prayers," *Worship* 43 (Jan. 1969): 6.

37. Ibid., 9–12.

38. See McKenna, *The Eucharistic Epiclesis*, 190–206; *Theological Studies* 36 (June 1975): 282–83; and the works cited in n. 13.

39. See, for example, Kavanagh, "Thoughts on the New Eucharistic Prayers," 8–9.

40. Geoffrey Wainwright, "The Nature of the Great Eucharistic Prayer," *Studia Liturgica* 11 (1976): 210. See also McKenna, "From 'Berakah,'" 97.

41. Ibid.

"we may say that we 'plead' Christ before God—that is, we entreat God on the basis of the sacrifice of Christ . . . we are *pleading* Calvary, not repeating it" and wondered whether Catholics and Protestants might find in such an understanding an avenue to agreement.[42] It is just such a dialogue that Talley himself suggested in light of our evolving understanding of eucharistic prayers.[43]

Talley also once again took up the placement of the popular acclamation that intervenes before the *anamnesis* and thus "forces a wedge between the narrative and the anamnesis" (17, see 16–18). He cited examples in the Anglican revisions and the Mass with Children, mentioned above, where this problem has been recognized and the acclamation has been placed after the *anamnesis* rather than before it. He expressed the hope that this is a harbinger of further revisions that will make the acclamation the fulcrum marking the shift from thanksgiving to supplication (18).

Finally, he addressed the theme of creation and comments, "if we are to see the eucharistic prayer as once again a primary proclamation of faith, creation must find a prominent place in such a prayer" (18). He recommended a position prior to the *Sanctus* rather than insinuating an allusion to creation afterward in a context that is primarily soteriological (19).

Talley concluded his odyssey up to that point by underlining the importance of the role we assign to the institution narrative. Other questions such as how or why the narrative is attached to the *anamnesis* and the relationship of the narrative-*anamnesis* unit to the prayer for consecration can only really be addressed in light of that role. He also remarked that we are unlikely to arrive at a quick agreement on the question of eucharistic sacrifice but we can at least strive to lower the "polemical heat" on the reference to the gifts in the *anamnesis*. Finally, he urged an analysis of the structure of the entire eucharistic prayer and not just elements in it. He contended that an analysis of tradition in all its variety "will reveal a rather consistent pattern of thanksgiving followed by supplication, that is, Eucharist and prayer. If we could agree on that, then we could be sure that we are addressing a single task, and that itself should serve the harder

---

42. Ibid., 210–11.

43. Talley, "Structures des anaphores anciennes et modernes," 40.

questions of the contents of each of those [elements], while leaving space for wide-ranging variety" (19).

Paul F. Bradshaw

Paul F. Bradshaw, Professor of Liturgy at the University of Notre Dame, is another prominent scholar who has focused on the issue of eucharistic origins and eucharistic prayers. He quotes Robert Wright's statement that there are two kinds of people, "lumpers" and "splitters."[44] "Lumpers" in liturgical scholarship like to arrange the data to emphasize a single unified line of development traceable from apostolic times to the fourth century. "Splitters" tend to emphasize the diversity in what we know about the earliest states of development—a diversity that was to yield later to a greater uniformity. Bradshaw is a self-avowed "splitter," and his study is an attempt to argue the case for the splitters' view of the earliest Christian worship.[45]

Challenging Findings

Bradshaw has challenged the prevailing theory stemming from Gregory Dix's classic *The Shape of the Liturgy*. This theory holds that the basic outline or shape of the earliest Eucharist was unified and of apostolic origin.[46] Simply put, Bradshaw argues that early Christian liturgy had great diversity and only later did it become more uniform.

In dealing with possible Jewish background of early Christian liturgy he cautions against two extremes. One is automatically accepting historical readings to be factually reliable. The other is to reject out of hand information proposed in rabbinical descriptions of their own religious traditions. For instance, one should be careful not to presume that numerous features of later Jewish worship would be familiar to Jesus and his disciples.[47] In examining the question of Jewish roots, Bradshaw limits himself to a brief treatment of four areas: elements of synagogue liturgy; daily prayer practice; forms of prayer

---

44. Bradshaw, *The Search,* ix.

45. Ibid., ix–x.

46. See Ibid., 6–8, and Paul F. Bradshaw, *Eucharistic Origins* (New York: Oxford University Press, 2004), vi.

47. Bradshaw, *The Search,* 31–33.

themselves; and grace at meals. In general he detects a diversity of practices rather than fixed formulas and uniformity.[48]

In dealing with worship in the New Testament Bradshaw also suggests caution but he does take stances. "Nevertheless in spite of all this uncertainty, those passages which have been identified by general consensus as hymns and prayers can legitimately be seen as reflecting the sort of liturgical material which early Christians would have used. . . . For example, early Christian forms of prayer reveal an apparently growing preference for *eucharisteo* over *eulogeo*. Although it is frequently said that these verbs are simply synonyms, our study of Jewish prayer-patterns has indicated that this is not the case, but that each word was used in a quite different liturgical construction. Thus the preference points to the dominance of the *hodayah/eucharistia* form over the *berakah/eulogia* in primitive Christianity."[49]

> From the point of view of liturgical scholars, the question of whether the Last Supper was a Passover meal does not seem particularly crucial. . . . In any case, we are far from certain about the precise details of the Passover meal in the first century, after the destruction of the Temple. To cite just one example, it seems likely that it did not become a true family meal until the Passover ceased to be a Jerusalem pilgrimage festival after 70 CE.[50]

Bradshaw also suggests that the institution narratives may have originally been used as teaching or catechetical devices. Only later (fourth century) were they inserted into the eucharistic prayers to help teach "half-converted and half-instructed" Christians the glory of God and the reality of Christ's presence in the Eucharist.[51]

In his treatment of the *Didache* Bradshaw notes that scholars are divided on the question whether or not chapters 9–10 are referring to a Eucharist. He gives four main explanations with the shortcomings of each: (1) it is only ancillary to the Eucharist proper; (2) it is a quite different kind of Eucharist; (3) it is an agape and not a Eucharist; (4) it is an early form of Eucharist.[52] He then provides an alternate explanation or paradigm, namely, that it is simply one of a

---

48. Ibid., 35–46.
49. Ibid., 59.
50. Ibid., 65.
51. Ibid., 62–63, 219.
52. Bradshaw, *Eucharistic Origins*, 26–31.

number of forms of Eucharist that coexisted in the early church. "As we shall see in the next chapter, there does exist other evidence that would lend some support to this notion of several parallel forms of Christian ritual meals that only gradually coalesced in the pattern that we recognize as the 'normal' Eucharist."[53]

Bradshaw acknowledges that he has purposely at times raised more questions than answers. "We must therefore be content to remain agnostic about many of the roots of Christian worship practices which we observe clearly for the first time in the following centuries."[54] This is in keeping with his use of the "hermeneutics of suspicion" throughout his study.

The *Apostolic Tradition*

In dealing with church orders, Bradshaw's position on Hippolytus and the *Apostolic Tradition* is particularly significant, given their role as a missing link of sorts between what went before and afterward. As we have seen above in discussing Thomas Talley, the common view was that Hippolytus was the author of that work which gave us a good picture of a liturgy in Rome around the year 215. The "sample" eucharistic prayer contained therein had a number of characteristics of the Jewish berakah and this understanding had an impact on the theology, the spirit, and the structure of modern eucharistic prayers. While acknowledging that the majority of scholars have supported this view, Bradshaw questions the prevailing assumptions on the place of origin, the date and the authorship of the *Apostolic Tradition*.[55]

Andrew McGowan also acknowledges that most scholars in the twentieth century held the traditional view but adds that Bradshaw is really proposing a paradigm shift. In this case it is a move

53. Ibid., 32. More recently, Bradshaw proposes, "Yet Another Explanation of *Didache* 9–10," *Studia Liturgica* 36 (2006): 124–28, that chapters 9 and 10 circulated independently of each other.

54. Ibid., 72.

55. Ibid., 80–83. See also Bradshaw, *Eucharistic Origins*, 19–20, 48–50, 135–38, who states that in its extant state the *Apostolic Tradition* dates from the fourth century or later. He adds, however (19–20), that does not mean that certain elements, for example, the institution narrative, contained in its eucharistic prayer did not exist as a teaching device long before it was inserted into the prayer. See also John F. Baldovin, "Hippolytus and the *Apostolic Tradition*: Recent Research and Commentary," *Theological Studies* 64 (Sept. 2003): 520–42; and Andrew B. McGowan, *Ascetic Eucharists: Food and Drink in Early Christian Ritual Meals* (New York: Oxford University Press, 1999), 28–29.

away from a single line development from earliest Christianity on to a theory of greater diversity in the beginning that gave way to greater uniformity, especially in the fourth century. "The work of scholars such as Paul F. Bradshaw has turned these specific doubts into what amounts to a challenge of the whole paradigm, although the shape of a new constructive approach to early Christian meals and early liturgy in general remains to be seen."[56] McGowan notes that usually such a shift reflects new data. Bradshaw and others are not basing the shift on new data so much as on old data viewed in a new light. He also seems less than optimistic that the debate over the *Apostolic Tradition* will soon end. Referring to his own study he comments: "The geographical extent of using milk in an initiatory cup remains somewhat obscure so long as the date and authorship of the *Apostolic Tradition* are also vexed, which may be forever."[57]

Bradshaw suggests further study of this and other church orders.[58] Meanwhile, given the advantages of the new eucharistic prayers mentioned above, shall we simply say we did the right thing for the wrong reason? John Baldovin shows balance in this regard:

> There is a very real possibility that the *Apostolic Tradition* describes liturgies that never existed. *A fortiori*, great caution must be employed in appealing to this document to justify contemporary rites. (I do not object to someone wanting to use the anaphora contained in the ordination rite for a bishop, for example, as the basis of a contemporary prayer. . . . But I do question the unjustifiable reason for using this prayer, namely the assumption that it was *the* eucharistic prayer of the early-third-century Church at Rome). . . . Many doubts have been expressed here, and many questions left open. Even if the liturgies described in the so-called *Apostolic Tradition* never existed in practice, they have had a major impact on the subsequent history of liturgical practice especially and perhaps even ironically in the West. The document addressed in this study has shaped the contemporary liturgies of initiation, ordination, and Eucharist. Of this there can be no doubt at all.[59]

---

56. McGowan, *Ascetic Eucharists*, 29.

57. Ibid., 111.

58. Bradshaw, *The Search*, 97.

59. Baldovin, "Hippolytus and the *Apostolic Tradition*," 542.

Evolution of Eucharistic Rites

Bradshaw, having examined the ancient church orders and other major liturgical sources, traces the evolution of eucharistic rites as we have done above in the context of Thomas Talley. He concludes that there are three major obstacles to real progress in seeking to understand the origins and development of early Christian liturgy. The first is the belief that we need to trace back to a standard fixed Jewish liturgy, for instance, a *Birkat Ha-Mason* with a text that was universally in use in the first century.[60] Second, is the attempt to locate all existing examples of early Christian liturgy in a single line of development. That leads to rejecting meal rituals that don't fit that pattern.[61] Third is assuming that early Christian eucharistic prayers would always have been "a single, flowing, seamless whole" rather than a diversity of patterns formed by combining small preexistent units.[62] It should not be surprising that we find a diversity of eucharistic prayer patterns in the first centuries of Christianity. Probably they involved putting together small preexistent units rather than creating a unified whole from scratch.[63] According to Bradshaw, what seems to have happened is a selective evolution whereby elements like the Sanctus, institution narrative, epiclesis, and intercessions from one tradition were added to elements from other traditions. This process led to the "classical shape" of the eucharistic prayer as we know it with its different regional variations.[64]

Further Findings

Turning to early Christian initiation rites he similarly concludes that "the traditional claim that early Christian initiation practice was fundamentally identical in every place cannot really be sustained."[65] What seems to emerge from his study is that "we cannot really talk

---

60. Bradshaw, *The Search*, 139–40.
61. Ibid., 140–41.
62. Ibid., 141–43.
63. Ibid., 142.
64. Ibid., 143.
65. Ibid., 146.

of a standard or normative pattern of early initiation practice in primitive Christianity."[66] So the norm once again is diversity.

The same is true of daily prayer and the liturgical year: "in the cases of baptism and Eucharist, the further one digs into the primary sources the more it is diversity rather than uniformity which is encountered in the first few centuries."[67] Bradshaw maintains that those shaping the Christian liturgy in the fourth century eventually chose to adapt, to some extent at least, to pagan language and symbols. The purpose of this was to help converts participate more fully in the liturgical celebrations. It also, however, meant the disappearance or transformation of some elements in earlier Christianity. Similarly, in order to keep doctrinal orthodoxy a variety of earlier practices were sacrificed. He concludes, "Although, as we have said, this development succeeded in strengthening the unity and catholicity of the Church, the price paid was a loss of some sense of local self-identity," or the very diversity that Bradshaw has discovered throughout his study.[68]

Growing Areas of Agreement

In his preface Bradshaw comments that it would be premature to claim that a consensus is emerging, but there is a growing number of scholars who would agree with him on a number of points.[69] First, if we were not already convinced of the complexity of examining the practices of the earliest Church, studies like his remind us how difficult it is. Moreover, the further back we go assertions of "what the early Church did" become more precarious.[70]

A growing number of scholars would agree that what we do know about that period point to much diversity rather than rigid uniformity. Bruce Chilton, for instance, would claim that there are six "Eucharists" or forms of celebrating Eucharist in the New Testament.[71]

---

66. Ibid., 169.

67. Ibid., 191.

68. Ibid., 229–30.

69. Ibid., x.

70. See McKenna, "From 'Berakah,'" 90–91, among many.

71. See Bruce Chilton, *A Feast of Meanings: Eucharistic Theologies from Jesus through Johannine Circles* (Leiden: Brill, 1994), and *Jesus' Prayer and Jesus' Eucharist: His Personal Practice of Spirituality* (Valley Forge, Pa: Trinity Press International, 1997).

Chilton contends that the diversities of emphasis in the Eucharist of the early Christian Church might teach us something about our own celebrations today.[72] Robert Daly picks up on a number of points in Chilton's thesis. While not necessarily agreeing with all the details, Daly sees Chilton's position as reflective of the work of modern historians of the liturgy and other exegetes. They question the "assumption that there was a somewhat unified line of development that one could trace from the established Eucharist of later centuries back close to the time of the historical Jesus."[73] Daly also agrees that we could learn something about our own Eucharist from the diversity in the early Church.[74]

Andrew McGowan is another scholar who would support Bradshaw's thesis of diversity in the early Church. McGowan's own study focuses not so much on the better known tradition of bread and wine but on diverse practices, for example, the use, in certain circles, of bread and water for the Eucharist. The "normative" tradition then becomes "one profound possibility among others."[75] In the context of questioning the ability of Gregory Dix's theory to meet the criteria of plausibility and inclusiveness that McGowan himself proposes, he states: "the issue with which this study is most directly concerned, [is] the use of food in Eucharistic meals and particularly the tradition in which the elements of the Eucharist were bread and water, not wine."[76] He contends that in some relatively significant areas wine was not used, partly at least because of its association with pagan sacrifices. Like meat wine came to be associated with sacrifice. Even though wine itself was not "sacralized" its use almost certainly was. Offering wine with a blessing was uniquely important even in a home setting. This was an echo of the more explicit cultic use of libations.[77]

---

72. Chilton, *Jesus' Prayer*, 94–97.

73. Robert J. Daly, "Eucharistic Origins: From the New Testament to the Liturgies of the Golden Age," *Theological Studies* 66 (March 2005): 9.

74. Ibid., 19–21.

75. McGowan, *Ascetic Eucharists*, 31.

76. Ibid.

77. Ibid., 64–66, and 182.

Bradshaw argues that instances of such diversity challenge scholars to ask not only what the early Church did but when and where and whether a practice was the only form in that place. This too is accepted by a growing number of scholars.[78] So, too, is a recognition that the "classical shape of the liturgy" is the result of a deliberate effort to assimilate different traditions during the fourth century rather than the survival of *the* one pattern of Christian liturgy from earliest times.[79] Finally, mainstream post-Nicene liturgical tradition was often the result of a compromise that took bits and pieces from different traditions and was probably unlike that of any single Christian community prior to the fourth century.[80]

What are some of the things we have learned? We should have learned to be humble or reserved in the face of the paucity of data about the earliest Church liturgy. Scholars in the twentieth century have generally agreed that Christian liturgy has roots in Jewish liturgical practice but we do not know in detail precisely how and that has led to numerous theories.[81] In dealing with the *Apostolic Tradition* questions have arisen not because there is much new data but because scholars like Bradshaw have looked at the old data in a new light.[82] McGowan as noted also believes the surrounding debate will not be resolved in the near future and says that Bradshaw's own reconstruction must stand the test of time.[83] Even if the questions are not settled, there is no need to scrap the structure and mood of our new eucharistic prayers.[84] There is much to be learned from the diversity of earliest Church liturgy (Bradshaw, Chilton, Daly, McGowan). Present eucharistic prayers continue to need examination, for example, for more emphasis on the creation theme.[85]

---

78. Bradshaw, *The Search*, x.

79. Ibid.

80. Ibid.

81. Ibid., 121–43.

82. McGowan, *Ascetic Eucharists*, 28–29.

83. Ibid., 29, and 111.

84. Baldovin, "Hippolytus and the *Apostolic Tradition*," 542.

85. Talley, "Eucharistic Prayers, Past, Present and Future," 18–19. See also Kevin W. Irwin, *Models of the Eucharist* (New York: Paulist Press, 2005), "Model One: Cosmic Mass," 39–66, for a fine presentation of this area.

The odyssey in the study of eucharistic prayers continues. An odyssey is described as a long wandering. Often it leads to new discoveries. The map of our documents and practices has great gaps and is sketchy at best. Yet we have learned that the turns of our theories can have practical repercussions. Some lead to dead ends. Others lead to progress, for instance, the sharp criticism of wording in Roman Eucharistic Prayer IV that led to recent revisions. Still others open up larger theological questions or vistas. Reflecting on over seventeen years of evolution in the study of eucharistic prayers, Thomas Talley was to muse that it is encouraging that we do "not have to get it right the first time, or even the second time. The dialogue between all the avenues of understanding—liturgiology, theology, pastoralia, and many others—themselves constantly developing, continues and will continue."[86] Meanwhile, we can hope and work for that day when the wonders our eucharistic prayers celebrate and pray for will finally become reality in our lives as well as on our lips.

---

86. Talley, "Structures des anaphores anciennes et modernes," 40.

Chapter 8

Changing Attitudes toward the Eucharist over the Centuries

Having seen in the previous chapter how complex the search for our eucharistic origins can be, we may better appreciate that attitudes toward the Eucharist have changed over time. As this chapter outlines those attitudinal changes in broad strokes, the reader's grasp of the historical details is less important than getting a sense of the shifting mentalities. This summary treatment is necessarily a simplification but, hopefully, not a distortion. The history of the Eucharist, the Mass, the Lord's Supper, as it is variously called, is a story of simple faith and theological speculation, of conflict and agreement, of change and resistance to change, of emperors and popes, clergy and lay people. It is a story of people—their hopes and fears, their faith and superstitions, their changing attitudes as nations and cultures changed.[1]

CREATIVE ORIGINS (FIRST 600 YEARS)

In the beginning, Christian communities were small. They had no churches, no temples—although at first some of those in Jerusalem continued to go to the Temple as Luke in the Acts of the Apostles reminds us: "They devoted themselves to the apostles' instruction and the communal life, to the breaking of the bread [a term for Eucharist] and the prayers. . . . Those who believed shared all things in

---

1. See John H. McKenna, *The History of the Mass*, a video, (Chicago: Liturgy Training Publications, 2001), for an example of such a broad stroke approach. See James F. White, *A Brief History of Christian Worship* (Nashville: Abingdon Press, 1993), 75, who notes that limiting oneself, as he does, to tracing the broad lines has its advantages "since most developments, once started, are consistent; reversals are uncommon."

common—they would sell their property and goods, dividing every-thing on the basis of each one's needs. They went to the temple area together every day, while in their homes they broke bread" (Acts 2:42–47 NAB).

Christians linked their celebrations closely to a rich Jewish heritage, infusing this heritage with new content, however, as they stressed the role of Christ, his death and Resurrection, and the role that they, the Christian community, played in this celebration. As sharers in Christ's Resurrection, *they* were the Church and the homes in which they celebrated were called "the house of the church of God." There they would blend, as did their ancestors, word, music, and ritual blessings.[2]

Indications are that they used ordinary bread and wine and "broke bread" in the setting of a meal, which symbolized deeper reali-ties. They seem to have presumed Christ's presence and stressed the signs (bread and wine), the action (eating and drinking), and espe-cially the goal of all this (nourishing the Christ-life already within them through baptism, preserving unity with each other in Christ, and laying claim to eternal life through a share in Christ's resurrec-tion). "Those who feed on my flesh and drink my blood have life eter-nal and I will raise them up on the last day. For my flesh is real food and my blood real drink. Those who feed on my flesh and drink my blood remain in me, and I in them" (Jn. 6:54–56).[3]

Paul the Apostle was just as clear on the reality and purpose of this meal: "Is not the cup of blessing we bless a sharing in the blood of Christ? And is not the bread we break a sharing in the body of Christ? Because the loaf of bread is one, we, many though we are, are

---

2. White, *A Brief History of Christian Worship,* 19–22. See also R. C. D. Jasper and G. J. Cuming, *Prayers of the Eucharist: Early and Reformed,* 3rd ed. (New York: Pueblo, 1987), 9–10; Louis Bouyer, *Eucharist,* trans. C. U. Quinn (Notre Dame, Ind.: University of Notre Dame Press, 1968), 50–135; Deiss, *Didache,* in *Springtime of the Liturgy: Liturgical Texts of the First Four Centuries,* trans. M. J. O'Connell (Collegeville, Minn.: Liturgical Press, 1979), 74–77, with fine introductions.

3. See White, *A Brief History of Christian Worship,* 24–26, 29. See also Edward Foley, *From Age to Age: How Christians Celebrated the Eucharist,* 2nd ed. (Collegeville, Minn.: Liturgical Press, 2008), 25–30, 43–47. See Andrew McGowan, *Ascetic Eucharists: Food and Drink in Early Christian Ritual Meals* (New York, Oxford University Press, 1999), for variations on this pattern as we have seen in chapter 7. See also Frank Senn, *A Stewardship of the Mysteries* (New York: Paulist Press, 1999). Of particular interest are chapter 7, "The Frequency of Celebration and Reception of Communion in Protestantism," 99–121, and chapter 8, "Roman Catholic Communion Practices: History and Present Challenges," 122–37, from a Lutheran perspective.

one body, for we all partake of the one loaf" (1 Cor. 10:16–17). And Ignatius of Antioch, just before his martyrdom in 107 AD, urged his people to live as they sang: in unison through Christ.[4]

They had a great hope in the world to come—a hope rooted in their experience of their risen Lord living among them and freeing them from death in all its forms. To express this belief they drew upon a host of symbols.[5] The risen Christ was life-giving water for their thirst, forgiveness for their sins, and healing for their sickness. Jesus was the bread of life who not only nourished them on earth, but who also held the promise of a risen life after death.[6] Texts like Acts 2:42–47 and James 2:1–5 also reflect a respect and concern for those who were poor. At least in earliest times, Christian homes could serve, as noted above, as "the house of the church of God." For the people realized that they were the "church."[7]

Justin Martyr's description of the Eucharist around 150 is one of the earliest and fullest accounts we have. One of the things he stressed was the link between the eucharistic service and social concern or service of others outside the liturgy. He speaks of a collection that is taken up so that the well-to-do can help those in need. "These gifts are collected and handed over to the one presiding. It is he who assists the widows and orphans. He assists those who are in want through sickness or for some reason, prisoners, and strangers passing through—in other words, he helps all who are in need."[8]

Justin describes the weekly Eucharist. It is still symbolic of deeper realities, very much shared in, and closely linked to the Resurrection. It is an assembly, a gathering of God's people. The structure of word, prayer, and ritual blessing is familiar to us, although it is not

---

4. See Foley, *From Age to Age,* 52, and White, *A Brief History of Christian Worship,* 37, 70. See also Senn, *A Stewardship,* 123–24.

5. See Josef Jungmann, *Pastoral Liturgy* (New York: Herder, 1962), 4–5, 359–62.

6. White, *A Brief History of Christian Worship,* 23, 25, 30. See also James J. Megivern, *Concomitance and Communion: A Study in Eucharistic Doctrine and Practice* (New York: Herder, 1963), 52–53, which remains a fine study on concomitance and communion practice.

7. See Foley, *From Age to Age,* 43–51, and Jungmann, *The Early Liturgy to the Time of Gregory the Great,* trans. F. A. Brunner (Notre Dame, Ind.: University of Notre Dame Press, 1959), 16–17.

8. Deiss, *Didache,* 93–94. See also Jasper-Cuming, *Prayers of the Eucharist,* 30.

certain that this was typical of the liturgies of his time.[9] In any event, for Justin this pattern was at the service of the community in its praise of God through Jesus Christ. Among its characteristics were a sense of participation, a close connection with the Resurrection, and a concern for those in need:

> On the day which is called Sunday, all, whether they live in the town or the country, gather in the same place. Then the memoirs of the apostles or the writings of the prophets are read for as long as time allows, after which the one presiding speaks, exhorting us to live by those noble teachings. Then we all stand and pray. . . . When we have finished praying, bread, wine, and water are brought up. Then the priest prays and gives thanks as well as he can. All the people respond with the acclamation "Amen!"[10]

Justin also declares that the food then shared in the assembly is the Body and Blood of the incarnate Jesus. The purpose of all this is "to nourish and transform our flesh and blood.[11]

The ties with creation and the Resurrection are clear: "It is on Sunday that we all assemble, because Sunday is the first day: the day on which God transformed darkness and matter and created the world, and the day on which Jesus Christ our Savior rose from the dead. . . . He appeared to his apostles and disciples and taught them what we have now offered for your examination."[12]

Inscriptions on gravestones around this time indicate that the early Christians took Communion in their hands. They also received standing, just as they prayed standing, to symbolize their belief that they had risen with Christ and were ready to greet him when he appears again.[13] Around this time St. Irenaeus (d. 202) expressed well the connection between Eucharist and Resurrection: "A shoot of a vine that is buried in the earth bears fruit in its proper season. A grain of wheat that falls to the ground and dissolves rises again. . . . So too

---

9. See, for example, Paul F. Bradshaw, *The Search for the Origins of Christian Worship: Sources and Methods for the Study of Early Liturgy*, 2nd ed. (New York: University of Oxford Press, 2002), 80–83.

10. Deiss, *Didache*, 93–94. See also, Jasper-Cuming, *Prayers of the Eucharist*, 29–30.

11. Deiss, *Didache*, 94, and Jasper-Cuming, *Prayers of the Eucharist*, 29.

12. Deiss, *Didache*, 94, and Jasper-Cuming, *Prayers of the Eucharist*, 30. See also White, *A Brief History of Christian Worship*, 26, 31.

13. Deiss, *Didache*, 94; A. Hamman, ed., *The Mass* (New York: Alba House, 1968), 184–85. See also *Instruction on Eucharistic Worship* 8 (May 25, 1967): 40–41, that picks up on this last theme.

our bodies fed by the Eucharist . . . shall rise again in due season since the Word of God will give them the grace of resurrection."[14]

Justin also writes that everyone shares from the gifts over which the thanksgiving has been spoken and that the deacons bring a share to those who are absent so that they can participate in the celebration.[15] Finally, the relatively small gathering place for the assembly could drive home visually the unifying effect of the Eucharist described by Ignatius of Antioch shortly before his martyrdom around 107 AD: "Take care then to partake of one Eucharist, for one is the flesh of Our Lord Jesus Christ, and one the cup to unite us with His blood, and one altar, just as there is one bishop."[16]

In the *Apostolic Tradition*, considered by a majority of twentieth-century scholars to have been written around 215 by Hippolytus of Rome, is a description of the Church's makeup and its liturgy.[17] According to this document Communion was still taken in the hand while standing, under the form of both bread and wine. Like those who had gone before him, Hippolytus stressed, in another work, the dynamic purpose of the Eucharist. It formed Christians into likenesses of Christ so that they became, with the help of the Holy Spirit, more perfect members of the Body of Christ.[18]

The Christians continued to link their celebration with a concern for the poor. An instruction at that time reads: "If a poor woman comes, or a poor man, whether they are from your parish or not, above all if they are advanced in years, and if there is no room for them,

---

14. Adversus Haereses V, 2, 3, as cited by Lucien Deiss, *It's the Lord's Supper: The Eucharist of Christians*, trans. E. Bonin (New York: Paulist Press, 1976), 104–5.

15. See White, *A Brief History of Christian Worship*, 29; Deiss, *It's the Lord's Supper*, 94; Jasper-Cuming, *Prayers of the Eucharist*, 30; and Senn, *A Stewardship*, 124.

16. Megivern, *Concomitance and Communion*, 55, citing Ignatius of Antioch, Epist. ad Philadelp. 4, ed. Solano, I 72 (PG 5:700).

17. As we have seen in chapter 7, a number of scholars now question the authorship, the date, and the place of origin of this work. See, for instance Bradshaw, *The Search*, 80–83. See also Bradshaw, *Eucharistic Origins* (New York: University of Oxford Press, 2004), 19–20, 48–50, 135–38, who states that in its extant state the *Apostolic Tradition* dates from the fourth century or later. He adds, however, that does not mean that certain elements, for example, the institution narrative, contained in its eucharistic prayer did not exist, possibly as a teaching device, long before it was inserted into the prayer. See also John F. Baldovin, "Hippolytus and the *Apostolic Tradition*: Recent Research and Commentary," *Theological Studies* 64 (Sept. 2003): 520–42, and McGowan, 28–29.

18. Megivern, citing Hippolytus on the Pascha iii, as cited by Gregory Dix, *The Shape of the Liturgy* (Westminster, 1945), 138.

make a place for them, O bishop, with all your heart, even if you have to sit on the floor."[19]

A profound change was to take place between the time of Hippolytus and that of Ambrose of Milan (d. 397). Constantine (d. 337) tolerated, and then embraced Christianity. Persecutions of Christians ceased. Converts streamed into the Church and that brought about change. Larger buildings were needed to house the larger numbers. Priests and bishops at times adopted imperial rank, customs and clothing. Latin had become the liturgical language.[20]

There were dark clouds on the horizon. Many of the converts were "unconverted" and "uneducated" in the ways of Christianity. In response preachers like John Chrysostom and Cyril of Jerusalem emphasized the awesome nature of the Eucharist perhaps to too great an extent at times. Phrases like the "dreadful sacrifice," "fearful moment," the "terrible table" used to describe the Eucharist were hardly the road to more frequent reception of Communion.[21] In addition, Arius (d. 336) denied the divinity of Christ and thus triggered a controversy that was to rage through the century. The effects of Arianism on Eucharistic attitudes (lasting far beyond the century) will be considered shortly. As often happens in a fight, it was difficult to maintain a balance doctrinally and pastorally.[22]

On the other hand, the emphasis on the dynamism of the Eucharist continued. Ambrose did not remain fixed on Christ's presence in the bread and wine. He pushed on to the effect this transformed nourishment had within his people.[23] The homilies of Augustine (d. 430) showed a keen sense of the ecclesial dimension as well as the dynamism of the Eucharist: "If you receive well, you are what you have received. . . . Since you are the body of Christ and His members, it is your mystery that is placed on the Lord's table; it is your mystery that you receive. . . . You hear the words: 'The body of Christ.' And you answer 'Amen.' Be therefore members of Christ, that your 'Amen' may be true. . . . Be what you see, and receive what

19. Deiss, *Didache,* 176, citing *Didascalia Apostolorum,* chapter 12.

20. See White, *A Brief History of Christian Worship,* 41–42, 72–73.

21. See Bradshaw, *The Search,* 216–21, and Senn, *A Stewardship,* 124.

22. Senn, *A Stewardship,* 124, citing Megivern, *Concomitance and Communion,* 63–66.

23. See Megivern, *Concomitance and Communion,* 67.

you are."[24] As Henri de Lubac was rightly to point out, Augustine's ecclesial realism presupposes eucharistic realism.[25] For Augustine, and those like him, Communion had the breathtaking purpose of more and more shaping those who received into what they already were—the Body of Christ. Eucharistic realism and ecclesial realism supported one another. Among ancient writers the accent was on the effect rather than on the cause. The faithful are united to one another because they are united to Christ in the Eucharist.[26] Pope St. Leo the Great (d. 461) was no less aware of the purpose of the Eucharist: "The partaking of the body and blood of Christ has no other effect than to make us pass over into what we receive."[27]

What we know of the first six hundred years indicates that Communion was taken in the hand and was ordinarily under both forms.[28] It was seen as food, nourishment, and a means of uniting the community.

It is true that seeds had been sown which would eventually lead to striking changes in attitudes regarding the Eucharist. The fight over Christ's divinity was a good example of this. Early Christian art, as well as its theology, while not denying his divinity, stressed the humanity of Christ. This humanity was, to be sure, risen, glorified, "irradiated with divinity," but precisely because of this the risen Jesus was considered to be close to the Christians, present and active among them. Christ is rarely pictured alone but rather surrounded by his Church—represented by apostles, sheep, deer, etc. He is their Shepherd, their Sun, their Healer, their Host. Despite, however, the efforts of the Council of Chalcedon (451) to reach a balance between Christ's divinity and his humanity, there was a strong reaction to the denial of Christ's divinity. Later generations were to lose sight of the *humanity* of the glorified, risen Lord. His glorified humanity became

---

24. Ibid., 68. See also Nathan Mitchell, *Cult and Controversy: The Worship of the Eucharist Outside Mass* (New York: Pueblo, 1982), 74.

25. Henri de Lubac, *Corpus Mysticum: L'Eucharistie et L'Église au Moyen Âge. Étude Historique* (Paris: Éditions Aubier-Montaigne, 1949), 284.

26. de Lubac, *Corpus Mysticum*, 283–84. His whole work is a fine treatment of the relationship between the Church as Body of Christ and the Eucharist as Body of Christ, especially 89–115, and 279–94.

27. Megivern, *Concomitance and Communion*, 72.

28. See Megivern, *Concomitance and Communion*, 5–26. McGowan's study, *Ascetic Eucharists*, makes a case for bread and water in some significant groups, as we noted in the last chapter.

swallowed up, as Josef Jungmann would say, in the godhead of the Trinity. The risen Jesus became a distant God.[29] As Christ became distant so would the clergy and the liturgy. Referring to the Eucharist with phrases like "the frightful mysteries," "which demand reverence and trembling," "a fearful and holy sacrifice" did not help.

But, for the most part, the Christians of this period stressed the communal aspect of the Eucharist; it was an action to transform and unify the community. Communion was still generally taken in the hand. The bread and the chalice were food and drink to nourish, to gladden the hearts of those partaking and to unite them in Christ. The architecture with its focus on the one table or altar tended to bring out these aspects.

With all the emphasis on unity, however, there was also much variety and participation. Bishops and priests were free to compose their own prayers or to choose from collections of texts. Each would take part in his or her own way—by taking part in entrance, Gospel, or communion processions, by presenting the gifts, singing, responding to prayers, reading, presiding, preaching, distributing Communion, etc.[30] Underlying much of this was the fact that people like Ambrose and Augustine rooted their preaching, their theology, and their spirituality in the Bible and in the actual celebration of the liturgy.

Middle Ages (roughly 600–1500)[31]

If we jump to the ninth century, the changes in attitude and practice are dramatic.[32] They stem from a number of factors. The reaction to Arianism continues to take its toll on the image of Christ, the Church, and the liturgy. The emphasis on Christ's divinity, almost to the exclusion of his humanity, leads to a sense of distance between him and the ordinary people. This in turn leads to a widening separation of the people from the clergy and from participation in the liturgy.

---

29. Jungmann, *Pastoral Liturgy*, 4–9, 57, 78, 360–62.
30. See White, *A Brief History of Christian Worship*, 52, 57.
31. White, *A Brief History of Christian Worship*, 75.
32. Ibid., 88.

There is a growing feeling that it is not the whole people of God who do the offering but rather the clergy who do it for them.[33]

The people themselves have changed. The barbarian invasion has run its course, leaving a firm Franco-Germanic influence in its wake. The people have a strong sense of an upper stratum of society who alone possess the power to rule. The fact that, for the most part, only the clergy and the more educated understand Latin, the liturgical language, further distance the clergy and the liturgy from the ordinary people. A love for the dramatic and the concrete has led to the use of candles in different places, the burning of incense, a special place for gospel reading, and additional prayers at the Offertory and Communion times. The subjective and individual are emphasized more than the objective and corporate.[34]

The preaching changes. Amalar, bishop of Metz (d. 853), conscious that the people no longer follow the Latin, turns to allegory to give them something to hold onto. For instance, the eucharistic prayer or Canon which was prayed aloud for 700 years is now recited silently. Amalar preaches that this symbolizes the "Holy of Holies" in the Jewish Temple that only the priest could enter. The priest raising his voice and striking his breast at the prayer "*Nobis quoque peccatoribus*" (in fact this raising of the priest's voice was a signal to the deacon to perform a particular liturgical function) becomes a reminder of the centurion's cry at the foot of the cross. This type of preaching, which was to dominate into the thirteenth century, moves away from the early Christian sense of entering into the dying and rising of Christ now made present. Instead, it focuses on the recalling of past events—sometimes viewed as quite separate from one another.[35]

One final factor underlies the dramatic change and shows the imbalance that follows upon a fight, whether over Christ's divinity or

---

33. See Bradshaw, *The Search*, 220; Jungmann, *The Mass of the Roman Rite*, trans. B. A. Brunner and revised by C. K. Riepe (New York: Benziger, 1959) 62–64. Reprinted as Christian Classics Reprint (Westminster, Md., 1980), and *Pastoral Liturgy*, 18–63. See also Mitchell, *Cult and Controversy*, 87–90, and Senn, *A Stewardship*, 125, citing Megivern, *Concomitance and Communion*, 29–33, 43.

34. Jungmann, *The Mass*, 58–59, and *Pastoral Liturgy*, 2–9, 59–62. See also Senn, *A Stewardship*, 126–27, who notes that the number of communicants also decreased in the Eastern churches that celebrated in the vernacular.

35. White, 99–100. See also Megivern, *Concomitance and Communion*, 80–82; Jungmann, *The Mass*, 67–69; and Mitchell, *Cult and Controversy*, 50–62, for the impact the move from symbol to allegory could have.

the reality of the Eucharist. To underline Christ's presence in the Eucharist, in reaction to an apparent denial of this belief, an appeal was made to an "overly physical approach," for example, bleeding hosts. As we have seen in chapter 1, Thomas Aquinas rightly argued that, however one explained the bleeding host phenomena, they did not prove our Lord's presence since his risen body does not bleed.[36] But in the ninth century these stories signaled a shift from a sense of an approachable Eucharist and eagerness to participate actively in the eucharistic meal to a sense of awe, fear, even superstition at times. In short, the Eucharist was becoming more an object than an action, more an awesome mystery that a joyful sharing.[37]

Changes in practice reflect the changes in attitude. Unleavened bread was becoming a requirement; it was whiter in appearance and had fewer crumbs. A tube or straw was used to share from the cup. The host was generally placed on the tongue instead of on the hand. The heavy decline in receiving Communion during this period indicates, not a better sense of reverence than the early Christians had, but rather an excessive sense of fear or extreme reverence.[38]

The architecture is also revealing. Where there was once only one altar in even the largest of basilicas, now there are many altars—some in small turrets or towers where only one or two people besides the priest could gather. This reflects the increase of private Masses and the lessening of an awareness of the communal character of the Eucharist. It has become mainly a source of favors, help and protection from demons, a means of "spiritual firepower."[39]

This represents a major shift in attitude from that of Christians in the first seven centuries. They had presumed the presence of Christ in the Eucharist and had focused on its power to transform the community. Now the stress is on trying to "prove" that presence, and

---

36. See Megivern, *Concomitance and Communion*, 40–45, and White, *A Brief History of Christian Worship*, 91, among others listed in chapter 1.

37. See White, *A Brief History of Christian Worship*, 88–92, for a description of medieval eucharistic piety. Whereas the early Church focused more on hope in the face of death, the Middle Ages emphasized more fear of damnation. See also Jungmann, *The Mass*, 56–70, and *Pastoral Liturgy*, 7–9, 18–63, and Megivern, *Concomitance and Communion*, 43, 78–84.

38. See White, *A Brief History of Christian Worship*, 96–97. See also Jungmann, *The Mass*, 64–65; Megivern, *Concomitance and Communion*, 29–33; and Senn, *A Stewardship*, 126.

39. Jungmann, *The Mass*, 62–64, 158–64, and *Pastoral Liturgy*, 59–63.

the focus is on the bread and wine rather than on the people to be nourished and transformed.

When in the eleventh century Berengar of Tours (d. 1088) did deny Christ's presence in the Eucharist, even more attention was placed on the bread and wine and on bleeding host stories. Theologians also began to emphasize that Christ is not only fully present in both forms, the bread and the wine taken together, but under each form separately. Thus the stage was set for the doctrine of concomitance that maintains that, since it is a question of a living Christ, wherever his body is there also is his blood and vice versa. This, and the fear of spilling, would eventually lead to Communion under one form.[40] In this century, too, a break takes place between the churches of East and West and, while both keep the basic elements of Word and Eucharist, their liturgies will reflect differing emphases.

In the West, Communion was still generally received under both forms of bread and wine into the twelfth century. In fact the popes continued to reject the practice of dipping the bread into the wine ("intinction") as a failure to follow our Lord's directive to "take and drink." But the "bleeding host" stories, and the awe they inspired, tended to reduce the frequency of Communion still further.[41]

As the altar gradually moved away from the people and eventually was positioned against the back wall, the priest's back was to the people.[42] Couple this with popular reaction to so-called bleeding hosts and the stage was set for another dramatic step in eucharistic attitudes and practices. By the thirteenth century, seeing and adoring the host had become more important than receiving it. To prevent the people from adoring the host prematurely, the bishop of Paris had his priests elevate the host after the institution narrative. This was the "signal" that the host was now "consecrated." Communion under one form also became the general rule in the thirteenth century.

The Gothic architecture, with its breathtaking beauty, also revealed a lessening awareness of the Eucharist as something to be

---

40. Jungmann, *The Mass*, 77–92. See also, Megivern, *Concomitance and Communion*, 37–39, and 102–4.

41. Megivern, *Concomitance and Communion*, 40–47.

42. See White, *A Brief History of Christian Worship*, 88.

shared and of the symbolism of food and drink. Instead we find greater emphasis on the Eucharist as a divine epiphany or appearance, as something to be adored, genuflected to, and looked at to receive grace. In short, the "mysterious" element comes to the fore. A screen or barrier often separated the laity from the main altar. A growing sense of remoteness and inaccessibility resulted.[43]

In the fourteenth and fifteenth centuries the centrality of the "moment of consecration" and the accompanying elevation led to the desire for what Jungmann termed "longer showings." This desire to view the host longer in turn led to a growing devotion to Exposition of the Blessed Sacrament, to "Benediction" and processions of the Blessed Sacrament. The feast of Corpus Christi, that first came to the fore around 1246 and was characterized by solemn processions through the streets, mirrored the trend of the time. In addition, zeal for honoring the Blessed Sacrament led to numerous other practices, such as genuflections before and after every touching of the sacrament.[44] There was also a great concentration on details, for instance, on Masses for special intentions, on fruits or benefits of the Mass, on stipends, and on the veneration of the saints and their relics. Along with their legitimate values these practices carried with them the danger of abuse.[45] Moreover, religious life in general and liturgical life in particular was becoming more and more complicated. There was a proliferation, a splintering taking place. If this was to be considered a flowering, it was, as Jungmann put it, "the flowering of autumn . . . a mighty facade, and behind it—a great emptiness."[46]

The architecture of the time reflected some of the splintering so prevalent in popular piety. "Late Gothic Church architecture had already revealed this. The house of God began to be split up into a multitude of chapels in which the separate guilds, separate families even, had their own guild or family altar and their own worship."[47]

---

43. Jungmann, *Pastoral Liturgy,* 67–68, 73–74.

44. See Jungmann, *The Mass,* 91–92. See also Mitchell, *Cult and Controversy,* 173–86, for a more thorough discussion of the origin and significance of these practices.

45. Jungmann, *The Mass,* 96–99, and *Pastoral Liturgy,* 71–72.

46. Jungmann, *Pastoral Liturgy,* 78.

47. Ibid., 79.

Reaction and Counterreaction: Trent (1545–63) to Pre-Vatican II (1960)

In the liturgical arena, as in others, the picture was bleak; the abuses were many. One has only to read some of the abuses listed by a Roman Catholic preparatory commission of the Council of Trent to sense the sorry state of affairs: "Masses celebrated with no assistants whatever; no one, not even the ministers, receiving communion at Mass; the rivalry of processions of the Blessed Sacrament from different churches which break out into brawls; priests puffing and waving signs of the cross furiously over the Host and Chalices as if these signs contained the power of consecration; the elevation of the chalice by placing it on top of the head; the laying of 'half-corrupt' cadavers on the altar during Mass (apparently it was felt that the closer to the altar, the more benefit to the deceased); the congregation assisting with their dogs, falcons and hawks."[48]

In addition to the abuses, the ensuing fight over such issues as Christ's presence in the Eucharist, the Eucharist as a sacrifice, the legitimacy of Communion under one species or form, and private interpretation of the Bible, left scars which remain with us today.[49]

Reformation and Renaissance (especially the sixteenth century)

In this context the Council of Trent moved toward reform. The Roman Missal of Pius V symbolized a centralized reform that was to last 400 years. It contained the prayers of, and the directions for, celebrating the Mass. No changes in the liturgy could be made without special permission from the pope.[50]

Communion under one form became the norm, although Rome never denied that both forms were the ideal. When people did

48. Joseph Powers, *Eucharistic Theology* (London: Burns & Oates, 1968), 32. See also Jungmann, *The Mass*, 99–103.

49. See White, *A Brief History of Christian Worship*, 120–22, on some of the issues.

50. See Jungmann, *The Mass*, 103–6, and Powers, *Eucharistic Theology*, 34–43. See also White, *Roman Catholic Worship: Trent to Today* (Collegeville, Minn.: Liturgical Press, 2003), 12–15, 23. Henceforth *Roman*.

receive they tended to view Communion as "co-union" ("Jesus and me") rather than "comm-union" ("union with one another in the risen Lord"). They received kneeling and on the tongue, and Roman Catholics were urged to receive more frequently, as were the Protestants in some churches.[51] The "rood screens" that in many churches had become a real wall between the people and the altar fell away but the many altars remained, at least in Roman Catholic circles. In Protestant circles the preaching of the Word and the pulpit generally became the focus. The new concern for the hearing of the Word eventually led to increased popularity of seating or pews in both Catholic and Protestant churches.[52]

Frank Senn, a Lutheran liturgical scholar, notes that the Middle Age practice of coming to the Eucharist to look at the host but not to receive it was the major eucharistic anomaly. He contends that all the reformers reacted against the practice of daily Mass coupled with such rare reception of Communion that a church law mandated receiving at least once a year. They all opposed Masses without communicants. Thus frequency of Communion became tied up with the question of frequency of celebration.[53]

Within Lutheranism, for instance, people were encouraged to receive even if they felt unworthy. In fact in the sixteenth, seventeenth, and early eighteenth centuries the number of communicants increased steadily.[54] However, even though before 1750 Holy Communion was celebrated on most Sundays and feast days, few individuals would receive more than four times a year.[55]

---

51. See Megivern, *Concomitance and Communion*, 246–50, 254–55. White, *A Brief History of Christian Worship*, 122–23, notes that both Luther and Calvin favored more frequent communion but it was difficult to break old habits of not receiving frequently. See also Senn, *A Stewardship*, 117.

52. Jungmann, *Pastoral Liturgy*, 365–66, and *The Mass*, 99–103. Due to a need for brevity I have limited myself after the Council of Trent primarily to the Roman Catholic Church. Very useful for Communion practices in Protestant churches is Frank Senn, *A Stewardship*. Of particular interest, as mentioned, are chapter 7, "The Frequency of Celebration and Reception of Communion in Protestantism," 99–121, and chapter 8, "Roman Catholic Communion Practices: History and Present Challenges," 122–37, from a Lutheran perspective.

53. Senn, *A Stewardship*, 99.

54. Ibid., 99–103.

55. Ibid., 105.

THE BAROQUE PERIOD (ESPECIALLY THE SEVENTEENTH CENTURY)

The next period was one of reaction and counterreaction. The controversy over real presence led to this aspect of the Eucharist receiving almost exclusive attention among Roman Catholics. Processions, exposition of the Blessed Sacrament and Benediction thus found new impetus as did devotion to Mary. The two keystones of Roman Catholic piety became devotion to the Blessed Sacrament and devotion to the Blessed Mother. This was legitimate in itself. To the extent, however, that the focus on Christ's presence in the species of bread and wine became one-sided—to the neglect of his presence in the people and the unity which was its purpose—some of the richness of the Eucharist was lost. [56]

More people received Communion, but frequent Communion was a rarity among Catholics. Also, it was often taken before or after Mass as an exercise independent from the rest of the celebration. [57] Legitimate and praiseworthy elements of piety were thus taken out of their proper setting. While there was a reawakening to the importance of preaching by Catholic and Protestant alike, the pulpit in the middle of the church and the choir in the organ loft also reflected the tendency to view the sermon and the singing as independent from the rest of the Eucharist. On the Protestant side, an almost exclusive emphasis on the Word led to a similar imbalance and a consequent sacramental impoverishment. This is not to deny, however, that many saints emerged from this period and that there was great devotion among the people despite liturgical tendencies that at times seemed far from the ideal. The architecture of this era was exuberant in honoring Christ as King while the music continued to enchant hearers. [58]

Once again time constraints prevent us from describing in detail the impact of the Enlightenment on the Eucharist and the subsequent reaction to the Enlightenment itself. In the eighteenth and nineteenth centuries Protestant worship underwent sweeping

---

56. See Jungmann, *Pastoral Liturgy*, 80–87, and *The Mass*, 106–13. See also Mitchell, *Cult and Controversy*, 163–86, and White, *A Brief History of Christian Worship*, 124.

57. See White, *Roman*, 36–37.

58. Jungmann, *The Mass*, 111–13. See also White, *A Brief History of Christian Worship*, 134–35, and *Roman*, 25–26; Senn, *A Stewardship*, 128

changes.[59] Liturgical scholars, however, tend to ignore the eighteenth century "Age of Reason," seeing little in it to study and even less to praise. For instance, there was a great decline of communicants in the period of Rationalism (the Enlightenment) toward the end of the eighteenth century. This probably stems from the fact that Rationalism tended to view worship primarily as instruction and so did not emphasize the sacramental aspect.[60] It has had, however, a great impact on following centuries. Despite the reaction in the nineteenth century to some of the excesses of Enlightenment rationalism, "the whole modern period is predicated on the supremacy of human reason against any form of external authority."[61]

The reactions to the Enlightenment mentality by "sacramental religions" was threefold: (1) ignore it for the most part (the approach of Roman Catholicism until the 1960s); (2) focus on the believer's nonrational or charismatic experience as opposed to a purely rational approach; (3) limit liturgical experience to a merely intellectual recalling of God's past actions.[62]

Interestingly enough, the demands that some of the rationalists were making at that time were amazingly close to liturgical reforms that were to occur much later.[63] Unfortunately, the desire for legitimate reforms became tainted with other tendencies that made the reforms themselves suspect.[64] The insistence on knowledge as the goal of human progress led to the sermon being regarded as predominately an appeal to moral conduct and as the central point of the liturgical celebration. The use of the vernacular or mother tongue was urged less as a means of entering into the sacramental re-presentation of Christ's dying and rising than as a way of instruction, of bringing people to greater knowledge. The "function" of liturgy would thus be one of teaching rather than reliving.[65]

---

59. White, *A Brief History of Christian Worship*, 142. Roman Catholics made even more radical changes in the twentieth century as if "making up for lost time."

60. See Senn, *A Stewardship*, 103.

61. White, *A Brief History of Christian Worship*, 142–43.

62. Ibid., 144–45.

63. Jungmann, *The Mass*, 113–15.

64. White, *Roman*, 54–56.

65. White, *Roman*, 47–48, 61–62, and Senn, *A Stewardship*, 103.

The Communion practice continued much the same as it had in the preceding century. Roman Catholics, for instance, received one form, on the tongue, and kneeling. Although the frequency of Communion increased somewhat with the passage of time, efforts from Trent on to encourage more frequent Communion met with resistance. It was considered a novelty and became linked with prior confession. In Protestantism in the beginning of the nineteenth century there was a liturgical revival, and monthly or quarterly celebrations of Communion became the norm in most Protestant churches. But here, too, there was resistance to more frequent reception.[66] In architecture "Rococo was replaced in the late eighteenth century by a cold archaeological Greek classicism, devoid of passion."[67]

The Liturgical Movement

As so often happens, a reaction to the preceding period, in this case to the Enlightenment, took place. To the Enlightenment's rationalism and questioning of Church authority, a Catholic restoration promoted tradition and reverence for authority. The clamor for a liturgy in the mother tongue met with a call to recognize Latin as the unchanging language. The cry for more participation in the liturgical action by the people ran into an approach that—more consciously than ever— reduced the people to spectators. In short, even healthy reforms, which the highest authority of the Church was to adopt a century later, fell under the shadow of suspicion because of their link with the Enlightenment.[68] Dom Prosper Guéranger, who founded the monastery of Solesmes in 1833, led the way in stressing a liturgy that was as traditional and monastic as it was beautiful and well executed. Guéranger and others like him, however, were to pave the way for the more pastoral stage that was to follow, spearheaded by people like Lambert Beauduin.[69]

At the beginning of the twentieth century Pope Pius X urged earlier and more frequent Communion and called for a renewal of Christian life, with active participation of the people in the liturgy as

---

66. White, *Roman*, 61. See also Senn, *A Stewardship*, 114, 117, 127.
67. White, *Roman*, 49.
68. Ibid., 71.
69. Ibid., 72–73.

its primary source. On November 22, 1903, in a special decree on church music, he stated, "Our people assemble for the purpose of acquiring the Christian spirit from its first and indispensable source, namely active participation in the most sacred mysteries and in the public and solemn prayer of the Church."[70] This became the guiding principle of a growing liturgical movement.[71] Advances in biblical and historical studies, new trends in theology, especially in the understanding of the Church and sacraments, and the ecumenical movement set the stage for dramatic changes in the liturgy following the Second Vatican Council.[72] Pius X also provided a milestone in liturgical history with his decree *Frequent and Even Daily Communion* (1905). It was to take about ten years before the desire to promote frequent Communion was to lead logically to a reaffirmation of the natural place for Communion, namely, within the Mass rather than before or after it.[73]

Among Protestants the liturgical movement strove to make Eucharist central to the life of the church. Official statements of some Protestant churches and theologians reflected this. Even appeals, however, to the wishes of Luther, Calvin, Cranmer, and Wesley did not at first lead to more frequent celebration and reception of Communion. Communion was, in the minds of many, something reserved for times of crisis. Senn contends that to some extent the reluctance to receive more frequently showed a high regard for Communion among Protestants. This led to "fencing the table" by insisting on a number of practices before receiving. Relaxing these disciplines and emphasizing positive aspects of the Eucharist has allowed more people to receive more frequently in a way similar to the reduction of fasting before receiving among Roman Catholics.[74]

In 1959 Pope John XXIII shocked the world by calling a council. In 1964 the Second Vatican Council approved the *Constitution on the Sacred Liturgy* and ushered in a new era, the story of which

---

70. *The Motu Proprio on Church Music*, Grail Translation (St. Meinrad, Ind.: Grail Publications, 1951), 4. See White, *Roman*, 80–81, 88–89.

71. For key figures and documents see White, *Roman*, 80–85, 103–12.

72. Jungmann, *The Mass*, 117–21. White, *A Brief History of Christian Worship*, 155–58, and *Roman*, 99–101.

73. Senn, *A Stewardship*, 129.

74. Ibid., 117–18.

is still being written. It is a story like the history we have just traced—of agony and ecstasy, of conflict and agreement, of change and resistance to change, of pettiness and greatness. It is a story that involved many changes in a relatively short time.[75]

It was an attempt to shape a liturgy that would help people better experience the nearness of Jesus Christ in his humanity and divinity, in his dying and rising; a liturgy which through Jesus Christ and in the Holy Spirit sanctifies people and worships the Father; a liturgy in which the *whole* Christ—Head and members, priest and people—actively take part; a liturgy that through understandable, meaningful symbols enables Christians to experience the richness of their past, the challenge of the present and the promise of the future.

What remains less clear is exactly how to achieve an active participation that goes beyond gathering in the same place, saying or singing the same words, and reading from the same revised books. What the final chapter or even the next chapter of our story will look like is also unclear. To a great extent that depends on the Christian people. It depends on their response to our times and to the movement of God's Spirit.[76]

In Roman Catholicism the Communion practice has of course changed. Once again the faithful can receive standing—as a sign of Christ's Resurrection and our share in it through baptism and the Eucharist. Once again we may take Communion in the hand and receive under both forms. The altar often looks more like a table than it had in recent centuries and is arranged so that the presider faces the people. The tabernacle has found a home other than on the main altar and frequently has its own chapel. The location of the presidet's chair, the lectern Ambo, and the altar generally express the difference as well as the organic connection between the introductory and concluding rites: the Liturgy of the Word and the Liturgy of the Eucharist. Often, too, those leading the singing and music do so from a position that integrates both them and their function within the rest of the assembly.

We have tried in this brief survey to understand the past, not condemn it. Each era produced saintly people. Had we lived in those

---

75. See White, *Roman*, 124–28, 138–42, for a catalogue of some of the changes after Vatican II.

76. See White, *A Brief History of Christian Worship*, 178–80.

times, we would probably have shared the same attitudes toward the liturgy. Many of the reforms begun at Vatican II still thrive and grow. Some, however, have been challenged and at times reversed. This is a living reminder that disagreement lives on and that changes tend to follow a zigzag pattern rather than a straight line.[77] The statement often attributed to Augustine is still a good starting point for any discussion: "In necessity, unity; in doubt, liberty; in all things, charity."

We hope all our efforts will lead beyond a better understanding of the Eucharist to a community which experiences more intensely, and therefore lives more faithfully, the dying and rising of Jesus Christ. Then the Eucharist will be what it is meant to be—a celebration of who we are in union with our Risen Christ and a source of resurrection power enabling us to be what we celebrate and become what we receive.

---

77. See White, *Roman*, 151–58. See also Keith F. Pecklers, "40 Years of Liturgical Reform: Shaping Roman Catholic Worship for the Twenty–first Century," *Worship* 79 (May 2005): 194–209, and Maxwell E. Johnson, "Liturgy and Ecumenism: Gifts, Challenges, and Hopes for a Renewed Vision," *Worship* 80 (January 2006): 2–29.

Chapter 9

Eucharistic Presence: An Invitation to Dialogue

Edward Schillebeeckx, in his introduction to his work *The Eucharist,* was somewhat apologetic for his narrowness in dealing only with the issue of eucharistic or "real" presence.[1] Self-limitation, however, is useful and necessary at times. I feel under a similar constraint in this chapter, which concentrates on the question of eucharistic presence.[2]

My purpose in this chapter is to help provide a basis for ecumenical dialogue. I am also convinced that our understanding of eucharistic presence has implications for our understanding of Eucharist and sacrifice. First, I shall briefly place the topic in the context of other crucial questions that lie at the heart of the discussion of eucharistic presence.[3] Then I shall give an overview of ways in which eucharistic presence has been understood in the course of Christian history, including transubstantiation. Finally, I shall discuss another model by which some theologians have attempted to understand eucharistic presence, the model of interpersonal encounter.

---

1. Edward Schillebeeckx, *The Eucharist,* trans. N. D. Smith (London: Sheed & Ward, 1967), 19–21.

2. Our chapter treats various views of eucharistic presence in general. For studies that focus on Christ's manifold presence in particular see Michael Witczak, "The Manifold Presence of Christ in the Liturgy," *Theological Studies* 59 (1998): 680–702, and Judith Kubicki, "Recognizing the Presence of Christ in the Liturgical Assembly," *Theological Studies* 65 (2004): 817–37.

3. See John H. McKenna, "Setting the Context for Eucharistic Presence," *Proceedings of the North American Academy of Liturgy* (Valparaiso, Ind.: Valparaiso University, 1998), 81–88.

SYMBOL AND REALITY

As we have seen in chapter 1, symbols are part and parcel of our existence as human beings. If we have deep feelings or experiences, we must
express them. Otherwise, they atrophy and die. Symbols facilitate this
expression and are basic to our knowing, our loving, our very being.

Symbols enable us to express both ourselves and our profound
human experiences, such as the birth of a baby, the death of a loved
one, falling in love, the sense of our own sinfulness. We sense God's
presence and the need to express the faith it inspires; we improvise, or,
more commonly, turn to already existing symbols to express the experience. This is what I think Jesus did, what the first Christians did and
what we do.[4]

We use symbolic actions. They have a meaning of their own
prior to, and independent of, any word proclaimed over them. We
embrace. We share a meal. We wash ourselves. We offer a forgiving
glance or gesture to someone. These actions, in themselves, are able to
express us powerfully and move us deeply. They are crucial to the experience. We also use words. We sing a song, recite a poem, say a prayer,
proclaim a blessing, or tell a story about ourselves and our experience.
Our words tell us in another way the same truth as our symbolic
actions to which they must always return if they are to be truthful.
Our words proclaim and give the deeper meaning of the symbolic
actions. Words also make that action somewhat less ambiguous.[5]
Finally, theological reflection tries in various ways to explain and illuminate the event or experience our symbolic actions and words sought
to express. Our symbolic actions, our words and our theological reflection are all meant to express the initial experience and, in expressing it,
to deepen it, much the same way as people in love do. And interaction
with others greatly affects the way we perceive all three.

For Karl Rahner, as we have seen in the first chapter, symbol
in the highest, most primordial fundamental sense is one reality rendering another present. It embodies or expresses the person or thing
so strongly, is so charged with meaning, that it renders the other

---

4. John H. McKenna, "Symbol and Reality: Some Anthropological Considerations,"
Worship 65 (Jan. 1991): 2–27, and chapter 1 for more complete documentation.

5. See Ernst Cassirer, *Language and Myth,* trans. Susanne K. Langer (New York: Dover,
1946).

present. It "allows the other to be there." It is the self-realization of one being in the other. This is what Rahner calls a "symbolic reality" ("Realsymbol").[6] Moreover, it is the symbolizer not the recipient who determines whether or not this is a symbolic reality. A consequence of this definition is that a symbol, for example, a ring or sexual intercourse, can lose its closeness to the symbolizer and sink to the level of mere sign or "symbolic representation" if the person no longer has his or her heart in it.[7]

A "symbolic representation" (signs, signals, codes) is not the self-realization of one being in another. It does not express or embody the person or thing so fully that it allows the other reality to be present in it. It is not so close to the person or thing signified. It is this lack of closeness that makes mere signs or symbolic representations. In addition, they are usually more arbitrary, for instance, red = stop, green = go. But arbitrariness, for Rahner, is not the key norm. Closeness to, or the presence of, the symbolizer is.[8]

Since it is the symbolizer, not the recipient, who determines whether or not this is a symbolic reality, the margin between sign ("symbolic representation") and symbol ("symbolic reality") is fluid. A symbol can become a mere sign if it loses its closeness to the symbolizer. So too, an arbitrary or conventional sign, for example, a ring, can become a symbol, if it is so charged with, so embodies, the other reality as to make it present. Once again the key is whether or not the symbolizer has his or her heart in it.[9] Strictly speaking, the symbol (the "symbolic reality") does not represent or point to an absent reality. The symbol itself has been formed (or transformed) by this reality. The symbol thus renders present what it reveals or symbolizes.[10] Symbols are then not simply things. They are actions involving rela-

---

6. Karl Rahner, "The Theology of Symbol," in *Theological Investigations* 4, trans. Kevin Smyth (Baltimore: Helicon, 1966), 225. It is interesting to compare the similarities to Rahner's approach in the work of a postmodern theologian Louis-Marie Chauvet, *Symbol and Sacrament: A Sacramental Reinterpretation of Christian Existence,* trans. Patrick Madigan and Madeleine Beaumont (Collegeville, Minn.: Liturgical Press, 1995), 112–24. Of course there are also great differences to which we shall refer below, for instance, the emphasis on the relational quality of symbolic language and the absence aspect as well as presence.

7. Rahner, "Theology of Symbol," 225. See also John Macquarrie, *Principles of Christian Theology* (New York: Scribner, 1977), 123.

8. Rahner, "Theology of Symbol," 225, 240–41.

9. Ibid., 240, 251–52.

10. Ibid., 235, 231–34.

tionships.[11] Some appreciation of symbol is necessarily part of the context for discussing eucharistic presence.

CHRIST'S RESURRECTION

The Resurrection is another crucial context for considering eucharistic presence. If our human understanding of our use of symbol is helpful, Christ's Resurrection takes this understanding and imagining into a "quantum leap" far beyond our dreams and expectations.[12] The love of God and the perfect human love of Jesus meet and they yield new life. Jesus' loving service and his confidence that his relationship with "Abba" would endure despite even death have borne fruit. Resurrection then implies, first of all, a relationship with "Abba." Jesus in a sense already stands in the future.[13]

To say that Jesus has been raised bodily is to say that his whole personality lives on. The totality of that which formed the center of expression and communication with others, of that which enabled him to enter into relationships with the world around him and the people in it, the source of his individuality and uniqueness, has undergone a radical transformation. This in turn involves some form of bodiliness unless one divides human beings into an ever existent "spirit" and a merely provisional body.[14] Describing what this entails is another matter. There is no question of a revivification or resuscitation. With all the stress on the continuity between the historical Jesus and the risen Lord, the witnesses leave no doubt that a radical transformation has taken place.[15]

Filled with God's Spirit the risen Jesus had a newfound freedom. This freedom is, however, not a freedom *from* the body; it is

---

11. See Chauvet, *Symbol and Sacrament,* 120–21. He prefers to speak of *symbolic* rather than *symbol* to avoid taking any symbol as adequate to express the divine or fixing on the symbol rather than on the one who comes to us through the symbol. (See Regis Duffy, Kevin Irwin, and David Power, "Sacramental Theology: A Review of Literature," *Theological Studies* 55 (1994): 657–705, at 684–85. Henceforth "Sacramental."

12. See chapter 5 for further documentation.

13. See Wolfhart Pannenberg, *Jesus—God and Man,* trans. Lewis Wilkens and Duane Priebe (Philadelphia: Westminster, 1968), 69, 82ff.

14. See McKenna, "The Eucharist, the Resurrection and the Future," *Anglican Theological Review* 60 (April 1978): 144–65, at 150, and Karl Rahner, "The Resurrection of the Body," *Theological Investigations* 2, trans. Karl Heinrich Kruger (Baltimore: Helicon, 1963), 203–16.

15. See McKenna, "The Eucharist," 151.

rather freedom *in* the body—in the "Spirit-ized" body of which Paul speaks in 1 Corinthians 15:44. Through the Spirit Jesus' body has been transformed into the perfect vehicle of his self-expression and communication. No longer does it impose the limits that it once did. He is free to give himself with absolute freedom. The appearance narratives witness to this facet of his new life. [16]

Furthermore, his risen body somehow embraces the whole universe, which has become the center of his self-expression and communication—his body. Teilhard grasped this point as if by intuition: "By virtue of Christ's rising again, nothing any longer kills inevitably but everything is capable of becoming the blessed touch of the divine hands, the blessed influence of the will of God upon our lives." [17] Rahner speaks of a sort of pancosmic relationship in which the universe is swept up to its fulfillment in and through the fulfillment of the personal human spirit. [18] Léon-Dufour spoke in similar terms. It is Christ's historic body, distinguishing him from others and transformed by the Resurrection, which plays an active, vital role in the transformation of the universe. [19]

Christ's risen or "Spirit-ized" body enables him to use individual elements of the universe as extensions of his presence. He is free to use words, especially those of Scripture, for a personal encounter with others. Natural symbols like water, bread, and wine suddenly become willing instruments in his free, total self-giving. People, too, are invited to enter into this process. They can become more or less willing extensions of his presence in the world. We can thus speak, in realistic terms, of people as members of Christ's body. Because Christ's Resurrection involves the universe and the people in it, what has taken place in him is still taking place in the persons and universe which he has swept up into his new life, his new freedom. [20]

---

16. Ibid., 151–52. This of course also raises the question of the "absence" of the risen One, a theme that runs through much of recent writing on Resurrection and on the Eucharist and one that we shall return to below. See for instance, Chauvet, *Symbol and Sacrament*, 48–62, and Jean-Luc Marion, *God Without Being*, trans. Thomas A. Carlson (Chicago: University of Chicago Press, 1995).

17. Pierre Teilhard de Chardin, *The Divine Milieu: An Essay on the Interior Life*, rev. ed. (New York: Harper & Row, 1965), 82–83.

18. Rahner, "The Resurrection of the Body," 210–15.

19. Xavier Léon-Dufour, *Resurrection and the Message of Easter*, trans. R. N. Wilson (New York: Holt, Rinehart and Winston, 1975), 241.

20. Ibid., 152–53.

As a result of his Resurrection then, Christ, the embodiment of God's gift of Self, lives in a tangible community. This community provides, or should provide, a context of individuals who mutually support, challenge, encourage, forgive, suffer for, and pray for one another. It is also a community that should resist evil and sin on the individual and institutional levels.[21] It seeks to create social structures that are just, confident that God's kingdom will someday come once and for all because the God who has begun this good work will see it to completion (see Phil. 1:6). This is grace, the embodiment of God's saving presence in Christ and his community. This is what our Eucharist seeks to celebrate in words and symbols and in celebrating to deepen. This is also the context in which I discuss eucharistic presence.[22]

CHANGING ATTITUDES TOWARD THE EUCHARIST

Another part of the context is the changing attitudes toward the Eucharist over the centuries. Initially, this celebration was clearly a communal experience with the meal character coming very much to the fore. The presence of Christ seems to be presumed.[23] The accent is on the symbols of bread and wine, the action of eating and drinking and, especially, the *purpose* of all this. This action was, among other things, to nourish the Christ-life within the participants by deepening their union with Christ, to unite them with one another in Christ[24] and to lead them toward eternal life by deepening their share in Christ's Resurrection begun in baptism. Believers' experience of the

---

21. This "ethical" dimension which witnesses to a personal and sociopolitical conversion is an important indicator of the Eucharist's transforming power. Chauvet puts it well: "of what value would the liturgical and *sacramental* celebrations be if they were not the living memory of the person whom the Scriptures attest as the crucified God and if they did not enjoin their participants to become concretely, by the practice of *agape*, what they have celebrated and received?" 177 (see 523, 535–36). See also Marianne Sawicki, *Seeing the Lord: Resurrection and Early Christian Practices* (Minneapolis: Fortress, 1994), 318, 323–24, 334–35; Duffy, "Sacramental," 674; McKenna, "The Eucharist," 163–65; A. Cameron-Mowat, "Liturgical Theology: Who's In Charge," *The Way* 35 (Oct.1995): 338–39.

22. See Wilhelm Breuning, "Die Kindertaufe im Licht der Dogmengeschichte," in Walter Kasper, ed., *Christsein Ohne Entscheidung*, (Mainz: Grünewald, 1970), 83.

23. See Paul Jones, *Christ's Eucharistic Presence: A History of the Doctrine* (New York: Peter Lang, 1994), 15.

24. Ibid., 14, n. 27, where he lists an impressive array of authors attesting to this.

risen Lord living among them and freeing them from death in all its forms gave them a great sense of hope in the world to come.[25]

They experienced a keen sense of the dynamism of the Eucharist, an action meant to nourish, gladden, transform, and unify the community. Many of Augustine's statements reveal the awareness of the transforming effect of the Eucharist which pervaded this period: "If you receive well you are what you have received." "Since you are the body of Christ and His members, it is your mystery that is placed on the Lord's table; it is your mystery that you receive. . . . You hear the words: 'The body of Christ,' and you answer 'Amen.' Be therefore members of Christ, that your 'Amen' may be true." "Be what you see, and receive what you are."[26] As Henri de Lubac was rightly to point out, Augustine's ecclesial realism presupposes eucharistic realism.[27] Pope St. Leo the Great (d. 461) is no less clear: "The partaking of the body and blood of Christ has no other effect than to make us pass over into what we receive."[28] Eucharistic realism and ecclesial realism supported one another. Among ancient writers the accent was on the effect rather than on the cause. The faithful are united to one another because they are united to Christ in the Eucharist.[29]

But attitudes began to shift. The Christological controversies led to losing sight of the humanity of the *glorified, risen Christ*. As Jungmann put it, his humanity was being swallowed up in the godhead of the Trinity. The risen Jesus was becoming a distant God.[30]

25. Josef A. Jungmann, *Pastoral Liturgy* (New York: Herder & Herder, 1962), 4–9, 57, 78, 359–62.

26. See James J. Megivern, *Concomitance and Communion: A Study in Eucharistic Doctrine and Practice* (New York: Herder, 1963), 68.

27. Henri de Lubac, *Corpus Mysticum: L'Eucharistie et L'Église au Moyen Âge* (Paris: Éditions Aubier-Montaigne, 1949), 284.

28. Megivern, *Concomitance and Communion*, 72.

29. de Lubac, *Corpus Mysticum*, 283–84. His whole work is a fine treatment of the relationship between the Church as Body of Christ and the Eucharist as Body of Christ, especially 89–115, and 279–94. See also, Nathan Mitchell, *Real Presence: The Work of the Eucharist*, 2nd ed. (Chicago: Liturgy Training Publications, 2001), 105: "In short, the church's celebration of a ritual meal launches a process of *becoming* eucharist, a process that is completed only when Christians recognize their own new identity as *Christ's body in the world*. That is why the epiclesis of the eucharistic prayer prays not only for a transformation of the gifts but also of the people. . . . Or as Augustine expressed it in Book VII of his *Confessions*, 'I am the food of grown men and women. Grow, and you shall feed upon me. You will not change me into yourself, as you change food into your flesh, but you will be changed into me" (book 7:10, trans. John K. Ryan [New York: Doubleday Image, 1960], 171).

30. See Jungmann, *Pastoral Liturgy*, 9–19, and Megivern, *Concomitance and Communion*, 63.

Social and economic factors, religious movements of dissent and reform,[31] the shift in liturgical genre from meal to ritual drama, from symbolic action to dramatic allegory also played a role.[32] The lingering effects of the Christological controversies, however, seem to have taken the heaviest toll. In any event, a shift was in progress in which the Eucharist was becoming more an object than an action transforming the community, more an awesome miracle than a joyful sharing. The debates over Christ's presence would only accelerate this movement.

EUCHARISTIC PRESENCE: A HISTORICAL OVERVIEW

During the apostolic times the reality of Christ's presence in the Eucharist is presumed. There may be a growing focus on the elements, as Marxsen has tried to point out,[33] but the emphasis continues to be on the action of eating and drinking and, especially, on the purpose of this action. Clearly this is no ordinary activity nor are the elements ordinary, as Paul points out: "Every time, then, you eat this bread and drink this cup, you proclaim the death of the Lord until he comes" (1 Cor. 11:26 NAB).

The dynamic, transforming aspect of this action continued to be stressed. Christians were at home with a notion of symbol that makes present the reality it symbolizes (a "symbolic reality" in Rahner's sense).[34] The words they use in their writings and in their prayers speak of a radical change. In Greek, for example, they use words like "*metastoicheiosis,*" ("*transelementation*").[35] The ancient liturgies do the same. Eastern Christians employed the terms "*metapoiestai,*" "*metaballesthai,*" "*meta-stoicheuousthai,*" and in the West we find the terms "*transformare,*" "*transfigurare,*" "*transfundere,*" "*transmutare.*" These terms seek to express a dynamism, like that of the Incarnation, in

---

31. David Power, *The Eucharistic Mystery: Revitalizing the Tradition* (New York: Crossroad, 1994), 186–87, 243–45.

32. Nathan Mitchell, *Cult and Controversy: The Worship of the Eucharist Outside Mass* (New York: Pueblo, 1982), 4–6.

33. Willi Marxsen, *The Lord's Supper as a Christological Problem,* trans. Lorenz Nieting (Philadelphia: Fortress Press, 1970), 13–33.

34. See McKenna, "Symbol," 8–11. For a good historical overview of some of the issues, see Kevin W. Irwin, *Models of the Eucharist* (New York: Paulist Press, 2005), 240–61.

35. Schillebeeckx, *The Eucharist,* 65–70.

which Christ "takes possession of" bread and wine, making them his Body and Blood. Thus eucharistic change is a change by appropriating a reality to oneself, "taking possession of" in that sense. In this setting "substantia panis" would mean the reality of the bread as opposed to the appearance or something abstract.[36]

When Jones, in his fine study of eucharistic presence, asks if Catholics need insist on an "ontological" change,[37] the response of authors like Schillebeeckx would be affirmative. The basis would be a tradition reflected in texts like those just mentioned. But once again they should be seen in a context which stresses the transformation of the community more than that of the elements.[38]

Augustine would be a prime example of this. But he is probably also at the root of the problem. His spatial conception of glorification and "reified" notion of the body provided the legacy of the West. Augustine lacked a suitable anthropology of the body and that leads to a dilemma. Either Christ has a glorified body localized in heaven or he possesses a divine ubiquity. Since Augustine was rightly convinced that Christ remains forever incarnate, he opted for a glorified body localized in heaven, which made it difficult for him to explain how Christ could be present in the Eucharist. His successors like Ratramnus, Berengar, and Calvin followed his theory more unrelentingly than he did. Augustine, basing his position on Christian tradition, clearly (although perhaps somewhat illogically) affirmed Christ's presence.[39]

In any event, up to the ninth century, Christian writers generally shared the view that a symbol made present the reality it symbolized, that sacraments were "symbolic realities." Augustine took a spiritualistic-symbolic approach which tended to be more speculative and intellectual. Ambrose tended to be more concrete, down to earth,

36. Ibid., 64–76, and John H. McKenna, *The Eucharistic Epiclesis: A Detailed History From the Partristic to the Modern Era,* 2nd ed. (Chicago: Hillenbrand Books, 2009), 7–70.

37. Jones, *Christ's Eucharistic Presence,* 235.

38. See Schillebeeckx, *The Eucharist,* 76–86; Chauvet, *Symbol and Sacrament,* 385–93; and Kevin Irwin, *Models,* 238–62.

39. See J. N. D. Kelly, *Early Christian Doctrines,* 5th ed. (New York: Continuum, 2000), 446ff. See also Josef Ratzinger, "Das Problem der Transubstantiation und der Frage nach dem Sinne der Eucharistie," *Theologische Quartalschrift* 147 (1967): 129–58, and especially, Gustave Martelet, *The Risen Christ and the Eucharistic World,* trans. R. Hague (New York: Seabury Press, 1976), 124–28.

more suited to the ordinary persons. But they differed only in emphasis; both approaches agreed on the reality present in the symbols. This sense of symbolic reality probably accounts for the remarkable fact that for the first eight centuries there was no dispute over Christ's presence in the Eucharist.[40]

THE NINTH CENTURY

In the ninth century a shift occurred. Maybe it was the lingering effects of iconoclasm or a more literal, earthy attitude that the barbarian invasion had brought with it. In any case, symbol and reality drifted apart in the minds of many. Amalar of Metz (d. 853), one of the key agents in that shift, combined in his preaching an exaggerated realism or an overly physical approach to the Eucharist and an "inveterate tendency toward allegory."[41] Whereas earlier writers viewed symbols as rendering present the reality symbolized, Amalar regarded them more as dramatic reminders of past events.[42]

Another key figure in the shift is Paschasius Radbertus (d. about 860). In the first scientific monograph on the Eucharist, he focused on the contents of the sacrament rather than its purpose. In his desire to underline the reality of Christ's presence, he downplayed symbolism to the point that his materialism "shocked the consciences even of his contemporaries, who were no strangers to a grossly realistic notion of the Eucharist."[43] For Paschasius "veritas" or reality seemed to mean physical reality.[44]

That put his opponent in the debate, Ratramnus (d. after 868) in the curious position of having to say that Christ's body was really

---

40. See Johannes Petrus de Jong, *Die Eucharistie Als Symbolwirklichkeit* (Regensberg: Friedrich Pustet, 1969), 28, 32–33; David Power, *Unsearchable Riches: The Symbolic Nature of the Liturgy* (New York: Pueblo, 1984), 46–47; Alasdair I. C. Heron, *Table and Tradition* (Philadelphia: Westminster, 1983), 70–74; and Megivern, *Concomitance and Communion*, 51–78, who rightly and repeatedly notes that the emphasis throughout this period is not on the reality of Christ's presence in the Eucharist but on the purpose of that presence, namely, transforming the community.

41. Megivern, *Concomitance and Communion*, 81.

42. Ibid., 79–81, and Power, *Unsearchable*, 56.

43. Megivern, *Concomitance and Communion*, 83.

44. de Jong, *Die Eucharistie*, 33. For a lucid treatment of what he terms a naïvely realist error see Avery Cardinal Dulles, "Christ's Presence in the Eucharist," *Origins* 34 (March 17, 2005): 627–31, at 628–29.

present "*in figura*," that is in a symbolic manner and not "*in veritate*," not as a physical or material reality. Taken out of context these words would seem to indicate that Ratramnus denied the reality of Christ's presence in the Eucharist, and he was in fact condemned by a Synod in Vercelli (1050). Today, however, most would agree that the issue between Paschasius and Ratramnus was not that one believed Christ to be present in the Eucharist and the other did not. The real problem was that the notions of symbol and reality were coming apart in the minds of many. This forced them to look elsewhere than to symbol to account for the reality of the Eucharist.[45]

This becomes increasingly evident in the case of Berengar of Tours (d. 1088). Reacting to an overly physical approach to the Eucharist, he taunted his opponents with teaching that we receive "little pieces of Christ's flesh." Embracing what he thought to be Augustine's and Ratramnus's position, he rightly returned to viewing sacraments as symbols. The problem was that the possibility of a symbol that actually makes present the reality symbolized never seemed to have crossed his mind. He ended up viewing the sacraments as representations without real content and thus denied the reality of Christ's presence in the Eucharist.[46]

His opponents, apparently unable to appeal to a notion of symbolic reality, found themselves at times pushed into an overly physical corner. An instance of this is the often cited oath demanded of Berengar by the Council of Rome (1059): "I, Berengar . . . believe in my heart and confess with my mouth that the bread and wine which are placed upon the altar, are, after the consecration, not only the symbol ("*sacramentum*") but also the real body and blood of our Lord Jesus Christ and physically ("*sensualiter*"), not only in symbol ("*in sacramento*"), but in truth ("*in veritate*"), are passed through the hands of the priest, broken and chewed by the teeth of the faithful."[47] This embarrassingly physical interpretation will be quietly left aside, benignly interpreted or attacked by later writers. Thomas Aquinas, for example, stated: "We don't chew Christ with our teeth; Christ isn't

---

45. See Megivern, *Concomitance and Communion*, 85–86; Heron, *Table and Tradition*, 93–94; de Jong, *Die Eucharistie*, 33–34, and McKenna, "Symbol," 13–14.

46. See Megivern, *Concomitance and Communion*, 89–90, and de Jong, *Die Eucharistie*, 34.

47. Henricus Denzinger and Adolfus Schönmetzer, eds., *Enchiridion Symbolorum*, 33rd ed. (New York: Herder, 1965), 690. Henceforth DS.

eaten in his own bodiliness nor is he chewed with the teeth—what is eaten and broken is the sacramental species."[48] On the popular level, the growing numbers of Bleeding Host stories were seen as bolstering the belief in the reality of Christ's presence. Thomas was equally forceful in rejecting this form of reasoning as overly physical and as failing to do justice to the manner of Christ's presence.[49] The absence of a healthy sense of symbolic reality coupled with a determination to preserve the reality of Christ's presence in the Eucharist led to a search for alternate ways of explaining this presence. Scholastic theology drew upon Aristotelian categories and put forward a change that did not take place in the physical structure of the bread and wine but in their metaphysical reality.

This theology reinterpreted ("transubstantiated") Aristotle by appealing to a real distinction between substance and accidents (they could therefore be separated from one another). This led to transubstantiation, an explanation in which the substance of the Body and Blood of Christ replaces the substance of bread and wine. According to this view, the appearances or "accidents" of the bread and wine remain and are supported by the substance of Christ's body and blood. In this context, substance is the being that underlies ("*substat*") any feature that may be added to it, that is, what a thing is. Accident is any feature added to that ("*ac-cidit*," lies next to it) or how a thing is.[50]

The irony is that in trying to fight materialistic notions with a metaphysical approach, the Scholastics, including Thomas, appealed to a basically physical analogy that left itself open to a physical understanding.[51] The focus is on the elements, the bread and the wine, and

---

48. ST, III, 77, 7, ad 3. See also "Christ's Presence in the Eucharist," 628–29.

49. See Megivern, *Concomitance and Communion*, 40–45, esp. 43, n. 2. See also, Joseph Powers, *Eucharistic Theology* (New York: Herder, 1967), 109–10. In addition to the question of symbolism, this raises the question of Christ's glorified body which is a key to understanding Christ's presence in the Eucharist or anywhere else, for that matter. De Jong, *Die Eucharistie*, 35–36, sees Berengar as a victim of a shift regarding symbol and reality from a Platonic-Augustinian approach to an Aristotelian approach.

50. See Schillebeeckx, *The Eucharist*, 57–58.

51. See Jones, *Christ's Eucharistic Presence*, 103. Even today "substance" means "matter" for many, if not most; for example, the Protestant reaction to Paul VI's encyclical *Mysterium Fidei* led to the following headline in the German newspaper *Frankfurter Algemeine*: "Pope maintains material presence of Christ in Eucharist." See also Owen Cummings, *Eucharistic Doctors: A Theological History* (New York: Paulist Press, 2005), 137: "In colloquial language today, 'substance,' 'substantial' and 'substantially' are not used in this precise, metaphysical sense. They mean, roughly

their change.[52] This change takes on an increasing, not to say supreme, importance. Moreover, when one maintained that the change is instantaneous,[53] the tendency was to focus on the "moment of consecration." That in turn led to a debate over the role of the epiclesis and the institution narrative that had pastoral implications.[54] In this respect, Thomas Aquinas was a product of his time. But it should also be noted that he did see Christ's bodily presence as a means to a fuller presence of Christ in his faithful and in that sense a transformation of the faithful. Nicholas Cabasilas, Aquinas's counterpart in the East, also saw eucharistic presence as a means to deepening Christ's presence in the faithful.[55]

John Wycliffe (d. 1384), an Aristotelian at Oxford, rejected the Thomistic distinction between substance and accidents and in so doing remained closer to the original Aristotle. He concluded that the accidents of bread and wine do not continue to exist without their subject or substance; that the substance of the bread and wine remains; and that there is no corporeal presence of Christ in the Eucharist. In adhering to an Aristotelian framework, Wycliffe had to interpret Christ's Eucharistic presence as "purely symbolic."[56] This earned a condemnation at the Council of Constance (1415). Those at the council felt they had to maintain a real distinction in order to maintain belief in "real presence." Unfortunately they went still further.

A contrast of the Fourth Lateran Council (1215) with the Council of Constance (1414–18) is interesting in this regard. As John Macquarrie rightly notes, the species became a veil, the agent of the consecration had become the priest, and substance had been identified with physical matter. Thomas would probably have been as uncomfortable with the last as a number of the reformers were. Once again, such an overly physical approach seems to ignore the sacramental, even the incarnational, principle that material realities or symbols,

speaking, what is physical and material, what is simply 'out there now.' That is not Thomas's understanding of the term or its cognates."

52. See DS 1642, 1652.
53. ST, III, 75, a. 7.
54. See McKenna, *The Eucharistic Epiclesis*, 70–78, and Chauvet, *Symbol and Sacrament*, 525.
55. See McKenna, *The Eucharistic Epiclesis*, 207–9.
56. See Schillebeeckx, *The Eucharist*, 58–59, and Jones, *Christ's Eucharistic Presence*, 101–2.

without ceasing to be material, can become another form of God's ontological presence.[57]

THE REFORMATION

Martin Luther (d. 1546) reacted to what he considered to be philosophy's taking over theology and argued for a return to basics, namely, the Bible. He also reacted to such practices as adoration of the Blessed Sacrament, the focus on the elevation, Benedictions, and processions of the Blessed Sacrament. While rejecting Zwingli's reduction of Christ's eucharistic presence to merely spiritual, he opposed the view that transubstantiation was an article of faith. Without using the word, he proposed a form of consubstantiation. He urged a return to Christ's institution, namely, "take and eat," which would allow for reservation for the sick but would avoid the practices just enumerated. He focused on the parallel between the Incarnation (hypostatic union) and the Eucharist. By appealing to the Body of Christ and a share in the divine ubiquity he restored eucharistic presence to its rightful Christological basis. But hypostatic union and consubstantiation are not really parallels.[58]

John Calvin (d. 1564) opposed adoration as too static and also opposed the overemphasis on Christ's divinity in eucharistic doctrine. In stressing the humanity of Jesus Christ, he sided with Zwingli's stance that Christ's body was localized in heaven and therefore not in the Eucharist. Instead, the Holy Spirit was seen as transporting us to heaven and thereby enabling our union with Christ. Calvin brought out the dynamism of the Eucharist and the role of the Holy Spirit. He left us, however, with a notion of Christ's risen body as localized.[59]

All this contributed to the context in which Trent's teaching on transubstantiation became, as Schillebeeckx has emphasized,

---

57. See John Macquarrie, *Christian Unity and Christian Diversity* (Philadelphia: Westminster, 1975), 74–76 and McKenna, "Symbol," 15.

58. See Jones, *Christ's Eucharistic Presence,* 117–34, and Ratzinger, "Das Problem der Transubstantiation,"137–45.

59. See Jones, *Christ's Eucharistic Presence,* 127, 134–46, and Ratzinger, "Das Problem der Transubstantiation," 133–37. See also Cummings, *Eucharistic Doctors,* 168–69, who quotes Max Thurian, *The Eucharistic Memorial* (Richmond: John Knox Press, 1961), part II, 114, as saying that Calvin had too carnal a conception of the risen Body of Christ. Calvin did not fully appreciate the difference between Christ's earthly body (pre-Resurrection) and his risen body.

highly polemical.[60] Schillebeeckx also demonstrated the legitimacy and value of exegeting the texts and examining their genesis. The following comparison should be useful in seeking the core reality that those at the council were trying to express.

The first draft stated: "If anyone should maintain that the sacrament of the Eucharist does not *truly* [*vere*] contain the body and blood of our Lord Jesus Christ, but (that these) are only there as a sign or a symbolic form, let him be excommunicated" [canon 1].[61] The second draft read: "If anyone . . . *truly* and *really* [*vere et realiter*].[62] The third draft read: "If anyone . . . *truly, really,* and *substantially* [*vere, realiter et substantialiter*].[63] That is the formulation adopted in the fourth and definitive text.[64] The adverbs have grown from "truly" to "truly and really" to "truly, really, and substantially." The effort to avoid any possibility of watering down the meaning is clear. Likewise, the first two drafts of canon 2 stated that there was a "unique and wonderful changing"; and the last two drafts mentioned a "wonderful and unique changing."[65]

The texts also relativized the Church's use of "transubstantiation." The first two drafts spoke of the change that "was very suitably called transubstantiation by our fathers."[66] The third draft spoke of the change that "our fathers and the universal Catholic Church have very suitably called transubstantiation."[67] The final definitive text, however, no longer claims that "our fathers" or the "universal" Church used the term, but simply states that it is very suitable [*aptissime*].[68]

Schillebeeckx has correctly argued that the genesis of these canons reveals three different levels in Trent's definition. The first is the core of the dogma. It lies in the affirmation of *a specific and distinctive eucharistic presence,* namely, the real presence of Christ's Body and Blood under the sacramental species of bread and wine (canon 1). The

---

60. DS 1632, 1642; cf. ST, III, 75–77.
61. Schillebeeckx, *Eucharist,* 31.
62. Ibid., 33.
63. Ibid., 36.
64. Ibid., 37.
65. Ibid., 31, 33, 36, 38.
66. Ibid., 31, 34.
67. Ibid., 36.
68. Ibid., 38.

insistence on the *lasting character of this presence* underlines its special and distinctive quality and thus distinguishes it from the presence in the other sacraments.[69]

The second level is an immediate theological reasoning that, if there is a distinctive mode of presence here, then there must be some real, ontological change in the bread and wine. Schillebeeckx contends that it is necessary to hold these two levels to be faithful to the Church's teaching. Given the historical circumstances and the scholastic framework in which they were operating, he maintains, the participants of the council *could not* establish or express this unless they insisted on acceptance of the change of the substance of bread and wine into the substance of Christ's Body and Blood (canon 2).[70] The third level makes use of the terminology, the way of explaining the other two levels. This was "very suitably" called "transubstantiation." This level is the most relative of the three.[71]

Both Thomas and Bonaventure had reasoned that way. They begin with an indisputable "fact of faith," namely, a distinctive, real presence in the Eucharist. Because of what that implied, they concluded, on the basis of theological reasoning, to a change in the substance of the bread and wine. To explain this change Thomas appealed to the Aristotelian categories of substance and accidents.[72]

Schillebeeckx contended that within the historical, and especially philosophical, framework the council members had to affirm a change in substance. Within the prevailing Aristotelian framework it was impossible to safeguard the distinctive character of Christ's eucharistic presence without affirming transubstantiation. Contrary to the claims of some that Trent was not influenced by any particular philosophy, he maintains that they were, they had to be, children of their times. One can raise the question today whether or not it is possible to have real, ontological change without having to appeal to transubstantiation. One can perhaps affirm true, real, substantial presence from another philosophical framework. But to expect Trent to have done so, he argues, is to expect too much.[73] In any

---

69. Ibid., 39–53.
70. Ibid.
71. Ibid.
72. See ibid., 49–51, 63.
73. See ibid., 51–53. Chauvet, *Symbol and Sacrament,* 7–8, 44, concurs.

event, transubstantiation became the Roman Catholic position for centuries to come.

The Reformation period failed to look to the ancient notion of a symbolic reality because this had been lost sight of. Zwingli (d. 1531) could acknowledge that the Eucharist was a fitting symbol but "merely" a symbol. On the other hand, the Counter Reformation approach was generally to look outside the symbol for a way of establishing the reality of the Eucharist. Numerous theories appeared on how the sacraments "caused," and a hardening emphasis on the words of the institution narrative as the "moment of consecration." No matter that Aquinas had combined the Augustinian notion of symbol with the Aristotelian concept of causality ("sacraments cause by signifying").[74] The late eighteenth and early nineteenth centuries saw a renewed interest in the realm of symbol. A painful clash within the Roman Catholic Church between theologians of renewal and a Neoscholasticism which seemed entrenched as "the" position of the church forced the former back to biblical, patristic, and liturgical sources. This, together with the contributions of the Catholic members of the Tübingen School, especially J. A. Möhler's *Symbolik* (1832) sowed the seeds to be nurtured by later theologians and eventually to be reaped in the Second Vatican Council.[75]

In the twentieth century, Odo Casel, the Benedictine scholar (d. 1948), Gerardus van der Leeuw (d. 1950), a Reform theologian and Anscar Vonier, a monk from Buckfast Abbey, helped to rediscover the ancient notion of symbol. Opponents often had to be reminded that although the eucharistic change was ontological it was not on the physical level.[76]

But a revised reading of Thomas Aquinas and a rediscovery of the ancient understanding of the relationship between symbol and reality led to a rehabilitation of the notion of symbol in recent

---

74. See de Jong, Die *Eucharistie*, 36; McKenna, *The Eucharistic Epiclesis*, 79–92; and Stephen Happel, "Symbol," in Joseph Komonchak, et al., eds., *The New Dictionary of Theology* (Wilmington, Del.: Michael Glazier, 1987), 999. See also Power, *Unsearchable*, 180–81.

75. Happel, "Symbol," 1000. See M. Schoof, *A Survey of Catholic Theology* (1800–1970), trans. N. D. Smith (New York: Paulist Press, 1970), 14–156, for an extensive treatment of the interactions of this period.

76. See de Jong, Die *Eucharistie*, 37–41; Power, *Unsearchable*, 181–84; and Jones, *Christ's Eucharistic Presence*, 203–4.

theology. Bernard Lonergan, John Macquarrie, Karl Rahner, Edward Schillebeeckx, and Paul Tillich, to name a few, made extensive use of this notion in their theology.

TRANSUBSTANTIATION

As an explanation transubstantiation has come under increasingly heavy fire. Some within the Roman Catholic Church maintain that transubstantiation is the ("only" implied) Catholic understanding of the eucharistic presence. They stress continuity with tradition. Without this formula, they argue, the Catholic understanding cannot be maintained. They appeal to the encyclical *Mysterium Fidei* 24, with its emphasis on Trent.

Others claim that transubstantiation once expressed a realistic understanding of the eucharistic presence but no longer does so. They seek other explanations that bring out the ecclesial dimension of this presence; that respect the context, namely, the communal celebration and reception of the Eucharist with its intended goals; that take into account the mentality of modern people, for example, with a stress on personalism. They appeal to *Mysterium Fidei* 25, with its openness to other more understandable explanations of the same reality.

The criticisms of transubstantiation are varied. It is not a question, within Roman Catholic circles at least, of denying a distinctive, objective eucharistic presence. Nor is it a question of denying that a real, ontological change takes place. What are being criticized are perceived weaknesses in the explanation. There has been and, continues to be, the danger of viewing the change in an overly physical way. Aquinas and others tried to avoid a materialistic interpretation and to place the issue on the metaphysical, sacramental level rather than on the physical level. In fact, however, the use of a physical analogy from Aristotelian natural philosophy (*like* one physical substance changing into another) runs the risk of ordinary people and even theologians thinking in physical terms. "Substance" in many people's minds and in science textbooks means material, physical.[77] There is also the danger of focusing on the elements and their change rather than the purpose

---

77. See Jones, *Christ's Eucharistic Presence*, 203–4, and McKenna, *The Eucharistic Epiclesis*, 188–92, for this and other criticisms. See also Cummings, *Eucharistic Doctors*, 137.

of the change, namely, "real presence" in the faithful, and an encounter with Christ.[78]

A Personalist Approach

These criticisms have led theologians to explain eucharistic presence through another analogy, that of an interpersonal encounter. The basic analogy is then the presence of one person, as a person, to another person, as a person. This analogy allows for degrees of presence and also accords a significant role to bodily presence in an interpersonal encounter.[79]

First, it allows for, even calls for, a distinction between different types or degrees of presence. There is a purely physical or local presence, such as water in a glass, a corpse in a coffin, or people in a crowded bus or subway car in which they are oblivious to one another despite the physical juxtaposition of bodies. Even when one person jostles another the awareness may only be of a thing, namely, an elbow in the ribs. You are still on the most primitive level, the physical. The presence may become more personal, if one says, "Excuse me but could you move your elbow" or smiles and gives a friendly greeting. Communication has begun. It may end there or it may continue and eventually lead to one person offering himself or herself in friendship to the other. Thus a presence far deeper than the purely local presence has been established. But one still does not have presence in its fullest sense.

Full, personal presence involves the response of the other. Presence in the deepest sense is mutual, interpersonal presence. It is not enough to have one offer. The other must to some extent reciprocate by accepting the offer and offering himself or herself. There are many different expressions, many different qualitative changes or intensities in this kind of presence. It involves mutual knowledge not just about, but of, the other as a person. On the deepest level this kind

---

78. See Macquarrie, 77–78, and McKenna, *The Eucharistic Epiclesis*, 188–91. See also Chauvet, *Symbol and Sacrament*, 392, 526. Dulles, "Christ's Presence in the Eucharist," 629, and 631, n. 10, sees Judith Kubicki, "Recognizing the Presence of Christ in the Liturgical Assembly," *Theological Studies* 65 (2004): 817–37, as saying that "Christ's primary presence is in the gathered assembly" and labels this a minimizing error. Kubicki might respond that she is merely trying to emphasize a dimension that has been neglected at times.

79. For what follows on the basic analogy, see McKenna, *The Eucharistic Epiclesis*, 192–95.

of presence involves love because only in a climate of love can a person reveal himself or herself for what he or she is. Although you cannot put this presence under a microscope, such a presence is no less real than the physical, local presence. In fact, it is this level or degree of presence, this interpersonal encounter, which is most real. For only in the context of mutual, reciprocal giving of persons to each other do you have real presence in the fullest sense.

Second, personal presence not only allows for degrees of presence; it also accords a significant role to bodily presence in an interpersonal encounter. Purely physical presence is the most primitive level or degree; it is secondary to full, interpersonal presence but in this analogy it is absolutely necessary. This corresponds to human nature. Every human exchange, every attempt of one person to communicate with another, takes place in and through that person's bodiliness. There is no way around it, given the human condition. Relationships start there, for instance, with a smile, a friendly greeting. They advance through words and gestures. They find expression through words and bodily gestures and this expression often intensifies the interpersonal presence or relationship. The woman who complains that, "You never say you love me anymore," may not be nagging. She may sense that what is not expressed is on its way to not being. The husband who responds, "I may not say it but I show it in many ways," may also be on to something. We don't always need words. We can use other symbols or symbolic actions. But the fact remains: we must express deep realities or risk losing them. And our bodies enable us to do just that.[80]

Third, this approach to presence situates this bodily presence in an anthropology of symbolic actions that is not dualistic. Remember what we said earlier. The notion of "symbolic reality" does not refer to a sign pointing to something else which is absent. Rather, a person's bodiliness, together with its modes of expression, make present what they express. A kiss, for instance, is not a sign of something else, of a person hidden behind it. It is, or should be, that person himself or herself expressing love for the other person. People can also extend their bodiliness or bodily presence by using material objects as expressions of themselves. A wedding ring, for example, although

---

80. See McKenna, "Symbol," 2.

there is no physical change, can be transformed. If the giver really has his or her heart in it, it now has a new reality. It personifies the person who gave it. It is the person expressing, in a concrete way, the gift of herself or himself to the person loved. And it is the symbolizer, the giver, who first and foremost determines the reality of the symbol.

Thus the explanation which uses an encounter of persons as its basic analogy denies neither the necessity nor the importance of bodily presence. It simply seeks to put it in perspective. It is always subordinate to the deeper personal presence to which it can lead and which it expresses and intensifies. Conversely, our bodiliness can even hinder deeper, personal presence. At times bodily limitations make it difficult, if not impossible, to express our free gift of self to another. A change in facial expression may force us to reveal ourselves in a way or at a time we don't want to. These limitations make it possible for others to "pin us down," to treat us as an objectifiable "thing," to be gazed at or to be pitied against our will. At these times our bodiliness deprives us of a freedom crucial to the self-giving necessary for a fully personal presence.

Application to the Eucharist

Obviously every analogy limps. It is difficult enough to describe the mystery of human relationships. It becomes even more difficult when we add to that the complexity and "mysteriousness" of God's dealing with people.

This personal analogy also needs to be seen in the context of a number of related issues we mentioned above, such as the nature of symbols and our understanding of Jesus Christ's glorified body, which retains a continuity with his body before death, yet has been radically transformed, "Spiritized." The risen body no longer has the limitations which at times hinder efforts to establish the deepest personal presence with people as well as the universe. It is the perfect vehicle of Christ's self-expression, and allows a sovereign, absolute freedom that enables an intimacy and intensity impossible before his death. Closely related to this is Christ's presence in the Church that has, among other things, become the embodiment of his ongoing presence in the world. The Eucharist in general and eucharistic presence, in particular, are meant to express and thereby intensify, that universal presence.

Also crucial is the issue of the manifold presence of Christ in the Eucharist, namely, in the whole believing community and in a special way when the faithful gather together in his name, in the presider and the assembly, and in the proclamation of the Scriptures in the assembly. Christ is really, personally present and active in all of these, although according to different modes. To understand Christ's presence in the bread and wine, it is necessary to situate this presence in the context of these other modes of presence.[81] Finally, there is the issue of the incompleteness of Christ's presence or his "absence" which makes us long for its fulfillment in the Parousia. It is only against the background of these related issues that the presence, often referred to as "real presence," has its place and meaning.

In this setting Roman Catholic theologians try to maintain the distinctive character of eucharistic presence. It is substantial in the sense that it is lasting as long as the bread and wine are still recognizable as food and drink. "Substantial" does not mean to deny the reality of the other modes of presence but simply affirms the distinctive character of Christ's presence in the gifts.[82]

Christ offers himself in the Eucharist. He takes hold of the bread and the wine (the "meal") and makes use of their bodiliness to offer himself in a "bodily presence" to the faithful. The bread and wine are not merely tokens or signs of Christ, pointing to him and reminding us of him. Rather, with a sovereignty and freedom that now belong to his glorified body, he identifies himself with the bread and wine. He uses them to embody and express his eternal giving of himself to the Father and to us. Christ will always "have his heart in it."[83]

What is the effect on the bread and the wine, according to this approach? While remaining unchanged on the physical level, the bread and wine have undergone a substantial change, a change that does not depend on the faith of the individual Christian. On the sacramental, ontological level they are no longer simply bread and wine; they are Jesus Christ offering to unite his faithful to himself in his

---

81. See *Instruction on Eucharistic Worship* (May 25, 1967) (Washington, D.C.: United States Catholic Conference, 1967), articles 9 and 55, and Kubicki, "Recognizing the Presence of Christ in the Liturgical Assembly," 821–26.

82. See McKenna, *The Eucharistic Epeclesis,* 197. See also Dulles, "Christ's Presence in the Eucharist," 628.

83. McKenna, ibid.

sacrifice and thus to unite them with the Father and with each other in the Holy Spirit.[84]

The change in the bread and wine is then a real, substantial change—no less real than had it taken place on the merely physical level. In fact, this change is more real, more substantial, than a merely physical change. The "bodily presence" of Christ in the bread and wine is also real—but no more real than the mutual presence of Christ and his faithful in the life of grace. In fact, it is this mutual, personal presence, this unity between Christ and his faithful and their unity with each other in Christ that the "bodily presence" of Christ in the gifts is to embody, express and intensify. It is this personal unity of the faithful with Christ, and, through Christ, with the Father and with each other in the Holy Spirit, which is the real presence. It is this presence that is the *raison d'être* of the "bodily presence" of Christ in the Eucharist and of the change in the bread and wine. And this presence is personal, and, therefore, reciprocal or mutual.[85]

Two points should emerge. First of all, the "bodily presence" of Christ and the change that accompanies it, while important and even necessary, are always subordinate to the deeper, personal presence which they are intended to express and intensify. They should not, therefore, be allowed to occupy the center of the stage in any discussion of the Eucharist. Secondly, even the personal presence of Christ offering himself to his Father and to his faithful does not constitute presence in the fullest sense since, as we have seen in examining the basic analogy, presence to be fully personal must be reciprocal. In the Eucharist, then, the Church must also respond by opening up to Christ's gift of himself; otherwise we do not have presence in its fullest sense. The sacramental sign becomes, therefore, simultaneously an embodiment of the mutual, personal presence of Christ and his Church and an invitation to every believer to participate personally in this presence. As Schillebeeckx states:

> The presence offered by Christ in the Eucharist naturally precedes the individual's acceptance of this presence and is not the result of it. It therefore remains an offered *reality*, even if I do not respond to it. My disbelief cannot nullify the reality of Christ's real offer and the reality of the

---

84. McKenna, 196–99. See also Dulles, "Christ's Presence in the Eucharist," 628.
85. McKenna, ibid.

Church's remaining in Christ. But, on the other hand, the eucharistic real presence also includes, in its sacramentality itself, reciprocity and is therefore completely realized only when consent is given in faith to the eucharistic event and when this event is at the same time accomplished personally, that is, when this reciprocity takes place, in accordance with the true meaning of the sign, in the sacramental meal.[86]

Once again it is on the sacramental, symbolic, metaphysical level that a change takes place. This involves the human mind, intention, and heart. We frequently act in this way. We take food and drink. We make them into a meal to express life, joy, agreement, forgiveness, welcome, friendship, interest, love—human self-giving. Is it any wonder that the self-giving of God in the Exodus event would find expression in a meal? Is it any wonder that the self-giving of God in the Christ event would also find expression in a meal?

By taking the bread and wine and making them a "symbolic reality" of himself and his own self-giving, Christ has given them new meaning in the Christian community. By doing this he has given them new being. They can no longer be called, they no longer are, what they were before. The food and drink (meal) are now symbol in its fullest, most primordial sense; namely, they embody Christ in his act of self-giving, allowing him to be present bodily. Schillebeeckx elaborates:

> The real, ontological meaning of the bread, that is, the bread itself, is thus radically changed—it is no longer orientated towards man as bread . . . even though nothing is changed physically. . . . A new object comes into being—the sacrament in which the reality of Christ is the *formally* constitutive element ("the substance as it were") together with the other elements which, subordinated to this new reality of Christ, are the *sign* of this reality and the *medium* by which it becomes accessible to us. The "new object" is thus the sacrament of Christ's body and blood.[87]

To describe the effect on bread and wine we need terminology of some sort. Unfortunately, the terminology in this area seems to be unusually fluid and ambiguous. The change is real, that is, in the person or thing itself, independent of the viewer's subjective attitude for its reality; for example, in the Eucharist the change is independent of

86. Schillebeeckx, *The Eucharist*, 141.
87. Ibid., 116–17.

the individual Christian's faith. To describe this we use the word "ontological" (or "ontic" for Rahner).[88]

The change is distinct from the other sacraments in that it is lasting (as long as humanly intelligible as food, drink)[89] and radical. A new reality comes into being (not alongside the bread and wine as in "companation"). "Substantial" is meant to express this distinctive character (others might use the terms "metaphysical," "essential"). As Schillebeeckx observed,

> An animal's eating is *essentially* different from a man's eating, even though the biological process is the same. A thing can become essentially different without being physically or biologically changed. . . . Remaining physically what it is, bread can be included in a sphere of meaning that is quite different from the purely biological. . . . [T]he bread *is* different, because the definite relationship to man at the same time defines the reality under discussion. . . . And such changes of meaning are more radical than purely physical changes, which are at a lower level and, in this sense, at a less real level.[90]

REACTIONS AND QUALIFICATIONS

In attempting an approach to eucharistic presence other than that of transubstantiation, Schillebeeckx and others have sought to preserve the traditional Roman Catholic values while bringing out values that seem to have been neglected in that framework. In effect they are trying to combine the ontological component of transubstantiation with such notions as "transfinalization" (a change in the purpose or finality of the elements and their reception) and "transsignification" (a change in the meaning or sign value of these realities).[91]

Naturally they are not without their critics. On the Catholic side, some wonder if the personal encounter analogy really does justice to the ontological change seen as so crucial. On the Protestant side, some question the insistence on an ontological or metaphysical

---

88. See Karl Rahner, "Christ in the Sacrament of the Lord's Supper," *Theological Investigations* 4, trans. Kevin Smyth (Baltimore: Helicon Press, 1966), 301.

89. Ibid., 315.

90. Schillebeeckx, *The Eucharist*, 131.

91. Ibid., 116–17. See Dulles, "Christ's Presence in the Eucharist," 630.

change.[92] Others ask if the analogy is not too individualistic by nature and fails to stress what Augustine would term the "whole Christ," head and members, with the individual swept up into the personal encounter between Christ and the Church as well as the "social justice" dimensions of the Eucharist.[93] Jones sees a need for "a social phenomenology of ecclesial presence" that will do justice to the presence of Christ to the community of believers prior to the eucharistic presence.[94] Perhaps the process of Christian Initiation of Adults with its emphasis on transformation through education, prayer, liturgical stages, and some form of social action could be helpful here. Still others, like myself, see challenges in the analogy but also positive implications for areas like the "moment of consecration," which in Roman Catholic circles, has dominated our thinking and piety for centuries.[95]

From a framework conventionally called postmodernity, which questions the "metaphysical determination" of God on the basis of the analogy of being,[96] a possibly more radical questioning has arisen. Louis-Marie Chauvet acknowledges that the sacraments are not the sum total of Christian life and should not be allowed to "elbow aside" Scripture or ethical involvement. He insists, however, that they occupy their rightful place as neither the unique center nor a mere appendage.[97] He challenges the ability of a metaphysics which views God in terms of "Being" to do justice to the sacraments, much less

---

92. See Jones, *Christ's Eucharistic Presence,* 234–35.

93. See, for instance, Sawicki, *Seeing the Lord,* 323–24, on Schillebeeckx's attempt, in his later writings, to apply his earlier view on symbol to the realm of human suffering and the "political" sphere. The critique of Rahner and Schillebeeckx seems to drive us back to the "Easter experience." It resists an image of a God "positioned outside creation and who reached into our reality to do something to us," a "divine intrusion" or "incursion." See Sawicki, *Seeing the Lord,* 323–25. See also John D. Laurance, "The Assembly as Liturgical Symbol," *Louvain Studies* 22 (1997): 127–52.

94. Jones, *Christ's Eucharistic Presence,* 236–37. See also Kubicki, "Recognizing the Presence of Christ in the Liturgical Assembly," 819–26.

95. See McKenna, *The Eucharistic Epiclesis,* 199–206, and Chauvet, Symbol *and Sacrament,* 472.

96. See Jean-Luc Marion, *God without Being,* trans. T. A. Carlson (Chicago: University of Chicago Press, 1995), xx–xxi, who proposes that we begin our approach to God not with the metaphysical notion of Being but rather with "love" or "*agape.*" "If to begin with 'God is love,' then God loves before being. He only is as He embodies himself—in order to love more closely that which and those who, themselves have first to be." See Power, "Sacramental," 684ff.

97. Chauvet, *Symbol and Sacrament,* 1.

to the mystery and Otherness of God. He quotes Heidegger: "To overcome metaphysics is nothing more than to reflect that 'perhaps part of the essential destiny of metaphysics is that its own foundation eludes it.'"[98] In fact Chauvet, as is evidenced in the following quotation, is not trying to do away with metaphysics but rather to recognize its limits and limiting quality.

> If we are going to free ourselves from a "productionist scheme" in regard to the sacraments we have to "overcome" the metaphysical view of the world (characterized by instrumentality and causality) and move into the symbolic (characterized by the mediation through language and symbol), where "revealer" and "operator" are indissolubly linked insofar as they are homogeneous. In this symbolic perspective, the relation of God and humankind is conceived according to the scheme of otherness which transcends the dualistic scheme of nature and grace undergirding classic onto-theology.[99]

This approach leads Chauvet to the ongoing, never fully achieved task of consenting (echoing Heidegger) to the "presence of the absence of God." "It is precisely in the act of respecting his radical absence or otherness that the risen one can be recognized symbolically."[100] The believer has to consent to the mediation of the Church as both the presence and absence of the Risen One. This requires a balance between forgetting that the Church is only a sacrament and denying that it is a sacrament.[101]

Chauvet's emphasis on absence (as well as presence) is really in service of God's mystery and otherness. He cites Heidegger:

> "This absence is not nothing; it is the presence of the hidden plenitude of what . . . is" and what the Greeks, the Hebrew prophets, and Jesus named "the divine."[102] Thus we are not talking about a deficiency but a fullness, a mystery, far beyond our ability to grasp or describe. The sacraments and the Church, for that matter, become "traces" of the

---

98. Ibid., 51–52
99. Ibid., 544. See also 84–88, 95–105, 128–40, esp. 139–40, 266–68, 444–46.
100. Ibid., 178.
101. Ibid., 178, 182–89.
102. Ibid., 62. See 48–62.

God who is never finished with coming, and therefore we are on a "transitive" way or journeying rather than in possession.[103]

Chauvet proposes an approach to eucharistic presence by way of symbolism which "is the exemplary expression of the *resistance* of God's mystery to every attempt by the subject to appropriate it."[104] The sacramental presence of Christ stands in relation to a twofold memorial: of the past in thanksgiving and of the future in supplication. This reminds us that we are not dealing here with "full" presence but rather with a certain absence. Christ's eucharistic presence "proclaims the irreducibility of God, of Christ, and of the gospel to our concepts, discourses, ideologies, and experiences." It discloses, even as it reveals, God's otherness.[105] Our task is to live with this absence in a presence that, like creation, is a gift—absolutely gratuitous and gracious and "always in excess."[106]

Chauvet's criticism of the Scholastic position on transubstantiation is that it speaks of presence in terms of a subsistent entity that simply is, like a thing, rather than being relational. He rightly notes that, even from the fourth century on when the Spirit's action on the elements was accented, the epiclesis always aimed at the transformation of the people through their participation in the "consecrated elements." It is for the Church, the "believing subjects," that the Spirit transforms the gifts, never for the gifts themselves. "We cannot be content here, under the pretext of 'realism' to imagine the reality at issue as the simple *esse* of a subsistent entity; the relation must be conceived precisely as 'presence,' that is, as *being-for, being-toward . . . the esse is constitutively ad-esse.*"[107]

103. Ibid., 54, 71, 75, 555.

104. Ibid., 383.

105. Ibid., 391, 403. See also Mitchell, *Real Presence*, 89–90.

106. Chauvet, *Symbol and Sacrament*, 549. See 108–9, 445–46, 550. See Marion's strong remarks on transubstantiation: "the substantial presence therefore fixes and freezes the person in an available, permanent, handy, and delimited thing. Hence, the imposture of an idolatry that imagines itself to honor 'God' when it heaps praises on his pathetic 'canned' substitute (the reservation of the Eucharist), exhibited as an attraction (display of the Holy Sacrament), brandished like a banner (processions) and so on" (164). "Presence is no longer measured by the excessiveness of an irreducibly other gift" (*God Without Being*, 166).

107. Ibid., 392. See 387–89, 526. See also, David Power, "Sacrament," in *A Promise of Presence* (Washington, D.C.: The Pastoral Press, 1992), 271–97, and McKenna, *The Eucharistic Epiclesis*, 207–10.

Chauvet vehemently opposes losing sight of the rich symbolism of bread. "Not only can one no longer say but one must no longer say, 'This bread is no longer bread.'" Such a statement had to be made when one remained on a metaphysical level since that was the only way to express the "necessary implication of the *conversio totius substantiae*" of Trent. But when you move to a symbolic terrain, to say that "This bread is the body of Christ" requires you to stress all the more that it is still bread, "but now *essential* bread, bread which is never so much bread as it is in this mystery. . . . The Eucharistic body of Christ at this level of thought, is indeed bread par excellence, 'the bread of life,' the *panis substantialis et supersubstantialis,* as the Church Fathers called it."[108]

Chauvet argues that his symbolic approach is compatible with, and preserves, the Church's faith in "real presence," which he shares. It takes into account all aspects of eucharistic presence. But this "does not necessarily require that one conceive it in the mode of metaphysical substance."[109]

He concludes with his key themes: "Sacraments are the bearers of the joy of the 'already' and the distress of the 'not yet.' They are the *witnesses of a God who is never finished with coming*: the amazed witnesses of a God who comes continually; the patient witnesses, patient unto weariness at times, of a God who 'is' not here except by mode of passage. And of this mode the sacraments are a trace."[110]

Chauvet and others remind us of the otherness, the mystery of the God we try to explain, a God in whom love, *agape,* precedes even "Being," a "crucified God" who continues coming to us with a "corporality" that was scandalous in Jesus and still is in the Church and the sacraments.[111] Their stress on "absence" as well as "presence" serves as

---

108. Chauvet, *Symbol and Sacrament,* 400.

109. Ibid., 401, 387.

110. Ibid., 555.

111. See, for example, Chauvet, *Symbol and Sacrament,* 82–83, 151–55. Marion, after criticizing an excessive focus on the present, suggests that the notion of *gift* would help: "the present must be understood first as a gift that is given" (*God Without Being,* 171). We need to view "eucharistic presence less in the way of an available permanence than as a new sort of advent" (*God Without Being,* 172). Each instant of the present, like manna, must be accepted as a gift which we cannot cling to but for which we can only pray and be thankful. This gift of presence and of the present, is rooted in God's gift in the past (memorial) and "strains" toward God's gift in the future (*epektasis*). All this in turn is anchored in God's "excessive" love for us shown on the cross and in the Eucharist and enabling us really to be transformed into Christ's body (see *God Without Being,* 172–82).

a healthy balance in dealing with eucharistic presence.[112] People in love will understand the difference between "face to face" and other forms of presence. But those other forms of presence are important and those in love know they are real.

The emphasis on balancing the importance of the sacraments with the Scriptures and "ethical" witness, on bread as symbol continuing to be bread, on the presence of Christ in the Scriptures and in the people,[113] on our need constantly to "co-respond" to God's continuing coming are helpful, though not entirely novel. But they are stated with a freshness that draws notice.

There are, however, still theologians who have not given up on the attempt to correlate reason and revelation.[114] Still others will question Chauvet's interpretation of Aquinas's metaphysics and view on causality as instrumental as opposed to relational.[115] The dialogue thus continues.

CONCLUSION

In this chapter I have attempted to situate the question of eucharistic presence in a broader context, especially a Christological and Trinitarian one. I have also tried to give the background and issues of eucharistic presence, as I now see them. I look forward to an ongoing dialogue. Even more, I look forward to "the day of the Lord" when we will no longer debate over the when and the how of the Eucharist but, in the fullness of Christ's presence, shall simply celebrate together the wonder of what God has done for us through Jesus Christ and in the Holy Spirit.

---

112. See Jones, *Christ's Eucharistic Presence*, 18–19, and throughout. Even Gerald O'Collins, *Christology* (New York: Oxford University Press, 1995), who proposes a Christology based on the analogy of presence acknowledges the absence dimension (312–13).

113. Marion is critical of explanations like transsignification which attempt to go "beyond, with real presence, the idolatrous reduction of 'God' to a mute thing," nevertheless look to transubstantiation to "ballast" themselves with reality. They thus constitute no real break with transubstantiation (165). Moreover, even shifting the focus of presence from a "thing" to the community draws his criticism since that seems to rely on a "collective consciousness" in the present. This effectively relegates the divine presence to the past. This according to Marion is another form of idolatry. At least transubstantiation did not rely on the limited attention span of the community for the presence of "the Other par excellence" (*God without Being*, 165–69). See Power, "Sacramental," 692.

114. See David Tracy's foreword to Marion's *God Without Being*, ix–xv.

115. See Power, "Event," 279–84.

Chapter 10

Eucharist and Sacrifice: An Overview

Perhaps nowhere in the realm of sacramental theology has the phrase "fighting words" been more fitting than in the case of Eucharist and sacrifice. This is true despite the fact that, as was also the case with eucharistic presence, the debate over Eucharist and sacrifice arose as a relatively late problem.[1] There was no magisterial teaching on the Mass as sacrifice until the Council of Trent.[2] While it would be interesting to discuss the negative and positive connotations of the term "sacrifice" today,[3] I will limit myself to the debate on the use of that term for the Eucharist. Gordon Lathrop, the noted Lutheran liturgi-

---

1. See John H. McKenna, "Eucharistic Presence: An Invitation to Dialogue," *Theological Studies* 60 (June 1999): 294–317, and his *The Eucharistic Epiclesis: A Detailed History from the Patristic to the Modern Era* (Chicago: Hillenbrand Books, 2008), 188–206.

2. See David N. Power, *The Eucharistic Mystery: Revitalizing the Tradition* (New York: Crossroad, 1994), 248. Henceforth EM.

3. See Robert J. Daly, *The Origins of the Christian Doctrine of Sacrifice* (Philadelphia: Fortress Press, 1978), 1–2; See also Daly's *Sacrifice Unveiled: The True Meaning of Christian Sacrifice* (New York: Continuum, 2009), 1–5, and "New Developments in the Theology of Sacrifice," *Liturgical Ministry* 18 (Spring 2009), 49–58, a shorter treatment of some of the key points in *Sacrifice Unveiled*; Louis-Marie Chauvet, *Symbol and Sacrament: A Sacramental Reinterpretation of Christian Existence,* trans. P. Madigan and M. Beaumont (Collegeville, Minn.: Liturgical Press, 1995), 290–91; Kevin Irwin, *Models of the Eucharist* (New York: Paulist Press, 2005), 217–37, and R. Kevin Seasoltz, "Another Look at Sacrifice," *Worship* 74 (September 2000): 386–90, who notes that feminists are at times particularly negative toward the notion of sacrifice since they feel it has been used to justify the suffering of women caused by all kinds of abuses (388–90). In addition to the authors he cites, see Marjorie Procter-Smith, *Praying With Our Eyes Open: Engendering Feminist Liturgical Prayer* (Nashville: Abingdon Press, 1995), 123–24, 133–34; Susan A. Ross, *Extravagant Affections: A Feminist Sacramental Theology* (New York: Continuum, 1998), 32, 120, 152–55, 163, 175, 180; and Kelley A. Raab, *When Women Become Priests: The Catholic Women's Ordination Debate* (New York: Columbia University Press, 2000), 106–40. But one also finds attempts among feminists to come up with some positive notion of sacrifice.

cal scholar, has rightly remarked that much energy and anger have gone into this "interconfessional struggle."[4]

The debate over Eucharist and sacrifice has also become intertwined with, and complicated by, the question of the ordained minister's role and identity. Within Roman Catholicism there is on one hand, anecdotally at least, a fear of a renewed clericalism fueled by an almost exclusive stress on the priest's sacramental role.[5] Lathrop, among others, also gives voice to the strong Protestant concern about linking sacrificial terminology with priesthood.[6] Among the more tradition-minded on the other hand, there is a fear of having the "priestly identity" swallowed up in the "priesthood of the people."[7] The question of Eucharist and sacrifice thus has ecumenical and *intra*ecclesial implications. My purpose is simply to offer a brief "state of the question" or overview as a basis for further dialogue.

THE "SPIRITUALIZATION" OF SACRIFICE

There is a strong scholarly consensus that a long process of "spiritualization"[8] of the understanding of sacrifice in the Jewish scriptures and also in the surrounding Hellenistic culture formed the backdrop for Christian usage. An evolution had taken place in which the notion of sacrifice had become less that of a material immolation (destruction) ritual and more that of a spiritual prayer form. This evolution seemed to stem from the exile experience and the prophetic opposition to formalistic rituals. It culminated in a situation in which a thanksgiving prayer form was accepted as a valid form of sacrifice.

---

4. Gordon W. Lathrop, *Holy Things: A Liturgical Theology* (Minneapolis: Fortress Press, 1993), 141. See also Robert J. Daly, "Robert Bellarmine and Post-Tridentine Eucharistic Theology," *Theological Studies* 61 (June 2000): 247–48.

5. See, for example, Diana Jean Schemo, "Priests of the 60s Fear Loss of their Legacy," *The New York Times*, September 10, 2000, 1, 46.

6. Lathrop, *Holy Things*, 155.

7. See Schemo, "Priests," 1, 46.

8. See Daly, *The Origins*, 6–7, and *Sacrifice Unveiled*, 69–74, who offers a number of synonyms for "spiritualization": dematerializing, sublimating, humanizing, deepening, ethicizing, rationalizing, interiorizing, symbolizing. "We are using the word spiritualization in a much broader sense than simply antimaterialistic. This sense includes all those movements within Judaism and Christianity which attempted to emphasize the true meaning of sacrifice, that is, the inner, spiritual, or ethical significance of the cult over against the merely material or merely external understanding of it"(7).

Therefore, no immolation was necessary. The psalms provide good examples of this process: "Offer praise as your sacrifice to God. . . . Those who offer praise as a sacrifice honor me" (Ps. 50:14); "I have made vows to you, God; with offerings I will fulfill them" (Ps. 56:13); "Save us, O Lord, our God. . . . That we may give thanks to your holy name and glory in praising you" (Ps. 106:47); "Let them offer a sacrifice in thanks, declare his works with shouts of joy. . . . Let them thank the LORD for such kindness" (Ps. 107:22, 31). Another example is the midrash on Psalm 56: "in the future (a messianic phrase) all prayers will cease, except the prayer of thanksgiving, which will never cease. Likewise, in the future every sacrifice will cease, except the sacrifice of thanksgiving."[9] In Jesus' time, for example, Philo of Alexandria ranked a thanksgiving or "eucharistic sacrifice" as the highest form of sacrifice.[10]

CHRISTIAN ADAPTATION

The limited evidence that we have[11] seems to indicate that the Gospels, remaining within the spiritualizing evolution, saw the Eucharist as a meal celebrating the renewal of God's covenant. The covenant motif or image appears in both the Marcan-Matthean and the Lucan-Pauline traditions but in a different form. Mark and Matthew link the Eucharist more with the Sinai covenant and its accompanying rites, for example, Moses' splashing blood on the altar and on the people. "This is my blood, the blood of the covenant, to be poured out on behalf of many." The emphasis on the covenant blood introduces sacrificial overtones in the Last Supper narrative and links it with the Sinai

---

9. *Let Us Give Thanks: Explanation and Texts of the New Eucharistic Prayers*, prepared by the Commission for the Sacred Liturgy of the Archdiocese of Chicago (Chicago: Liturgy Training Program, 1968), 26. The section on Eucharist—Sacrament of a Sacrifice—is based on the study of the late Salvator Marsili, OSB.

10. See Daly, *The Origins*, 22, 28, 44, 85, 96, 132, 134, and *Sacrifice Unveiled*, 29, 49, 70, 72; Power, *The Eucharistic Mystery*, 56, 114; Chauvet, *Symbol and Sacrament*, 241–44; *Let Us Give Thanks*, 25–26, and Jean Laporte, *Eucharistia in Philo* (New York: The Edwin Mellen Press, 1983), especially 93–97.

11. Robert J. Daly, "Eucharistic Origins: From the New Testament to the Liturgies of the Golden Age," *Theological Studies* 66 (March 2005): 3–22, argues for the diversity in what we know of the development of the early history of the Eucharist and against the notion that there was a one-line development (7). For a more in-depth treatment of the New Testament materials see Daly, *Sacrifice Unveiled*, 51–69.

covenant. Christ is the new Moses. The "liturgy" of Christ's life and death is presented as a covenant sacrifice which raises the Mosaic event to a higher plane and gives it new meaning. The stress here is on cultic sacrifice.[12]

Luke and Paul, on the other hand, take a different tack. They mention the blood: "This cup is the new covenant in my blood, which will be shed for you." The accent, however, is not on the Sinai covenant but on the new covenant foretold by Jeremiah who, in keeping with the prophetic stress on inner attitudes, makes no mention of blood. "The days are coming, says the Lord, when I will make a new covenant with the house of Israel and the house of Judah. It will not be like the covenant I made with their fathers. . . . But this is the covenant which I will make. . . . I will place my law within them, and write it upon their hearts; I will be their God, and they shall be my people" (Jer. 31:31–33). Luke and Paul thus link the Eucharist more forcefully with the prophetic concept of "spiritual sacrifice." The emphasis here is on the notion of a spiritual prayer form and the fulfillment of eschatological prophecy rather than on cultic immolation.[13]

Both traditions, however, see Jesus' death as redemptive and connect it with the Suffering Servant. The "for many" phrase in Mark 14:24 and Matthew 26:28 and the phrase "which is poured out" (or "shed") in Mark 14:24, Matthew 26:28, and Luke 22:20 are also a direct allusion to Isaiah 53:12b. The Servant theme thus provides a convergence point for the two traditions. Whomever Isaiah has in mind[14] that figure goes beyond bloody sacrifices or immolations and achieves what they failed to do. "He achieves all that sacrifice cannot, with its attempts at substitution, its shedding of blood and its making of offerings."[15] The Servant is the one who interiorizes the Law. He is

---

12. See William R. Crockett, *Eucharist: Symbol of Transformation* (New York: Pueblo, 1989), 17–20, and David N. Power, "Words That Crack: The Uses of 'Sacrifice' in Eucharistic Discourse," *Worship* 53 (Sept. 1979): 391–92.

13. See Crockett, *Eucharist*, 18–20, and Power, "Words That Crack," 391.

14. See Richard J. Clifford, "Isaiah, Book of, (Second Isaiah)" in David Noel Freedman, et al., eds., The *Anchor Bible Dictionary*, 6 vols. (New York: Doubleday, 1992), 3: 499–500. See also Daly, *Sacrifice Unveiled*, 53–54, 67, on Christ's attitude as portrayed by the Gospels, and H. Wheeler Robinson, *Corporate Personality in Ancient Israel* (Philadelphia: Fortress Press, 1964), 1–3.

15. Power, "Words That Crack," 390–92.

faithful to his covenant relationship with Yahweh and the commitment to Yahweh's people that implies. He also suffers for this relationship and gives his life for Yahweh and the covenant.[16]

In "Christologizing" these themes, Christians made use of the language of metaphor, which has been described as "'the transposition of an alien name' (Aristotle) or a 'deliberate yoking of unlikes' (Owen Barfield) [or] a play between identity and difference."[17] The sacred and cultic terms of the Old Testament when not being used of Jewish and pagan rites and ministers were used only in relationship to Christ and to the daily life of Christians. This enabled the Christians to distance themselves from those other rites, indicate that what they were doing was *true worship*, and also to "stretch" the meaning of words like "sacrifice" to include obedience to the Gospel, works of charity, prayer, and thanksgiving, all of which gave honor to God. The people themselves were called a living sacrifice, a royal priesthood, a temple holy to God.[18]

Paul expands this into a missionary perspective. The universal priesthood of the faithful is to go beyond the Church to the world. It is a ministry to be God's presence in the world. "But I have written to you rather boldly in some respects to remind you, because of the grace given me by God to be a minister of Christ Jesus to the Gentiles in performing the priestly service of the gospel of God, so that the offering up of the Gentiles may be acceptable, sanctified by the holy Spirit" (Rom. 15:15–16). *That* is the Christian "spiritual sacrifice."[19] The notion of propitiation certainly did not dominate the early Christian understanding of Eucharist, as Power remarks, but was present, as Chauvet notes.[20]

Thanksgiving clearly dominates the scene. *Didache*, Justin, and Irenaeus all refer to Malachi 1:11 ("For from the rising of the sun, even to its setting, my name is great among the nations; and everywhere they bring sacrifice to my name, and a pure offering") to

---

16. See ibid., 390–92, 403.

17. Ibid., 388.

18. See Chauvet, *Symbol and Sacrament*, 254, and Power, *The Eucharistic Mystery*, 115–18, 142–43. Daly, *The Origins*, 36–52, sees this kind of "stretching" already within Jewish tradition thanks to the "spiritualization" process.

19. Chauvet, *Symbol and Sacrament*, 257.

20. Ibid., 297, and Power, *The Eucharistic Mystery*, 143. For a more thorough treatment of the Fathers see Daly, *Sacrifice Unveiled*, 75–98.

explain Christian sacrifice in general and eucharistic sacrifice in particular as one of thanksgiving. Justin's use of metaphorical language in this regard is particularly forceful. A thanksgiving over bread and wine is the form Christians use to commemorate Christ's suffering and death. Early eucharistic prayers also pick up on this notion of a sacrifice of thanksgiving.[21]

Thus in the second century what Chauvet terms the "anti-sacrificial" tendency continues to hold sway. Anthologies of anti-sacrificial biblical quotations witness to that. Chauvet concludes that examining the New Testament and afterward reveals "an undeniable anti-sacrificial and anti-priestly subversion." In other words, "From now on, the new priesthood is the priesthood of the people of God . . . the temple . . . the body of Christians. . . . And the sacred work, the cult, the sacrifice that is pleasing to God, is the confession of faith lived in the agape of sharing in service to the poorest, of reconciliation and of mercy."[22]

SHIFTING TRENDS

Only at the beginning of the third century are the terms "sacrifice" and "priest" used to describe the Eucharist and the presiding ministers, for instance, by Tertullian and Cyprian. Those terms were to impose themselves more forcefully in the fourth century.[23] In light of the earlier bias against such cultic terminology being used of the liturgy, one wonders what brought on the change.

Maybe it reflects the thesis of R. Girard. He contends that competing desires between individuals for some object tend to shift from the object to a conflict between the parties involved. Eventually this conflict disrupts the community. The community resolves the conflict by selecting and sacrificing a victim or scapegoat. This eventually leads to a ritual repetition of a "scapegoat mechanism." But to mask the underlying violence of this process a deity is brought into the picture. The group tends to use sacrifice and sacrificial terminology as a means of unburdening itself of its internal violence and the guilt that inspires. The "sacrificial process" also enables the group to avoid

---

21. See Lathrop, *Holy Things*, 139–55, and Power, *The Eucharistic Mystery*, 96–97.

22. Chauvet, *Symbol and Sacrament*, 260. This is also the central theme of Daly's *The Origins*.

23. Chauvet, *Symbol and Sacrament*, 258–59, and Power, *The Eucharistic Mystery*, 118.

taking responsibility for its own ethical behavior. Judaeo-Christian
Scriptures in general and Jesus in particular, by freely choosing
against violence unmask and reject the violence of such primitive sacrificial behavior. They thus become "anti-sacrificial" in that sense.
Jesus' innocent death, especially, reveals the arbitrariness of violence
and where it leads. There is, however, a continuing cultural pressure to
overturn this revelation and return to the "old ways." This may
account, in part at least, for the reemergence of the language of
immolation, victim, etc.[24]

Be that as it may, Chauvet, while maintaining the legitimacy
of sacrificial and sacerdotal language in regard to the Eucharist and its
ministers, points out some other factors which may have influenced
the return to a "sacrificial" (= immolation) mindset among Christians.
After the conversion of Constantine and the end of persecutions
against Christians, there was an influx of pagan converts into the
Church. The clergy also began to function as civil leaders as well as
religious leaders and would appear to new converts from paganism to
exercise a role comparable to pagan priests.[25] Closely connected with
this was the tendency to regard the cultic ("priestly") activities of the
clergy as defining their whole existence. Later on in the Middle Ages
the majority of priests no longer exercised the ministry of the word at
all.[26] The gradual lessening of the participation of the people in the
liturgy (what Chauvet calls the "confiscation of the baptismal priesthood of the entire people of God by the priests")[27] also led to a one-
sided focus on the cultic role of the clergy. This was later to be
compounded by the multiplication of Masses and "Mass priests"
ordained exclusively to offer the "sacrifice of the Mass" as expiation

---

24. See Chauvet, *Symbol and Sacrament*, 303–6. See also René Girard, *The Scapegoat*, trans.
Yvonne Freccero (Baltimore: Johns Hopkins University Press, 1986), and *Violence and the Sacred*
(Baltimore: Johns Hopkins University Press, 1977); M. B. Agnew, "A Transformation of Sacrifice:
An Application of René Girard's Theory of Culture and Religion," *Worship* 61 (Nov. 1987):
493–509, who offers a fine summary of Girard's theory, of the lack of clarity in the way the term
"sacrifice" is used, and of the implications of Girard's theory for liturgy and the "victims of
persecution, of distorted economic systems, of war, of oppression" (507–8). See also Patrick T.
McCormick, *A Banqueter's Guide to the All-Night Soup Kitchen of the Kingdom of God* (Collegeville,
Minn.: Liturgical Press, 2004), 115–18, for another clear presentation of Girard's position and its
implications for today.

25. See Chauvet, *Symbol and Sacrament*, 308.

26. Ibid., 309, citing P. M. Gy, "Evangelisation au Moyen Âge," in *Humanisme et Foi
Chretienne* (Paris: Beauchesne, 1976), 572.

27. Chauvet, *Symbol and Sacrament*, 309.

for the deceased.[28] Perhaps, too, there is an anticipating of the move away from symbolic, metaphorical language as less real to more physical, literal language as more real.[29]

POST-NICENE CONTRIBUTIONS

Nevertheless, later writers like Chrysostom, Cyril of Jerusalem, and Augustine continued and refined what their predecessors had left them. Chrysostom, for example, echoed Justin's emphasis on the moral implications of sharing Eucharist. He found it strange that people provide precious vessels for the Body and Blood of Christ while neglecting the poor who are also the Body of Christ.[30] Cyril could speak on the one hand of the eucharistic prayer as the Church's spiritual sacrifice. But he also spoke of the Eucharist as a "sacrifice of propitiation" in which we offer Christ crucified to appease the merciful God on behalf of the living and the dead.[31]

Furthermore, "while an older theology thought of sacramental participation in historical events in terms of spiritual configuration and fruit, fifth-century mystagogy speaks of an event that, taking on supraterrestrial form, is here and now present in sacramental form."[32] What began on the cross now goes on as an eternal exercise of Christ's priesthood. These writers found, in the Neoplatonic perception that symbols share in the reality symbolized, something in their contemporary world view which helped them explain the sacrament's relation to historical and eternal reality. It did not completely satisfy their desire to identify the gift with the reality in sacramental form, but it helped. For them Christ's saving action had a "transhistorical quality." His suffering and death only reached completion in his passage to the Father and his continuing priestly activity.[33]

---

28. Ibid., 309–10. See also Frank Senn, *Christian Liturgy: Catholic and Evangelical* (Philadelphia: Fortress Press, 1997), 258.

29. See Chauvet, *Symbol and Sacrament,* 291–97.

30. See Power, *The Eucharistic Mystery,* 149.

31. Ibid., 147.

32. Ibid., 148.

33. Ibid., 149–51.

Augustine is particularly helpful for the present discussion on sacrifice. For him Christ's passion was complete surrender to God and thus a perfect sacrifice. He echoed Chrysostom and Theodore of Mopsuestia in saying that Christ's sacrifice is perfected in his ascension to God's right hand where he continues his priestly mediation.[34] He makes it clear that God has no need of human sacrifices and what honors God profits humankind, not God. In that context he describes the function of the eucharistic *sacramentum*: It is the "visible sacrifice, that is, the sacrament or sacred sign of the invisible sacrifice."[35] But maybe the greatest contribution he made to the discussion is connecting his notion of Eucharist as sacrifice with his ecclesial sense that all are one with Christ, united to him in the Eucharist as his body.[36]

Augustine's ecclesiology is a key to understanding his eucharistic theology. Chauvet provides a couple of examples of this: "Because you are the body of Christ and his members, it is your own mystery that lies on the altar, it is your own mystery that you receive. . . . Be what you see, and receive what you are." "This [Eucharistic] sacrifice is the symbol of what we are."[37] Augustine spoke of "the reality itself of which it [the Eucharist] is the sacrament." He said that Jesus "wished to make the sacrifice of the Church a daily sacrament of this reality, for the Church, being the body of which he is the head, learns thereby to offer itself through him."[38] For Augustine the *sacramentum* was the rite of the Church. In it he distinguished the sign (*signum*) and the reality (*res*) which included both the Body and Blood offered in communion and the Body, the communion between head and members in the Holy Spirit.[39] For him, too, the *sacramentum* was what we might call a "symbolic reality": it made the reality present.[40]

---

34. See ibid., 154–55.

35. Augustine, *City of God*, 10:5–6, as cited by Chauvet, *Symbol and Sacrament*, 312, and Archdiocese of Chicago, *Let Us Give Thanks*, 27.

36. See Crockett, *Eucharist*, 72, and Power, *The Eucharistic Mystery*, 153–55.

37. Cited by Chauvet, *Symbol and Sacrament*, 291–92, citing Augustine, Sermon 272 (PL 38:1246–1248), and 227 (PL 1099–1101).

38. Ibid., 296, citing Augustine with no reference except M. Lepin, *L'idée du sacrifice de la Messe d'après les théologiens depuis l'origine jusqu'à nos jours*, 2nd ed. (Paris: Beauchesne, 1926) 79.

39. Power, *The Eucharistic Mystery*, 155.

40. See McKenna, "Eucharistic Presence," 300–2, 295–96, and Power, *The Eucharistic Mystery*, 149–50.

Later generations would lose sight of this understanding of symbol, and therein lies a significant piece of our present-day problem of explaining how Christ's sacrifice can be present in the Eucharist. The shifting attitudes toward the Eucharist in the centuries to come took their toll on the understanding of the nature of eucharistic presence. This in turn would have its impact on the link between Eucharist as sacrament and Eucharist as sacrifice.[41]

It is interesting in this regard to note that both Thomas Aquinas and Bonaventure linked the sacramental presence of Christ to the notion of sacrifice. Thomas gives the presence of the Christ who suffered, Christ the victim, as a reason for calling the Eucharist a sacrifice. In receiving the mediator *himself,* the communicant receives the grace of his passion.[42] Bonaventure also gives as one reason for the real, abiding presence of Christ in the sacrament the need for a "placatory sacrifice, satisfied by the offering of Christ's very body and blood."[43] Luther, too, strongly defended eucharistic presence but, like so many others, especially in the Protestant tradition, does not seem to have seen the link between that presence and the notion of Eucharist as effective "memorial" and Eucharist as sacrifice. He did, however, allow for an understanding of eucharistic sacrifice in a manner reminiscent of Augustine, as the offering of the members of the body in union with Christ their head.[44]

A number of practices connected with medieval eucharistic piety did not help to keep the focus on the people offering themselves in union with Christ. Receiving Communion as part of a communal celebration had given way to looking at the host instead of receiving it ("ocular communion"). This is a far cry from Augustine's stress on

41. See McKenna, "Eucharistic Presence," 295–306; Chauvet, *Symbol and Sacrament,* 291–97; and Senn, *Christian Liturgy,* 256–63.

42. *Summa Theologiae* III q. 73, art. 4 as cited by Power, *The Eucharistic Mystery,* 227–30. See also Crockett, *Eucharist,* 119–24.

43. Power, *The Eucharistic Mystery,* 239.

44. See Crockett, *Eucharist,* 124, 130, 132–33. Some of the new eucharistic prayers, especially in the Protestant tradition, express well this last trait. For instance the anamneses in the Methodist Great Thanksgiving Prayers: "and so, in remembrance of these your mighty acts in Jesus Christ, we offer ourselves in praise and thanksgiving as a holy and living sacrifice, in union with Christ's offering for us, as we proclaim the mystery of faith," *The United Methodist Book of Worship* (Nashville: The United Methodist Publishing House, 1992), 57.

204 BECOME WHAT YOU RECEIVE

participation: "it is clear to the church that she herself is offered in union with Christ her head. . . . Christians also make the memorial of this sacrifice in the holy offering and partaking of the body and blood of Christ."[45]

In addition, the practice of fasting and praying for others' sins as well as one's own extended itself to the deceased. A growing emphasis on purgatory gave rise to an increasing desire for Masses for the dead. This led to the ordination of "Mass priests" who were ordained exclusively for offering such Masses. This in turn led to stressing the role of the priest as mediator and intercessor and the attaching of special importance to the prayer of the priest, especially during the Mass. A comparison between the Fourth Lateran Council (1215) with the Council of Constance (1414–18) illustrates the emphasis on the role of the priest. The Fourth Lateran in speaking of the eucharistic transformation states that the body and blood of Jesus Christ are really (*veraciter*) contained under the species of bread and wine, the bread having been transubstantiated (*transubstantiatis*) into the body and the wine into the blood *by the divine power* (*potestate divina*).[46] The Council of Constance, on the other hand, states "after the *consecration by the priest* there is under the veil of bread and wine no material bread and wine, but the very same Christ who suffered on the cross and sits at the right hand of the Father."[47] As Macquarrie points out, the species have become a veil, *the agent of the consecration is the priest* and substance has now become identified with physical matter.[48] Finally, the dimension of "propitiation" (understood as "reconciliation" or "pardon") was so focused on that, in the popular imagination at least, the Eucharist came to be seen as a sin offering in its own right. Some saw this as a threat to the once-for-all character of Christ's atonement.[49]

---

45. Augustine, *City of God,* 10:6, and *Against Faustus,* 20:18, as cited by Crockett, *Eucharist,* 72.

46. DS, 430 (802).

47. DS, 666 (1256).

48. John Macquarrie, *Christian Unity and Christian Diversity* (Philadelphia: Westminster, 1975), 74–78.

49. See Chauvet, *Symbol and Sacrament,* 309–11; Power, *The Eucharistic Mystery,* 170–71; Crockett, 72; and Senn, *Christian Liturgy,* 258.

Trent and the Reformation

Needless to say, the context of Trent was highly polemical whether the issue was eucharistic presence or the Eucharist as sacrifice.[50] Among the problems the reformers raised in regard to the question of sacrifice were:

> 1) An apparently automatic application of Christ's satisfaction without faith or devotion on the part of the recipient; 2) The idea that the Eucharist could benefit noncommunicants, even those absent from the celebration, and not only the living but also the dead; 3) The importance given the actions of the celebrating priest apart from the community's participation, e.g., "private" Masses; 4) The propitiatory character of the Mass as leading to a "works theology"; 5) Invoking the saints and celebrating Masses in honor of them as a seeming substitution of their works for the satisfaction of Christ.[51]

The position of Trent combined doctrine and practice. It fostered a sacramental memorial and re-presentation intended to exclude, among other things, a purely subjective remembrance. It stressed the act of the priest in realizing this memorial. Therefore, a benefit arises from the priestly action distinct from eucharistic Communion. It maintained that offering the sacrifice for living and dead expressed the communion between both.[52] Interestingly, the theologians at the Council of Trent did not suggest that the Mass contained any real immolation (destruction) nor was there any trace of theories of immolation. These were to arise among the theologians *after* Trent. The council in effect affirmed that the Eucharist was a sacrifice but did not define what it meant by "sacrifice."[53]

The opposition to offering the Mass for the living and the dead and all that went with it (stipends, "private" Masses, etc.) had stirred up the controversy over the Eucharist as sacrifice. The Catholic emphasis on Eucharist as a sacrifice of propitiation for the living and

---

50. See, for example, Edward Schillebeeckx, *The Eucharist,* trans. N. D. Smith (London: Sheed & Ward, 1968), 30–33, and Daly, "Robert Bellarmine," 247–48.

51. David N. Power, *The Sacrifice We Offer: The Tridentine Dogma and Its Reinterpretation* (New York: Crossroad, 1987), 48–49.

52. Power, *The Eucharistic Mystery,* 260.

53. Daly, "Robert Bellarmine," 247–48. For a more in-depth study of sacrifice during the Reformation and the post-Reformation periods see Daly, *Sacrifice Unveiled,* 141–88.

the dead, for the remission of sins and for other needs was, at least in part, to bolster the role of the ordained priest. The reformers strongly opposed giving special value to the priest's action in applying Christ's merits to the church.[54]

The Protestant side then accented the sacrament and the gift aspect, while the Catholic side accented the offering and sacrifice. Unfortunately, Trent separated the doctrine on sacrament and the doctrine on sacrifice into two separate decrees. The Thirteenth Session (1551) treated the Eucharist as sacrament. The Twenty-Second Session (1562) a full decade later treated the Eucharist as sacrifice. Edward Kilmartin observed: "The separation of the question of real presence and sacrifice is a clear sign that the Council did not see the inner connection between the sacramentality and the sacrificial character of the Mass. Rather an accidental connection between the two was to a great extent simply taken for granted."[55] The word *sacrifice* was allowed to dominate the discussion of the eucharistic celebration. Some of the images used in the decree on sacraments, like eschatological banquet and Passover, might have helped in the decree on sacrifice.

Neither side had a sense of liturgical history that might have enabled them to see the link between the entire eucharistic prayer and the sacramental re-presentation and also between the eucharistic prayer and the communion rite. Both sides tended to isolate the institution narrative from the rest of the eucharistic prayer. Therefore they were unable to get back to the notion of memorial in the biblical and liturgical sources.[56] Finally, they both seemed to equate sacrifice with immolation. This was the "fatal flaw" and led to all kinds of theories on how an immolation took place in the eucharistic rite.[57] It also makes it difficult to maintain that we are not dealing with a new sacrifice but in some way the one sacrifice of Christ. It would have been far better to question the equation of sacrifice with immolation.[58]

54. Ibid., 257–58, and Lathrop, *Holy Things*, 155.

55. Edward Kilmartin and Robert Daly, *The Eucharist in the West: History and Theology* (Collegeville, Minn.: Liturgical Press, 1998), 178.

56. Power, *The Eucharistic Mystery*, 257, 259, and *The Sacrifice We Offer*, 151–54.

57. See Daly, "Robert Bellarmine," 258, and 249–57, where he outlines some of the resultant theories.

58. See ibid., 248; Archdiocese of Chicago, *Let Us Give Thanks*, 24–27, and Power, *The Eucharistic Mystery*, 249–50.

The "fatal flaw" was actually twofold. One weakness was to use as a starting point the notion that sacrifice necessarily meant immolation or destruction of some sort (this is what Daly calls "the-history-of–religions" sense of the word).[59] The other weakness was to fail to focus on Jesus' personal sacrifice as doing away with or over-turning the understanding of "sacrifice" as requiring "immolation" or destruction. Instead the theologians might have made their starting point the relationship between Jesus and the Father and, in the Spirit, between Jesus and his body the Church. The outward form of meal would then be the efficacious sign or symbolic embodiment of those relationships.[60]

Looking at Christian sacrifice from a Trinitarian and liturgi-cal perspective might have enabled them to see that sacrifice "is, in the first place, the self-offering of the Father in the gift of his Son, and then the free self-offering response of the Son in his humanity, and in completion, the faithful, in the power of the Spirit, being taken up into that Father-Son relationship."[61] Given the circumstances, how-ever, such an understanding was beyond reach. In fact, as good as it is, it might be difficult in certain circles to appreciate even today.

On the other hand, in Trent's mind faith and repentance were clearly necessary to benefit from the "propitiatory" effects of the Eucharist. The council also made progress in promoting more fre-quent communion by the faithful. And the conciliar debates effec-tively put an end to any respectable Catholic theory that would see the Mass as a sacrifice in any way distinct from the cross.[62] But, given the context, the differences in mentality and emphases between Catholics and Protestants were too great to overcome. Senn makes the interest-ing point that Cardinal Cajetan, the Dominican theologian, had offered an explanation that incorporated a notion of making present Christ's redemptive sacrifice. "The victim is one and the same, but there are two manners in which he is immolated. The first, the original, unique and proper manner of immolation, was by way of

59. Daly, "Robert Bellarmine," 248.

60. Ibid.

61. Robert J. Daly, "Sacrifice Unveiled or Sacrifice Revisited: Trinitarian and Liturgical Perspectives," *Theological Studies* 64 (March 2003): 24–42, at 24 (editor's summary), and at 27, for another version. See also Daly, *Sacrifice Unveiled*, 6–23, and 223–29, and Daly, "New Developments," 51–58.

62. Power, *The Eucharistic Mystery*, 258–59.

shedding of blood; that is, under natural appearances (*in propria specie*), when his blood was shed and his body broken on the cross. The second manner, which recurs every day, a manner which is extrinsic and accessory to the first (*externus accesoriusque*), is unbloody—re-presenting in an immolatory manner (*immolatitio modo repraesentans*), under the appearance of bread and wine, Christ offered on the cross."[63] Senn adds: "Here was an understanding of memorial and sacrifice that could have profitably entered into dialogue with the reformers' views."[64] Cajetan's position went without much notice in his own day and exercised little or no significant influence in the following centuries.

MORE RECENT DEVELOPMENTS

Where have we come since then? Among other things to a convergence of the question of Eucharist as presence, Eucharist as sacrifice, Eucharist as memorial in the biblical sense, and Eucharist as "symbolic reality" in the early Christian sense.[65] If Christ is personally risen, as we believe he is, if he is personally present in the Eucharist, "in sacrament," "in symbol," "in memorial," then his attitude of giving himself to the Father and of being accepted by the Father, his attitude of giving himself to and for us is being embodied in the "visible sacrifice, that is, the sacrament or sacred sign of the invisible sacrifice," as Augustine put it.

What form would it take? As Aquinas long ago reminded us, it is up to the institutor of the sacrifice to determine the form, and the form Jesus made use of was that of a meal. If Christ's life and death can be called a sacrifice, then it is present in him as he comes to us in the ongoing exercise of his priestly ministry.[66] But this sacrifice is

---

63. Senn, *Christian Liturgy,* 261, citing *De missae sacrificio et ritu adversus Lutheranos.*

64. Ibid.

65. See McKenna, "Eucharistic Presence," 300–8, and Senn, *Christian Liturgy,* who notes that "the ancient Christian concept of Mysterium was lost in medieval theology: 'Symbol' and 'truth,' 'sacrament' and 'reality' were torn asunder. . . . The result was a 'historicizing' of the sacrifice of the cross in both medieval and Reformation theologies. Any discussion of the mass as a propitiatory sacrifice could only suggest to the reformers that the all-sufficiency of Christ's once-for-all atoning sacrifice was being undermined," 262–63.

66. See Edward Schillebeeckx, *Christ the Sacrament of the Encounter with God,* 32; Roger Haight, *Jesus Symbol of God* (Maryknoll, N.Y.: Orbis Books, 1999), 147–51; Seasoltz, "Another Look at Sacrifice," 401; Chauvet, *Symbol and Sacrament,* 298: Jesus' life as well as his death can be

unlike any other. It was really, as Chauvet puts it, an "anti-sacrifice," his *kenosis*, his "letting-be" of God, to use a phrase from Heidegger. "The 'sacrifice' of his life given unto death is that of *consent to his condition as Son-in-humanity and as Brother of humanity* . . . where he consents to taste humanity to its extreme limit, death experienced in the silence of a God who would not even intervene to spare the Just One this death."[67] The Resurrection is God's acceptance of Jesus' "letting-be."

The notion of memorial, especially its biblical foundations, has helped recent ecumenical dialogue on eucharistic sacrifice as has the role of the eucharistic prayer in keeping memorial. A better understanding of this prayer helps churches put aside the dichotomy between subjective and objective commemoration and between sacrifice of thanksgiving and sacrifice of propitiation.[68] The link between the eucharistic prayer and the Communion rite is also clearer. The presence of an epiclesis in the eucharistic prayers has made us more aware of the role of the Holy Spirit and of the fact that the assembly is always a *praying* assembly.[69]

The power and reality of metaphorical language is better appreciated than before. "My hypothesis . . . is that metaphor is the key to the interpretation of Christian sacrificial language, whether it be used of Christian life, Christian celebration, or of Christ's death," as Power puts it.[70] Senn seeks to strike a balance in this area:

> Lutherans need to understand that sacrifice is a polysemous concept in the eucharistic tradition that refers variously to the offering of bread and wine, the self-offering of the faithful, and the saving act of Jesus Christ. Roman Catholics need to remember that sacrifice is one metaphor for the saving act of Christ along with others, such as ransom and purchase, victory over

---

viewed as a sacrifice. "His dying for us is the ultimate expression of his living-for." See also Power, *The Eucharistic Mystery*, 55.

67. Chauvet, *Symbol and Sacrament*, 301.

68. See Senn, *Christian Liturgy*, especially his section on "The Relevance of the Study of Eucharistic Prayer in Transcending the Ecumenical Impasse over Eucharistic Sacrifice," 477–79.

69. See Power, *The Eucharistic Mystery*, 260, and McKenna, *The Eucharistic Epiclesis*, 215–17, 224, for a critique of the positioning and splitting of the epiclesis as well as Daly, "Robert Bellarmine," 242–43.

70. D. Power, "Words That Crack," 389. See also Lathrop, *Holy Things*, 139–58, and J. Pierce, "The Eucharist as Sacrifice: Some Contemporary Roman Catholic Reflections," *Worship* 69 (Nov 1995): 401–3.

sin, death, and the devil, and the restoration of immortality through the incarnation of the Word.[71]

Furthermore, just as the recovery of the ancient notion of a "symbolic reality," that is, a symbol which enables the reality to be present, has helped the dialogue, so, too, a realization that metaphor and reality are not opposed but complementary is useful. The metaphor reveals an underlying reality. "Mere symbol" and "mere metaphor" need rethinking in light of history. The greater, more active participation of our people in the liturgy, especially in Communion as a response to Christ's offer of himself, and an awareness of the ethical implications of eucharistic celebrations are also hopeful signs.

The Future

Of course there continue to be "sore spots" like the role of the priest. This might lessen if the clear Catholic doctrine that the merits or personal mediation of the priest add nothing to the mediation of Christ was placed in the context of memorial remembrance and prayer. This would make it even clearer that it is the Paschal mystery of Christ that operates through the liturgical actions of the priest. Couple this with Protestant theology and practice that acknowledges the importance of commemorative prayer, and our differences might not be as radical as they once appeared.[72]

There have been attempts by Roman Catholic theologians to take a fresh look at the question of Eucharist and sacrifice. Robert Daly, following the late Edward Kilmartin, has been critical of the position of the "contemporary Roman Catholic magisterium." Daly argues that "*in persona Christi*" has been interpreted in such a way as almost to eliminate the ecclesiological dimension of the Eucharist, and the Christological perspective has been stressed almost to the exclusion of the Trinitarian dimension, especially of the role of the Holy Spirit. In addition, he contends that there is still too strong a focus on the words of institution and that the dynamic of the eucharistic action is seen as flowing from Christ to the priest to the Eucharist to the Church. This leads to an overemphasis on priestly power,

---

71. Senn, *Christian Liturgy*, 479.
72. Power, EM, 262–63.

position, and privilege. He adds that much of the magisterial teaching fails to stress that the Christ event did away with sacrifice in the history-of-religions sense of the word (as demanding some immolation or destruction). He urges a rethinking of this approach in light of contemporary theological consensus which would emphasize the ecclesiological and Trinitarian dimensions, focus more on the whole eucharistic prayer and its accompanying ritual action, and see the role of the priest as embedded in the Christ-Church relationship rather than standing between Christ and the Church.[73]

Such inner Church discussions can only help to further ecumenical dialogue as does Frank Senn's call, from a Lutheran perspective, to focus on eucharistic prayers as a way around an ecumenical impasse.[74] And as forceful as he is on the question of sacrifice, Gordon Lathrop can acknowledge, "If the purpose of sacrifice is carefully circumscribed, eliminating the cruder meanings, if worship and moral life are invited by the talk of 'offering' into self-giving, if such self-giving acts are seen as reflecting and celebrating the all-sufficient self-gift of Christ rather than in any sense adding to it, the language can be and has been used to speak the Christian gospel."[75]

Another very helpful approach to the question of sacrifice is that of R. Kevin Seasoltz. After sketching attitudes toward the notion of sacrifice in our contemporary world, he examines the place of sacrifice in a theology of creation, incarnation and soteriology, and in eucharistic theology. He seeks to maintain the centrality of sacrifice in Christian life but also in the very makeup of creation.[76]

Seasoltz sees creation itself as a continuous sacrificial act on the part of God, involving as it does costly love, self-limitation, and surrender.[77] Regarding redemption, he places the emphasis on God's activity in Jesus Christ. Christ's action of self-giving is an eternal action and Calvary manifests the eternally present sacrificial disposition of the Godhead.[78] Following Schillebeeckx, he maintains that

---

73. Daly, "Robert Bellarmine," 239–40, 245, 246–48. See also Edward Kilmartin, The Eucharist in the West, 365–83.

74. Senn, *Christian Liturgy*, 477–79.

75. Lathrop, *Holy Things*, 141.

76. Seasoltz, "Another Look at Sacrifice," 387.

77. Ibid., 392.

78. Ibid., 400–1.

suffering does not enter the being of God. Rather, God enters into compassionate solidarity with Jesus on the cross (and with all who suffer) and, after evil has run its course, overcomes sin and death by raising Jesus from the dead.[79] By emptying himself, Jesus in turn reveals the very character of God as totally self-giving.[80] In treating the Eucharist, Seasoltz expresses well the utter giftedness for us of any exchange with God and the key role of the Holy Spirit in transforming both the gifts and the people receiving them.[81] These themes can only aid the discussion of Eucharist and sacrifice.

Finally, attention to some of the themes that postmodernist theologians like Chauvet and J.-L. Marion have raised might help further the discussion.[82] To whatever extent Chauvet reflects postmodern thought, he is clear that while sacrificial language is legitimate it must also be "anti-sacrificial" in the sense of moving beyond an immolation notion to a "spiritual sacrifice" which serves to transform the world. "The ethical practice of reconciliation between human beings, constitutes the premier place of *our* sacrifice. That is what the anti-sacrifice of the Eucharist shows us and enjoins us to do."[83] He and Marion also stress the presence and absence of the Risen Christ, the "irreducibility of God, of Christ, and of the gospel to our concepts, discourses, ideologies, and experiences,"[84] the absolutely gratuitous, gracious and "always in excess" character of God's gift to us,[85] and the "being-for, being-toward" of Christ's presence.[86] These are all humbling reminders of the limits of our dialogue.

In any event, the question of Eucharist and sacrifice refuses to go away. As Chauvet notes, the language of sacrifice, while not the only way to express the meaning of Jesus, nevertheless has its place. In fact it is hard to avoid its overtones in a ritual that speaks of eating

---

79. Ibid., 404.

80. Ibid., 405.

81. Ibid., 406–10.

82. Jean-Luc Marion, *God Without Being*, trans. Thomas A. Carlson (Chicago: University of Chicago Press, 1995).

83. Chauvet, *Symbol and Sacrament*, 309.

84. Ibid., 403.

85. Ibid., 549, and Marion, *God Without Being*, 164–66.

86. Chauvet, *Symbol and Sacrament*, 392, 387–89, 526.

and drinking the body and blood of Christ. We are "dealing here with a 'sacrifice-in-sacrament,' but a very singular sacrifice."[87]

The morsel of bread and sip of wine remind us that complete fulfillment lies in the future. We can nevertheless still dream of, and work toward, the day when we will no longer debate about the *how*, but celebrate together *what* God has done for us through Jesus Christ and in the Holy Spirit.

---

87. Ibid., 302.

Chapter 11

Eucharist and the Holy Spirit

A Catholic expert at Vatican II was quoted as saying that the Holy Spirit was "the great unknown" among Roman Catholics.[1] A rediscovery of the Spirit has been helped by a renewed interest in a prayer in the eucharistic celebration called the epiclesis or invocation of the Holy Spirit. This chapter is an attempt to highlight the role of the Holy Spirit by reflecting on the epiclesis historically, theologically, pastorally, and ecumenically.

HISTORICAL REFLECTIONS

Historically,[2] the epiclesis has possible forerunners in the Christian Scriptures and in the Jewish *berakoth* or blessings.[3] In the *Apostolic Tradition* (c. 215), until relatively recently attributed to Hippolytus,

---

1. Boris Bobrinskoy, "Le Saint-Esprit, vie de l'église," Contacts 18 (1962): 195. David J. Kennedy, *Eucharistic Sacramentality in an Ecumenical Context: The Anglican Epiclesis* (Burlington, Vt.: Ashgate, 2008), 225–26, more recently echoes a similar complaint. See also Patrick Regan, "Quenching the Spirit: The Epiclesis in Recent Roman Documents," *Worship* 79 (September 2005): 386–404. The author offers a powerful presentation of the role of the Spirit in "The General Instruction of the Roman Missal," in the *Catechism of the Catholic Church* (2000), and the apostolic letter *Dies Domini*. He then outlines the inherent weakness of a change in view of the encyclical *Ecclesia de Eucharistia* and the *Lineamenta* or "Guidelines for Preparing for the Synod of Bishops in October 2005."

2. For the overall historical background, see John H. McKenna, *The Eucharistic Epiclesis: A Detailed History from the Patristic to the Modern Era*, 2nd ed. (Chicago: Hillenbrand Books, 2009). Paul F. Bradshaw, ed., *Essays on Early Eastern Eucharistic Prayers* (Collegeville, Minn.: Liturgical Press 1997); E. G. Atchley and F. Cuthbert, *On the Epiclesis of the Eucharistic Liturgy and in the Consecration of the Font*, Alcuin Club Collections 31 (London: Oxford University Press, 1935); F. Cabrol, "Epiclèse," DACL 5/1 (1922): 142–84; S. Salaville, "Epiclèse eucharistique," *DThC* 5/1 (1913): 194–300; Edward Schillebeeckx, *De Sacramentele Heilseconomie* (Antwerp, 1952), 307–54; and G. C. Smit, "Epiclèse et Théologie des Sacrements," MSR 15 (1958): 95–136. See also John H. McKenna, "Eucharistic Prayer: Epiclesis," in Andreas Heinz and Heinrich Rennings, eds., *Gratias Agamus: Studien Zum Eucharistischen Hochgebet* (Freiburg: Herder, 1992), 283–85.

3. McKenna, *The Eucharistic Epiclesis*, 3–7.

the epiclesis asks that the Holy Spirit be sent upon the church's offering that those partaking may be gathered together into one and filled with the Holy Spirit for the strengthening of their faith in truth.[4] The later fully developed form, however, traditionally contained three elements: (1) an appeal for the Holy Spirit; (2) to transform or sanctify the bread and wine; (3) so that they might benefit those who partake of them worthily. This is the form that the present study presupposes. An ancient example of this form is the epiclesis found in the Anaphora of St. Basil:

> Therefore, Holy Lord, we, sinners and your unworthy servants . . . offering the images of the holy Body and Blood of your Christ, pray and call upon you, O Holy of Holies, that through your good pleasure the Holy Spirit might come upon us and upon these gifts which we offer and bless them and sanctify them and make this bread the precious Body of the Lord and God and our Savior, Jesus Christ. Amen. And this cup the precious Blood of the Lord and God and our Savior, Jesus Christ. Amen. . . . And all of us who partake of the one bread and cup unite us with one another in the communion of the one Holy Spirit and see to it that none of us partakes of the holy Body and Blood of your Christ unto judgment and punishment, but rather that we find mercy and grace with all the saints who have been pleasing to you from the beginning.[5]

The epiclesis was eventually to become entangled in the question of eucharistic consecration. In this regard, two questions could be raised for the patristic period: Did the patristic writers consider the epiclesis to be consecratory? If so, in what sense?[6]

4. A. Hänggi and I. Pahl, eds., *Prex Eucharistica* (Fribourg-Suisse: Éditions Universitaires, 1968), 236, 238. See also R. C. D. Jasper and G. J. Cuming, *Prayers of the Eucharist: Early and Reformed*, 3rd ed. (New York: Pueblo, 1987), 31–38. As we have seen in earlier chapters, a number of scholars now question the authorship, the date, and the place of origin of this work. See, for example, Paul F. Bradshaw, *The Search for the Origins of Christian Worship*, 2nd ed. (New York: Oxford University Press, 2002), 80–83. See also Bradshaw, *Eucharistic Origins* (Oxford: University of Oxford Press, 2004), 19–20, 48–50, 135–38, who states that in its extant state the *Apostolic Tradition* dates from the fourth century or later. He adds, however, that does not mean that certain elements, for example, the institution narrative, contained in its eucharistic prayer did not exist, possibly as a teaching device, long before it was inserted into the prayer. See also John F. Baldovin, "Hippolytus and the *Apostolic Tradition*: Recent Research and Commentary," *Theological Studies* 64 (Sept. 2003): 520–42, and B. McGowan, *Ascetic Eucharists: Food and Drink in Early Christian Ritual Meals* (New York: Oxford University Press, 1999), 28–29.

5. Hängii and Pahl, *Prex*, 81. See also Jasper-Cuming, *Prayers*, 119–20.

6. For a fuller development of the data from the patristic period, see McKenna, *Eucharistic Epiclesis*, 42–70.

At first glance, a number of texts seem to be clear. When subjected to closer scrutiny, however, they allow for interpretation and have in fact received widely varying interpretations. Some of the early Christian writers, Ambrose and Augustine for instance, seem to stress the consecratory value of the institution narrative. Others, Cyril of Jerusalem and John Damascene, for example, seem to stress the consecratory value of the epiclesis. The frequent uncertainty as to the exact meaning of the patristic texts, therefore, tends to make one wary of overly categorical and overly consistent interpretations of pertinent patristic passages.

Some clear lines do, however, emerge from an examination of the patristic texts. In the eyes of the patristic writers, the action of the Holy Spirit is an absolute necessity for the realization of the Eucharist. There is also general agreement that they regarded the whole eucharistic prayer as consecratory. It is possible that they viewed the words of institution and the epiclesis as two consecratory "moments" or high points within this larger framework of the entire eucharistic prayer. Despite all the ambiguities, one thing is certain. The "moment of consecration" was not an issue for the early Christian writers. As a consequence, there was for them no problem of the epiclesis and the "moment of consecration." In fact, up to the beginning of the fourteenth century we find little or no evidence of a conflict over the epiclesis. Neither Photius nor Michael Cerularius, neither Thomas Aquinas nor the Council of Lyons made an issue of the eucharistic epiclesis.[7]

The rise of Scholasticism had, however, brought with it a growing interest in the precise "moment of consecration." Thomas Aquinas is a case in point. A number of papal statements and the reaction of western missionaries against the eastern use of the epiclesis, which in their minds wrongly prayed for the changing of the gifts after the "moment of consecration," also reflect this interest.

A response from the East was inevitable. Nicholas Cabasilas, who was to set the tone for later Orthodox thought on the epiclesis,

---

7. See Robert F. Taft, "Mass without the Consecration? The Historic Agreement on the Eucharist between the Catholic Church and the Assyrian Church of the East Promulgated 26 October 2001," *Worship* 77 (2003): 482–509. He argues that respected theologians have historically seemed comfortable with viewing the whole eucharistic prayer as consecratory and/or a prayer, after the institution narrative, calling for transformation of the gifts (496–503, 509).

ought to be understood against a backdrop of Scholasticism. He inveighed against making the words of institution alone sufficient for consecration. In stressing the need for prayer (the epiclesis), however, he does not appear to have denied all consecratory value to the words of institution. Both East and West, immersed as they were in the political tensions of the time, found it difficult to approach their basic differences of mentality objectively. The events subsequent to the Councils of Florence and Trent reflect a hardening of position on both sides. The Orthodox tradition perhaps in overreaction to the Roman position, increasingly stressed the epiclesis and at times revealed an untraditional precision in regard to the "moment of consecration." The Roman tradition, on the other hand, continued to mirror the precision-oriented Scholastic mentality and to insist on the exclusive consecratory value of the words of institution. The conciliar and papal statements to this effect thus reflect the Scholastic appreciation of the sacramental formula and ought to be interpreted in the light of that appreciation.

Moreover, Robert Taft, a noted ecumenical scholar, has published a series of articles on a historic agreement that he considers "the most important magisterial teaching since Vatican II."[8] The context is an agreement on Guidelines for Admission to the Eucharist between the Chaldean Church and the Assyrian Church of the East (Oct. 26, 2001).[9] The purpose of the agreement was to make sure that Catholics of the Chaldean Church not be deprived of the Eucharist in the absence of a Catholic priest. Catholics could be sure that when, under certain circumstances, they received Communion in an Assyrian Eucharist using the ancient eucharistic prayer of Addai and Mari they would be receiving the Body and Blood of Christ.[10]

The startling fact is that the eucharistic prayer of Addai and Mari does not have an explicit institution narrative. Thus the agreement indicates that the Vatican acknowledges that this eucharistic prayer is valid and legitimate despite the absence of an explicit institution narrative. The Pontifical Council for Promoting Christian Unity, the Congregation for the Oriental Churches, the Congregation for

8. Taft, "Mass without the Consecration?" *America* 188, no. 16 (May 12, 2003): 7–11, citing 11. Henceforth America. See also Taft, "Mass," 482–509.

9. Taft, "Mass," 483–84, and *America:* 8.

10. Taft, "Mass," 483–86, and *America:* 8.

the Doctrine of the Faith, and Pope John Paul II himself all approved the agreement.[11]

The agreement has a number of implications. First, it reminds us that the shape of both the liturgical action and the liturgical word ("matter" and "form") have undergone such far-reaching changes that the actions and words in themselves cannot be the substance of the sacrament which Trent said the Church cannot change. Trent's *salva substantia illorum* could best be understood as: "except for the sacramental signification, manifested by *some* words and *some* gestures which according to the faith judgment of the Church are suited for the expression of this sacramental signification."[12]

Within this view the Church could change the *specific* "form" of the sacrament and still leave the "substance" untouched. Within such a view it is conceivable, for instance, that the Church could declare that the epiclesis, in addition to the institution narrative, would henceforth belong to what is called the "form" of the Eucharist.[13]

Second, the agreement is significant for the century-old debate over the "moment of consecration." It makes it more difficult to argue that the institution narrative is the only possible agent of change.[14]

Third, the agreement could favor the view of a growing number of theologians that the early Christians saw the entire eucharistic prayer as consecratory. In addition to ancient texts, they would point to recent documents that seem to lean toward such an interpretation. They cite, for instance, the *General Instruction of the Roman Missal* (November 18, 1969), no. 54: "Now begins the summit and center of the whole celebration, namely the Eucharistic Prayer itself, that is, the prayer of thanksgiving and sanctification" and the *Catechism of the Catholic Church*, no. 1352: "with the eucharistic prayer, the prayer, namely, of thanksgiving and consecration, we come to the heart and culmination of the celebration."[15]

---

11. Taft, "Mass," 483, and *America:* 8. See also Mark Plaiss, "This, Too, Is My Body," *Commonweal* 133, no. 10 (May 19, 2006): 9, for a good brief summary of some of the issues.

12. See McKenna, *The Eucharistic Epiclesis,* 152–66.

13. Ibid., 165–66.

14. See Taft, "Mass," 484–86, and *America:* 8–10.

15. Taft, "Mass," 501–3, and *America:* 10.

In addition, Taft affirms strongly that the words of institution are always consecratory, even in the eucharistic prayer of Addai and Mari, "because Jesus' pronouncing of them at the Last Supper remains efficaciously consecratory for every Eucharist until the end of time."[16]

Taft has demonstrated an "ecumenical theology," that is, "a new way of studying Christian tradition in order to reconcile and unite, rather than to confute and dominate. Its deliberate intention is to emphasize the common tradition underlying differences, which, though real, may be the accidental product of history, culture, and language rather than essential differences in the apostolic faith."[17]

THEOLOGICAL REFLECTIONS

It would be presumptuous to think that one could propose all-embracing, definitive solutions to the complex questions surrounding the epiclesis. In a fine study on the epiclesis, David Kennedy cautions against limiting the Holy Spirit's role to sanctifying the elements and thereby "marginalizing" the Spirit's role in creation, in the present life of the Church, and in the hope for the final future.[18] The relationship of the epiclesis to the Holy Spirit's role in the Eucharist is a case in point. A proper grasp of the Spirit's activity in the Eucharist would involve a study in itself. Even the decrees of Vatican II leave much to be desired here.[19] Nevertheless, it is necessary to broaden the horizons on the epiclesis question to include the role of the Holy Spirit in saving history and in the Eucharist as well as in creation and the final future. The need to reconcile the activity of Christ with that of the

---

16. Taft, *America:* 11, and "Mass," 503–8.

17. Taft, *America:* 9, and "Mass" 486–89.

18. David J. Kennedy, *Eucharistic Sacramentality,* 225–26. Kennedy illustrates his point by noting (236–38) that the image of creator-Spirit is a central pillar of Old Testament pneumatology and the New Testament hope for the eschatological re-creation (Romans 8:19–23) is "by the power of the Spirit who once brooded upon the waters of chaos."

19. See J.-M.R. Tillard, "L'Eucharistie et le Saint-Esprit," NRTh 90 (1968): 363–64, who notes that the Decree on the Ministry and Life of Priests (Dec. 7, 1965; AAS 58 [1966]: 991–1024), no. 5, and the *Instruction on Eucharistic Worship* (May 25, 1967; AAS 59 [1967]: 539–73), nos. 3, 6, 8, 38, 50, made a more conscious effort there. Nathan Mitchell, *Real Presence: The Work of the Eucharist* (Chicago: Liturgy Training Publications, 2007), 29–31, also notes that Pedro Rodriguez, ed., *Catechismus Romanus* (Vatican City: Libreria Editrice Vaticana, 1989), makes no reference to the Holy Spirit when speaking of the eucharistic consecration but the *Catechism of the Catholic Church* corrected that flaw (n. 1333, 1357). See also 1105–6, 1375, and 1412.

Holy Spirit in the Eucharist is inherent in the view that sees the epi-clesis as an expression of the Spirit's role in the Eucharist. It is first necessary, however, to view this activity against the broader back-ground of the saving economy. Consequently, a brief sketch of the interaction of Christ and the Spirit in saving history and in the Eucharist will precede applying insights in these two areas to the epiclesis question.

The Holy Spirit and Saving History[20]

If Christ is the sacrament of encounter between God and ourselves, it is because he bears within his body-person the fullness of the Spirit.[21] One may speak of a Johannine-Alexandrian approach, which stresses the Incarnation or the descendent, Logos-Flesh movement. In this approach the emphasis is on the fact that the Logos became one of us and by so doing divinized us.[22] One may also speak of the Pauline-Antiochean approach, which stresses the death-Resurrection (glorifi-cation) or the ascending, human-divine movement. Here the emphasis is on the fact that the Son of God become human is made *Kyrios* or Lord only at the moment of his Resurrection.[23]

Nevertheless, here as elsewhere it is a question not of exclusiv-ity but of complementarity. Incarnation is not simply the fact that the Logos or Second Person of the Trinity took on human flesh through birth. Incarnation, in its fullest sense, is a lifetime process of becom-ing human, fully human. For Christ, it involved a progressive opening up in loving obedience to his Father and out of love for us. Corre-sponding to this opening up on the part of Christ was his progres-sively being filled with the Holy Spirit; put another way, the fullness of the Holy Spirit, which he possessed from the beginning, was grad-

20. See McKenna, *The Eucharistic Epiclesis,* 218–20.

21. See Schillebeeckx, *Christ the Sacrament of the Encounter with God.* Stagbook edition, trans. P. Barrett and N. D. Smith (London: Sheed & Ward, 1963), esp. 5–54, and J.-M.R. Tillard, *Flesh of the Church, Flesh of Christ: At the Source of the Ecclesiology of Communion,* trans. M. Beaumont (Collegeville, Minn.: Liturgical Press, 2001), 2–13, especially 4–6. See also McKenna, *The Eucharistic Epiclesis,* 218–20.

22. See Tillard, *The Eucharist: Pasch of God's People,* trans. D. Wienk (New York: Alba House, 1967), 71–102.

23. Ibid., 102–12.

ually being unveiled in him. The culmination of this dynamic process took place in his death, Resurrection, and glorification.[24]

Thus, whether one looks upon the redemptive process as a gradual filling up of Christ with the Spirit or as a gradual unveiling of the fullness of the Holy Spirit that Christ possessed from the first moment of the Incarnation, a number of common factors emerge. First, a progressive "transformation" of the human Christ is involved. Secondly, the whole process involves an interaction between Christ and the Spirit. It is not a question of an either-or. This becomes especially clear when one views the activity of Christ and the Spirit in relationship to the sanctification of humankind. We have here a double presence, a double service and mediation, a double action of Christ in the Spirit and the Spirit in Christ serving as "the two hands of the Father" in drawing us into a new life.[25] Moreover, it is no question of a watered-down notion of "appropriation" in which the distinctive divine personalities become lost in the common *ad extra* work of the Trinity. It is "appropriation" in the strong sense which the Greek tradition and writers like Aquinas within the Latin tradition have given this notion.[26] Drawing us up into the Trinitarian life is indeed a common work. In achieving it, however, the Persons keep their own characteristics; the operation comes from the Father, through the Son, and is accomplished in the Holy Spirit. Finally, both approaches to the redemptive process agree in seeing the Resurrection—or, perhaps more exactly, the Paschal mystery—as the event that enables Christ to dispense to us the Spirit with which he is filled, the Spirit of new life. It is the Holy Spirit who accomplishes our sanctification, who carries the work of Christ to its fulfillment. To put it another way, it is Christ, filled with the Holy Spirit, who, through his own Resurrection and exaltation as Lord (*Kyrios*), is now able freely to communicate this life-giving Spirit to us.

---

24. See Schillebeeckx, *Christ the Sacrament*, 20–27, and Tillard, *Flesh of the Church*, 4–6, for an outline of the Spirit's role in various stages of Christ's saving mission.

25. See Bobrinskoy, "Le Saint-Esprit", 186–87, 191.

26. See Tillard, *The Eucharist*, 89–90, 94–95. See also "Trinity," in Karl Rahner and Herbert Vorgrimler, *Dictionary of Theology*, 2nd. ed (New York: Crossroad, 1981), 513–17, and *Catechism of the Catholic Church* (Vatican City: Libreria Editrice Vaticana, 1994), nn. 257–60.

One can regard the Paschal mystery as the event which enables Christ to radiate the fullness of the Spirit which he possessed from the very first moment of incarnation;[27] or one can see this Paschal mystery as the event through which Christ is transformed and receives the fullness of the Spirit which he, as *Kyrios,* shares with us.[28] It seems, however, to be basically a case of different emphases.[29] In both approaches, moreover, it is clear that Christ, as *Kyrios,* as triumphant Lord, exercises his saving activity only in the Spirit (*en pneumati*). Thus in the saving economy, while each has a distinct role, the activity of Christ and the activity of the Holy Spirit are inseparably entwined. This symbiosis holds true for any saving activity but especially for that of the glorified Lord. As Tillard puts it, "One understands, then, that for Paul, whenever it is a question of the blessings of the kingdom and it is necessary to designate the agents, the titles *Kyrios* and *Pneuma* are interchangeable. Jesus is Lord in the Holy Spirit."[30] This "pneumatological Christology," as Nissiotis calls it,[31] has important implications for the Eucharist and for the eucharistic epiclesis as well.

The Holy Spirit and Eucharist

The first implication of what we have just seen concerning the relationship of Christ and the Spirit in the saving economy flows from the fact that the Eucharist is an activity of the triumphant Lord, the glorified *Kyrios.*[32] To say that the glorified Lord is at work is automatically to say that the Holy Spirit is at work, since the glorified Lord is the Spirit-filled Lord, the "pneumatic Christ."[33] It is the penetration

---

27. Tillard, *The Eucharist,* 72–73.

28. Ibid., esp. 104–5.

29. Ibid., 111–12.

30. Tillard, "L'Eucharistie et le Saint-Esprit," 367, 376, and *Flesh of the Church,* 2–13, esp. 4–6. See also Peter Brunner, "Zur Lehre vom Gottesdienst der im Namen Jesu versammelten Gemeinde," *Leiturgia* 1 (1954); K. F. Müller and J. Blankenburg (Kasel, 1952), 355–56, who speaks of the "dynamischer Identifikation" of Christ and the Holy Spirit since Christ's resurrection and glorification.

31. See N. Nissiotis, "Pneumatological Christology as a Presupposition of Ecclesiology," *Oecumenica* 2 (1967): 241.

32. See McKenna, *The Eucharistic Epiclesis,* 220–22.

33. See Tillard, "L'Eucharistie," 366–69, and *Flesh of the Church,* 4–6. See also O. Casel, "Mysteriengegenwart," *Jahrbuch Fur Liturgiewissenschaft* (1938), 8, 161–63.

of Christ by the Spirit that has brought about Christ's glorification, and it belongs to the Holy Spirit to bring the work of Christ to its fulfillment. It belongs to the Holy Spirit to take the historical and objective work of Christ, the summit of which is the Paschal mystery, and to actualize it in the lives and destinies of the faithful and of all humanity.[34]

In the Eucharist the Spirit does this not only by realizing the so-called fruits of the Eucharist in the faithful; the Spirit is also intimately bound up with the transformation of the bread and wine into the Body and Blood of the Lord. The testimony that it is the Holy Spirit who realizes this transformation—apart from any question about the moment in which he does so—is unimpeachable. Theodore of Mopsuestia, Cyril of Jerusalem, John Chrysostom, Augustine, Paschase Radbert, and Thomas Aquinas, not to mention many of the early epicleses, are among the numerous witnesses to this fact. [35]

The bread and wine have become "spiritual" nourishment in the fullest sense of that word. They are filled with the Holy Spirit; for they are no longer ordinary bread and wine but the Body and Blood of the glorified Christ, who has become "Spiritized," filled with the Holy Spirit.[36] They are radically different, just as Christ after his Resurrection and Ascension is radically different, since they, as he, have been impregnated with the Holy Spirit. They are the "Spirit filled Lord," the *Kyrios*. As Tillard puts it,

Everything becomes clear once one discovers, along with the great tradition, that the body and the blood thus present are the body and blood of the risen Lord. They are, therefore, the "Spiritized" (*pneumatiques*) body and blood. Moreover, since, after the Ascension, it is only in and by the Holy Spirit that Christ is present to his Church, the intervention of the Holy Spirit is indispensable for the accomplishment of this "Eucharistic wonder."[37]

---

34. See Tillard, *The Eucharist,* 120, and his "L'Eucharistie," 367.

35. See Salaville, "Epiclèse eucharistique," 235–47; Tillard, "L'Eucharistie," 378–83.

36. Tillard, "L'Eucharistie," 376.

37. See Tillard, *The Eucharist,* 112–27. It is, however, especially from the Orthodox theologians that one receives, if not a grasp, at least a glimpse, of the richness of the relationship of Christ's glorified body, the Holy Spirit, and the Eucharist in the light of the Resurrection and Ascension. See esp. Sergius Bulgakov, "Das eucharistische Dogma," Kyrios 3 (1963): 47–55, and Paul Evdokimov, "Eucharistie—Mystere de L'Eglise," *La Pensée Orthodoxe* 2 (1968): 59–62.

The real wonder, however, has yet to take place. The whole purpose of the humanization of the Logos is our divinization. Evdokimov sums it up well when he says: "God became incarnated in man and man became Spirit-ualized in God. To the Incarnation, the humanization of God, corresponds the pneumatization, the divinization of man."[38] The purpose of Christ's Resurrection and Ascension was, similarly, not to take Christ away from his disciples; it was to make him present to them in a new way. His presence was to be interiorized. No longer was he to stand before them; he was to live on within them. This is the goal of the Eucharist. And it is precisely this interiorization and divinization that is the task of the Holy Spirit in the Eucharist. The Spirit is not simply to "Spiritize" the bread and wine by making the glorified Body and Blood of Christ present in them. Even more, the Spirit is there to "Spiritize" those who partake of the bread and wine by deepening the glorified Lord's presence in them.

This "Spiritizing" of those partaking involves two aspects. First, the Holy Spirit makes the Body and Blood of Christ, in a sense, capable of achieving its saving effects in the faithful. Second, the Holy Spirit works in the hearts of the faithful to open them to the action of the sacramental Body and Blood of the Lord. If either the presence of Christ offering himself or the acceptance of the assembled faithful is lacking, the fullness of the intended encounter is not present.[39] Now it is the Holy Spirit who makes possible not only the offer and the attitude of acceptance but also the joining of the two here and now in the celebration of the Eucharist.[40]

Finally, it should be emphasized once more that it is in no way a question of the Holy Spirit replacing Christ in the Eucharist. It is permissible, even necessary at times, to concentrate on one or the other for the purpose of obtaining a better theological grasp of their distinct roles in the Eucharist. One should, however, never lose sight

---

38. Paul Evdokimov, *L'orthodoxie* (Neuchâtel: Delachau et Niestlé, 1959), 251.

39. See McKenna, *The Eucharistic Epiclesis*, 192–99, 208–9.

40. See Tillard, "L'Eucharistie," 378; also Boris Bobrinskoy, "Présence réelle et communion eucharistique," RSPT 53 (1968): 414. See Robert F. Taft, "A History of the Liturgy of St. John Chrysostom," in *The Communion, Thanksgiving and Concluding Rites 6*, OCA 281 (Rome: PIO, 2008), for a treatment of "communion in the Holy Spirit as a fruit" of the Eucharist.

of the fact that the Eucharist is inseparably an action of the *Kyrios,* the glorified Lord, and of the *Pneuma tou Kyriou,* the Spirit of the Lord. It is the risen Lord exercising his Lordship in the Spirit; put another way, it is the Spirit of the Lord at work.[41]

The Holy Spirit and Epiclesis

The effort to view the epiclesis against the broader context of the Holy Spirit's activity in saving history and in the Eucharist has a number of important consequences for the epiclesis question.[42] First, a glance at the Spirit's activity in saving history indicates the value of attempts to parallel the epiclesis with the Incarnation, the Resurrection, the Ascension, and Pentecost. As long as such attempts do not lose sight of the basic unity of the Spirit's activity in saving history, as long as they avoid an either-or exclusivity in regard to the Spirit's role in the Incarnation, Resurrection, etc., they can shed much light on the Spirit's role in the Eucharist by situating this role in the broader perspective of saving history. For the Holy Spirit forms a unifying thread between the Incarnation, as we have explained it above, the death, Resurrection, Ascension, and the crown of all these, Pentecost. The Spirit does so by "Spiritizing" Christ, by transforming Christ into a "life-giving Spirit"[43] for us and by carrying this life-giving function of Christ to its fulfillment.

It is, moreover, the epiclesis proper that (1) gives voice to the Spirit's role in the accomplishment of Christ's life-giving function in the Eucharist, (2) makes it clear that without the Holy Spirit the eucharistic, "pneumatic"[44] Body and Blood of Christ are not present, (3) underscores the Holy Spirit's role in "Spiritizing" the bread and wine and making them objective means of salvation for those who properly partake of them. Furthermore, it is the epiclesis proper,

---

41. See Tillard, "L'Eucharistie," 369, 375–77; also Bobrinskoy, "Le Saint-Esprit dans la Liturgie," 58, 56; J. G. Davies, *The Spirit, the Church and the Sacraments* (London: SCM Press, 1954), 136–40; R. N. S. Craig, "Nicholas Cabasilas: An Exposition of the Divine Liturgy," in *Studia Patristica* 2 (Berlin: 1957), 22, 25–28, who points out that Cabasilas took this complementarity into account.

42. See McKenna, *The Eucharistic Epiclesis,* 222–23.

43. See Rom. 1:4 and the accompanying footnote (d) in *The Jerusalem Bible;* also Rom. 8:11, Acts 2:32–36, 2 Cor. 3:18.

44. See Tillard, *The Eucharist,* 105ff.

especially the Antiochean type, which invokes and expresses the Spirit's activity not only upon the eucharistic gifts but also upon the assembled faithful. The eucharistic epiclesis thus makes it clear that the Eucharist is there so that the Holy Spirit may fill, may "Spiritize" the faithful as the Spirit has already "Spiritized" Christ and the gifts. In fact, it would be hard to find a better expression of the Spirit's role in the Eucharist than a fully developed epiclesis proper.

To raise the objection that such a stress on the role of the Holy Spirit downgrades Christ's role in the Eucharist is to miss the interplay of Christ and the Holy Spirit in the saving economy. To ask "Is it Christ or is it the Holy Spirit who consecrates?" is to ask a false question. The very fact, however, that this question has been asked in conjunction with the epiclesis indicates the need to place the epiclesis in the context of a "pneumatological Christology."[45] It also indicates the truth of Evdokimov's contention that the real issue is the theology of the Holy Spirit to which the epiclesis gives voice.[46]

In addition to highlighting the role of the Holy Spirit, the epiclesis can serve as a reminder that God realizes the Eucharist for the assembly and in particular for the partaking assembly. The ancient texts of the epiclesis almost invariably speak of a transformation of the gifts so that those partaking might receive such benefits as unity, forgiveness, and life in the present and in the eschatological future. This underlines the unity between the transformation of the gifts ("consecration") and the transformation of the communicating assembly ("communion"). Such a relationship reflects the thought of such classical writers as Thomas Aquinas and Nicholas Cabasilas, as well as modern personalistic thought which sees Christ's "bodily presence" in the Eucharist as a means to fuller presence of Christ in his faithful and, in this sense, a transformation of the faithful.[47]

The epiclesis also brings out the fact that God realizes the Eucharist through the believing assembly. That it is God who takes the initiative, that God remains absolutely free and sovereign in realizing the Eucharist, is undeniable. It is also undeniable that the

---

45. Nissiotis, "Pneumatological Christology," esp. 235–36, 239, 240–44.

46. Evdokimov, L'orthodoxie, 250.

47. See McKenna, The Eucharistic Epiclesis, 207–8; B. Bobrinskoy, "Présence réelle et communion eucharistique," 408; and Judith Kubicki, The Presence of Christ in the Gathered Assembly (New York: Continuum, 2006).

church plays a role, however subordinate, in the realization of the sacrament. Without the church's faith there is no sacrament and no sacramental encounter. The epiclesis affirms that it is normally, ideally, the faith of the church here and now present, that is, the local assembly, which shares in the realization. It does so, however, by praying. In the epiclesis the assembly, having recalled the events of saving history and having made thankful acknowledgment of these events, confesses its own helplessness. It appeals to God to act upon the bread and wine in view of those about to partake of them. The assembly appeals to God to transform both the gifts and the communicants so that this celebration of the Eucharist may bring about a mutual eucharistic presence.[48]

The epiclesis, and the theology implied therein, thus tends to broaden the context in which eucharistic or "real" presence is viewed. In the liturgical sphere this takes place by viewing, as patristic writers often did, the entire eucharistic prayer as "consecratory." Within this consecratory eucharistic prayer one would then see two high points or essential moments, namely, the institution narrative and the invocation of the Holy Spirit or the epiclesis. Within the Roman Catholic tradition, Odo Casel, for example, argued for this approach as early as the first quarter of the twentieth century as did the *Faith and Order Studies 1964–67*.[49]

As we have seen, in the theological or more speculative sphere, a number of theologians, while not denying an ontological change, have suggested a more personalistic approach to "real presence," that is, an approach which uses as the basic analogy the intersubjective relationship between two persons rather than the change of one physical substance into another. Such an approach stresses the ultimately reciprocal nature of "real presence" and thus makes it more difficult to pinpoint the exact moment in which this reciprocal or mutual presence takes place.[50]

There is a clear tendency, then, in both liturgical and theological spheres to de-emphasize the "moment of consecration." This is helpful, since the "moment of consecration" has been a constant

---

48. See McKenna, *The Eucharistic Epiclesis*, 215–17.
49. See McKenna, *The Eucharistic Epiclesis*, 202–6.
50. See McKenna, *The Eucharistic Epiclesis*, 192–99.

stumbling block to a satisfactory solution of some vital questions raised by the eucharistic epiclesis.

Pastoral Reflections

Pastorally, one might look at the need for an epiclesis, its position in the eucharistic prayer, and some modern attempts at expressing this prayer. As to the need, there can be no doubt that the intervention of the Holy Spirit is absolutely necessary. Nor can there be any question that the assembly, while playing a necessary role in the realization of the sacramental encounter, must always approach the Eucharist as a praying assembly, acknowledging its own helplessness, appealing for the realization here and now of God's promises, while believing firmly that God will answer its appeal. In other words, the "epiclesis attitude" is also an absolute necessity in the realization of the Eucharist, even when it is not made explicit in an epiclesis proper. It belongs to the nature of human beings, however, to give some expression to their deepest beliefs and feelings or risk their stagnation. It would seem, therefore, to be a practical necessity for the eucharistic assembly to express its awareness, for instance, of the need for the intervention of the Holy Spirit and its own need for a praying or epicletic attitude. Otherwise, it risks having this awareness die or fall into the oblivion of forgetfulness. The epiclesis proper is not the only means of expressing these important aspects of the eucharistic celebration, but it is a preeminent one—historically and theologically. This is one reason modern eucharistic prayers have included an epiclesis proper.[51]

Where should it be positioned? One cannot exclude the possibility of placing the epiclesis, or part of it, before the institution narrative. Nevertheless, the weight of evidence favors a position after the institution narrative. Two reasons seem particularly forceful. First, such a position would emphasize the basic helplessness of the assembly in the realization of the Eucharist and thus help avoid a magical understanding of the words of institution. Positioning the appeal for the transformation of the gifts before the institution narrative, on the other hand, could allow the impression that the "magic" words of

---

51. See Schillebeeckx, *Christ the Sacrament,* 87, 92–95, 117–22; and McKenna, *The Eucharistic Epiclesis,* 224–26. See also Taft, "Mass," 503–8 and *America*: 8.

institution are alone responsible for the realization of the Eucharist. Secondly, such an arrangement would avoid a split epiclesis, that is, one in which the appeal for the transformation of the gifts is separated from the appeal for the benefits to those partaking in the gifts. The split epiclesis sacrifices one of the traditional advantages of the epiclesis proper, namely, its ability to underline the unity between consecration and communion.[52]

ECUMENICAL REFLECTIONS

A study of modern attempts, in North America, to express the epiclesis is revealing liturgically, theologically, and ecumenically.[53] Our starting point is the epiclesis in the early Christian eucharistic prayers. While in no way being an inflexible norm, these texts can serve as a basis for comparison. Some general characteristics are evident. One is the reference to some change in the bread and wine in the direction of Christ's Body and Blood. Another is the frequent appearance of the eschatological dimension and the rich variety of "other benefits." Finally, there is almost always a reference to partaking of the gifts.

The epicleses in the *Book of Common Prayer* seem to exhibit no significant variances from the pattern just mentioned. One might simply note that had the term "word" been left as Cranmer intended it, as a reference to the institution narrative rather than to the Incarnate Word, we might have a compromise form which would draw us closer to the early Christian emphasis. As noted above, this viewed the eucharistic prayer in its entirety as "consecratory" with two high points: the institution narrative and the epiclesis.

The Lutheran epicleses also reveal a significant variation. There is no reference to a change of the bread and wine into the Body and Blood of Christ—a reference that is characteristic of most early epicleses. Is its absence due to an emphasis on the institution narrative as "consecratory" or a desire to avoid the implications of certain terms, for instance, "make them be for us the body and blood of Christ";

---

52. See McKenna, *The Eucharistic Epiclesis*, 226–27.

53. For a detailed treatment of what follows, see John McKenna, "The Epiclesis Revisited: A Look at Modern Eucharistic Prayers," *Ephemerides Liturgicae* 94 (1985): 314–36, and chapter 10 in F. Senn, ed., *New Eucharistic Prayers: An Ecumenical Study of Their Development and Structure* (New York: Paulist Press, 1987).

"may they be for us"; "that they become"; "to change"—or both? On the other hand, the Lutheran prayers show a strong sense of the eschatological dimension so prevalent in early epicleses.

The Methodist epicleses reveal an emphasis on calling down the Spirit upon the people. The eschatological note is missing in the first six Great Thanksgivings but is present in the next sixteen—mainly because they use number seven as a prototype. The text made official in May 1984 has a strong eschatological emphasis and, while it makes no explicit mention of partaking of the gifts, is probably the most complete résumé of elements traditionally associated with the epiclesis. It also forcefully underlines the transformation of the assembly as well as the gifts. The text reads:

> Pour out your Holy Spirit on us, gathered here, and on these gifts of bread and wine. Make them be for us the body and blood of Christ, that we may be for the world the body of Christ, redeemed by his blood. By your Spirit make us one with Christ, one with each other and one in ministry to all the world, until Christ comes in final victory and we feast at his heavenly banquet.

The Presbyterian prayers also show a great awareness of the calling down of the Spirit upon the people as well as the gifts. The eschatological dimension is lacking in most of these epicleses. The option to say the institution narrative with the breaking of the bread—thus placing the epiclesis before the institution narrative—is a significant variant from the ancient pattern.

The Roman Catholic pattern also has difficulties when compared to the early Christian epicleses.[54] We do find the stress on the unity of those partaking that is common to many modern epicleses and a good number of the ancient ones. The split epiclesis, that is, praying for the transformation of the gifts before the institution narrative and for the effects on the people (of partaking) after the institution narrative, is found only in the Alexandrian type of earlier prayers and is an isolated phenomenon among more modern ones. Perhaps this is a vestige of the old (but not ancient) "moment of con-

---

54. See Kevin Irwin, *Models of the Eucharist* (New York: Paulist Press, 2005), 280–89, for a fine treatment of the epiclesis in Roman Catholic eucharistic prayers.

secration" question and the fear that mentioning a change in the gifts after the institution narrative would somehow rob the latter of its consecratory power.

Unfortunately, this pattern has several disadvantages. It neglects the stronger of the ancient traditions. It also interrupts the flow of the narration of the wonderful things God has accomplished in creation and in history. It fails to emphasize the basic helplessness or praying attitude of the assembly and thus may unwittingly foster a "magical" notion of the institution narrative. Finally, as mentioned above, this pattern could rob the epiclesis of one of its greatest strengths, namely, the ability to underline the unity between "consecration" and communion. The fact that this pattern continues to be normative for Roman Catholic eucharistic prayers invites reconsideration.

The changing of the gifts into Christ's Body and Blood finds forceful emphasis in the Roman Catholic epicleses, bringing out the reality of Christ's presence in the Eucharist. There is no trace of an eschatological dimension (although it does appear in the intercessions following the epiclesis). Except for unity, other benefits to those partaking are extremely sparse.

A comparison of the epiclesis in different traditions is revealing. At times, it shows contrasting mentalities, if not theological biases. At other times, it reveals the fruit of ecumenical dialogue and scholarship. One can only hope that this latter will yield further enrichment for all traditions and lead us closer to that day when Christ's final victory and the unity for which the epiclesis so often prays will become a reality.

Obviously, the epiclesis with all its richness is only one element in the eucharistic prayer, and to isolate it is to risk being one-sided.[55] But even this brief examination of the epiclesis underscores the unmistakable importance of the Holy Spirit in the eucharistic celebration. It invites us to a richer and more nuanced appreciation of our liturgical traditions as well as fuller, more conscious participation in worship.

---

55. See Kennedy, *Eucharistic Sacramentality*, 244.

Bibliography

Achtemeier, Paul J., Roger S. Boraas, HarperCollins, and Society of Biblical Literature. *The HarperCollins Bible Dictionary.* 2nd ed. New York: HarperCollins, 1996.

Ahern, Barnabas M., Édouard Dhanis, and G. Ghiberti. *Resurrexit: Actes du Symposium International sur la Résurrection de Jésus, Rome 1970.* Vatican City: Libreria Editrice Vaticana, 1974.

Aland, Kurt, and Frank Leslie Cross. *Studia Patristica: Papers Presented to the International Conference on Patristic Studies. Vol. 2.* Papers Presented to the 2nd International Conference on Patristic Studies. Held in Oxford, 1955. Part 2 in Berlin, 1957.

Atchley, E. G., Cuthbert, F. *On the Epiclesis of the Eucharistic Liturgy and in the Consecration of the Font.* Alcuin Club Collections 31. London: Oxford University Press, 1935.

Baldovin, John F. "Hippolytus and the *Apostolic Tradition*: Recent Research and Commentary." *Theological Studies* 64 (September 2003): 520–42.

Barth, Karl, Geoffrey William Bromiley, and Thomas Forsyth Torrance. *Church Dogmatics.* Edinburgh: T. & T. Clark, 1956–77.

Benedict XVI. Encyclical Letter, *Deus Caritas Est: To the Bishops, Priests and Deacons, Men and Women Religious, and all the Lay Faithful, on Christian Love.* Boston: Pauline Books, 2006.

Bishops' Committee on the Liturgy. *Music in Catholic Worship.* Rev. ed. Washington, D.C.: National Conference of Catholic Bishops, 1983.

Bokser, Baruch M. in "Unleavened Bread and Passover, Feasts of." *The Anchor Bible Dictionary* 6. New York: Doubleday, 1992.

—. *The Origins of the Seder: The Passover Rite and Early Rabbinic Judaism*. Berkeley: University of California Press, 1984.

Bouley, Allan. *From Freedom to Formula: The Evolution of the Eucharistic Prayer from Oral Improvisation to Written Texts*. Washington, D.C.: The Catholic University of America Press, 1981.

Bouyer, Louis. *Eucharist: Theology and Spirituality of the Eucharistic Prayer*. Translated by C. U. Quinn. Notre Dame, Ind.: University of Notre Dame Press, 1968.

—. *Eucharistie, Théologie et Spiritualité de la Prière Eucharistique*. 2nd ed. Paris: Desclée, 1966.

Bradshaw, Paul F. *Eucharistic Origins*. New York: Oxford University Press, 2004.

—. *The Search for the Origins of Christian Worship: Sources and Methods for the Study of Early Liturgy*. 2nd ed. New York: Oxford University Press, 2002.

—. *Essays on Early Eastern Eucharistic Prayers*. Collegeville, Minn.: Liturgical Press, 1997.

—. and Lawrence A. Hoffman, eds. *Passover and Easter: The Symbolic Structuring of Sacred Seasons*. Notre Dame, Ind.: University of Notre Dame Press, 1999.

Brown, Raymond Edward. *The Death of the Messiah: From Gethsemane to the Grave: A Commentary on the Passion Narratives in the Four Gospels*. New York: Doubleday, 1994.

—. "The Importance of How Doctrine is Understood." *Origins* 10/47 (7 May 1981): 737, 739–43.

—. *The Gospel According to John (XIII–XXI)*. Garden City, N.Y.: Doubleday, 1970.

Brunner, Peter. *Zur Lehre vom Gottesdienst der im Namen Jesu versammelten Gemeinde*. Kassel: J. Staudaverlag, 1954.

Bultmann, Rudolf Karl. *Theology of the New Testament*. London: SCM Press, 1965.

Burkhart, John E. *Worship*. Philadelphia: Westminster Press, 1982.

Cassirer, Ernst. *Language and Myth*. Translated by S. Langer. New York: Dover, 1946.

Chauvet, Louis Marie. *Symbol and Sacrament: A Sacramental Reinterpretation of Christian Existence*. Translated by Patrick Madigan and Madeleine Beaumont. Collegeville, Minn.: Liturgical Press, 1995.

Childs, Brevard S. *Memory and Tradition in Israel*. London: SCM Press, 1962.

Chilton, Bruce. *Jesus' Prayer and Jesus' Eucharist: His Personal Practice of Spirituality*. Valley Forge, Pa.: Trinity Press International, 1997.

———. *A Feast of Meanings: Eucharistic Theologies from Jesus through Johannine Circles*. Leiden: Brill, 1994.

Clifford, Richard J. *Fair Spoken and Persuading: An Interpretation of Second Isaiah*. New York: Paulist Press, 1984.

Collins, Raymond F. *First Corinthians*. Collegeville, Minn.: Liturgical Press, 1999.

Commission for the Sacred Liturgy of the Archdiocese of Chicago. *Let Us Give Thanks: Explanation and Texts of the New Eucharistic Prayers*. Chicago: Liturgy Training Program, 1968.

Crockett, William R. *Eucharist: Symbol of Transformation*. New York: Pueblo, 1989.

Cummings, Owen F. *Eucharistic Doctors: A Theological History*. New York: Paulist Press, 2005.

Daly, Robert J. *Sacrifice Unveiled: The True Meaning of Christian Sacrifice*. New York: Continuum, 2009.

————. "Eucharistic Origins: From the New Testament to the Liturgies of the Golden Age." *Theological Studies* 66 (March 2005): 3–22.

————. "Sacrifice Unveiled or Sacrifice Revisited: Trinitarian and Liturgical Perspectives." *Theological Studies* 64/1 (March 2003): 24–42.

————. "Robert Bellarmine and Post-Tridentine Eucharistic Theology." *Theological Studies* 61 (June 2000): 239–60.

————. *The Origins of the Christian Doctrine of Sacrifice.* Philadelphia: Fortress Press, 1978.

Davis, Stephen T., Daniel Kendall, and Gerald O'Collins. *The Resurrection: An Interdisciplinary Symposium on the Resurrection of Jesus.* New York: Oxford University Press, 1997.

Deiss, Lucien. *Springtime of the Liturgy: Liturgical Texts of the First Four Centuries.* Translated by M. J. O'Connell. Collegeville, Minn.: Liturgical Press, 1979.

————. *It's the Lord's Supper: The Eucharist of Christians.* Translated by Edmond Bonin. New York: Paulist Press, 1976.

Deissler, Alfons, and Karl Lehmann. *Das Opfer Jesu Christi Und Seine Gegenwart in Der Kirche : Klärungen Zum Opfercharakter d. Herrenmahles.* 2nd ed. Freiburg im Breisgau: Herder, 1983.

de Jong, Johannes Petrus. *Die Eucharistie Als Symbolwirklichkeit.* Regensburg: F. Pustet, 1969.

de Lubac, Henri. *Corpus Mysticum: L'Eucharistie et l'Église au Moyen Âge. Étude Historique.* 2nd. ed. Paris: Éditions Aubier-Montaigne, 1949.

Donovan, Vincent J. *Christianity Rediscovered.* 2nd ed. Maryknoll, N.Y.: Orbis Books, 1982.

Durkheim, Emile. *The Elementary Forms of the Religious Life.* New York: Free Press, 1965.

Eliade, Mircea. *Rites and Symbols of Initiation: The Mysteries of Birth and Rebirth.* New York: Harper & Row, 1975.

————. *Images and Symbols: Studies in Religious Symbolism.* New York: Sheed & Ward, 1961.

Evdokimov, Paul. *L'Orthodoxie.* Neuchâtel: Delachaux et Niestlé, 1959.

Feeley-Harnik, Gillian. *The Lord's Table: Eucharist and Passover in Early Christianity.* Philadelphia: University of Pennsylvania Press, 1981.

Fink, Peter. "Three Languages of Christian Sacraments." *Worship* 52 (November 1978): 561–75.

Fiorenza, Francis Schüssler, and John P. Galvin. *Systematic Theology I: Roman Catholic Perspectives.* Minneapolis: Fortress Press, 1991.

Fischer, Balthasar, Andreas Heinz, Heinrich Rennings, and Deutsches Liturgisches Institut. *Gratias Agamus : Studien Zum Eucharistischen Hochgebet: Für Balthasar Fischer.* Freiburg: Herder, 1992.

Fitzmyer, Joseph A. *The Acts of the Apostles.* New York: Doubleday, 1998.

Foley, Edward. *From Age to Age: How Christians Celebrated the Eucharist.* 2nd ed. Collegeville, Minn.: Liturgical Press, 2008.

Freedman, David Noel, et al., eds. *The Anchor Bible Dictionary.* 6 vols. New York: Doubleday, 1992.

————. Allen C. Myers, and Astrid B. Beck. *Eerdmans Dictionary of the Bible.* Grand Rapids, Mich.: Eerdmans, 2000.

Garsoïan, Nina G., Thomas F. Mathews, and Robert W. Thomson. *East of Byzantium: Syria and Armenia in the Formative Period.* Washington, D.C.: Dumbarton Oaks, Center for Byzantine Studies, 1982.

Girard, René. *The Scapegoat.* Baltimore: Johns Hopkins University Press, 1986.

————. *Violence and the Sacred.* Baltimore: Johns Hopkins University Press, 1977.

Gregg, David William Austin. *Anamnesis in the Eucharist.* Bramcote Notts, England: Grove Books, 1976.

Guardini, Romano. "A Letter from Romano Guardini." *Herder Correspondence* 1:1 (special issue 1964): 24–26.

Gy, Pierre-Marie. *La Liturgie Dans l'Histoire.* Paris: Éditions du Cerf, 1990.

Hall, Jerome M. *We Have the Mind of Christ: The Holy Spirit and Liturgical Memory in the Thought of Edward J. Kilmartin.* Collegeville, Minn.: Liturgical Press, 2001.

Hänggi, Anton. *Prex Eucharistica; Textus e Variis Liturgiis Antiquioribus Selecti.* Edited by I. Pahle. Fribourg: Éditions Universitaires, 1968.

Heron, Alasdair I. C. *Table and Tradition.* Philadelphia: Westminster Press, 1983.

Hoffman, Lawrence A. "A Symbol of Salvation in the Passover Seder." In Paul Bradshaw and Lawrence Hoffman, eds. *Passover and Easter.* Notre Dame, Ind.: University of Notre Dame Press, 1999, 109–13.

Hunsinger, George. *The Eucharist and Ecumenism: Let Us Keep the Feast.* New York: Cambridge, 2008.

Irwin, Kevin W. *Models of the Eucharist.* New York: Paulist Press, 2005.

Jasper, R. C. D., and G. J. Cuming. *Prayers of the Eucharist: Early and Reformed.* 3rd ed. New York: Pueblo, 1987.

Jenni, Ernst, and Claus Westermann. *Theological Lexicon of the Old Testament.* Peabody, Mass.: Hendrickson Publishers, 1997.

Jones, Paul H. *Christ's Eucharistic Presence: A History of the Doctrine.* New York: P. Lang, 1994.

Jung, C. G., and Marie-Luise von Franz. *Man and His Symbols.* New York: Dell, 1964.

Jungmann, Josef A. *Pastoral Liturgy.* New York: Herder & Herder, 1962.

————. *The Early Liturgy to the Time of Gregory the Great.* Translated by Francis A. Brunner. Notre Dame, Ind.: University of Notre Dame Press, 1959.

————. *The Mass of the Roman Rite, its Origins and Development (Missarum Sollemnia).* New rev. and abridged ed. New York: Benziger Bros., 1959.

Kasper, Walter. *Jesus the Christ.* New York: Paulist Press, 1976.

————. *Christsein Ohne Entscheidung: Oder Soll Die Kirche Kinder Taufen?* Mainz: Matthias-Grünewald-Verlag, 1970.

Kavanagh, Aidan. *On Liturgical Theology.* New York: Pueblo, 1984.

————. "The Norm of Baptism: The New Rite of Christian Initiation of Adults." *Worship* 48 (1974): 143–52.

Kelly, J. N. D. *Early Christian Doctrines.* 5th ed. New York: Harper & Row, 2000.

Kereszty, Roch A. *Jesus Christ: Fundamentals of Christology.* Rev. updated ed. New York: Alba House, 2002.

Kilmartin, Edward J., and Robert J. Daly. *The Eucharist in the West: History and Theology.* Collegeville, Minn.: Liturgical Press, 1998.

Komonchak, Joseph A., Mary Collins, and Dermot A. Lane. *The New Dictionary of Theology.* Wilmington, Del: Michael Glazier, 1987.

Kubicki, Judich M. *The Presence of Christ in the Gathered Assembly.* New York: Continuum, 2006.

Lane, Dermot A. *Keeping Hope Alive: Stirrings in Christian Theology.* Dublin: Gill & Macmillan, 1996.

———. *Christ at the Centre: Selected Issues in Christology.* New York: Paulist Press, 1991.

Lathrop, Gordon. *Holy Things: A Liturgical Theology.* Minneapolis: Fortress Press, 1993.

Lawler, Michael G. *Symbol and Sacrament: A Contemporary Sacramental Theology.* New York: Paulist Press, 1987.

Ledogar, Robert J. *Acknowledgment; Praise-Verbs in the Early Greek Anaphora.* Rome: Herder, 1968.

Léon-Dufour, Xavier. *Sharing the Eucharistic Bread: The Witness of the New Testament.* Translated by M. J. O' Connell. New York: Paulist Press, 1987.

———. *Resurrection and the Message of Easter.* New York: Holt, Rinehart and Winston, 1975.

Ligier, Louis. "The Origins of the Eucharistic Prayer: From the Last Supper to the Eucharist." *Studia Liturgica* 9 (1973): 185.

Macquarrie, John. *A Guide to the Sacraments.* New York: Continuum, 1999.

———. *Principles of Christian Theology.* 2nd ed. New York: Scribner, 1977.

———. *Christian Unity and Christian Diversity.* Philadelphia: Westminster Press, 1975.

Marion, Jean-Luc. *God Without Being.* Translated by Thomas A. Carlson. Chicago: University of Chicago Press, 1995.

Martelet, Gustave. *The Risen Christ and the Eucharistic World.* Translated by R. Hague. New York: Seabury Press, 1976.

Marxsen, Willi. *The Lord's Supper as a Christological Problem.* Translated by L. Nieting, Philadelphia: Fortress Press, 1970.

———. *The Resurrection of Jesus of Nazareth.* Philadelphia: Fortress Press, 1970.

———. and C. F. D. Moule. *The Significance of the Message of the Resurrection for Faith in Jesus Christ.* Naperville, Ill.: Allenson, 1968.

Mazza, Enrico. *The Origins of the Eucharistic Prayer.* Collegeville, Minn.: Liturgical Press, 1995.

———. *The Eucharistic Prayers of the Roman Rite.* Translated by M. J. O'Connell. New York: Pueblo, 1986.

McCormick, Patrick T. *A Banqueter's Guide to the All-Night Soup Kitchen of the Kingdom of God.* Collegeville, Minn.: Liturgical Press, 2004.

McGowan, Andrew Brian. *Ascetic Eucharists: Food and Drink in Early Christian Ritual Meals.* New York: Oxford University Press, 1999.

McKenna, John H. *The Eucharistic Epiclesis: A Detailed History from the Patristic to the Modern Era.* 2nd ed. Chicago: Hillenbrand Books, 2009.

———. "From 'Berakah' to 'Eucharistia' to T. Talley and Beyond." *Proceedings of the North American Academy of Liturgy.* Valparaiso, Ind.: Valparaiso University, 1995, 87–100.

———. "The Eucharist, the Resurrection and the Future." *Anglican Theological Review* 60 (April 1978): 144–65.

Megivern, James J. *Concomitance and Communion: A Study in Eucharistic Doctrine and Practice.* New York: Herder, 1963.

Mitchell, Nathan. *Real Presence: The Work of the Eucharist.* Chicago: Liturgy Training Publications, 2001.

———. *Cult and Controversy: The Worship of the Eucharist Outside Mass.* New York: Pueblo, 1982.

Moltmann, Jürgen. *Theology of Hope: On the Ground and the Implica-tions of a Christian Eschatology.* Translated by J. W. Leitch. New York: Harper & Row, 1967.

Morrill, Bruce T. *Anamnesis as Dangerous Memory: Political and Litur-gical Theology in Dialogue.* Collegeville, Minn.: Liturgical Press, 2000.

Mussner, Franz. *Die Auferstehung Jesu.* München: Kösel-Verlag, 1969.

Neuner, Josef, and Jacques Dupuis. *The Christian Faith in the Doctrinal Documents of the Catholic Church.* Rev. ed. New York: Alba House, 1982.

Nissiotis, Nikos. "Pneumatological Christology as a Presupposition of Ecclesiology." *Oecumenica* 2 (1967): 235–52.

O'Collins, Gerald. *Easter Faith: Believing in the Risen Jesus.* Mahwah, N.J.: Paulist Press, 2003.

———. *Christology: A Biblical, Historical, and Systematic Study of Jesus Christ.* New York: Oxford University Press, 1995.

Pannenberg, Wolfhart. *Jesus—God and Man.* Translated by L. Wilkens and D. Priebe. Philadelphia: Westminster Press, 1968.

Perkins, Pheme. *Resurrection: New Testament Witness and Contempo-rary Reflection.* Garden City, N.Y.: Doubleday, 1984.

Petuchowski, Jakob Josef, and Clemens Thoma. *Lexikon Der Jüdisch-Christlichen Begegnung.* Freiburg: Herder, 1989.

Power, David Noel. *The Eucharistic Mystery: Revitalizing the Tradition.* New York: Crossroad, 1994.

———. *The Sacrifice We Offer: The Tridentine Dogma and its Reinterpre-tation.* New York: Crossroad, 1987.

———. "Words That Crack: The Uses of 'Sacrifice' in Eucharistic Discourse." *Worship* 53 (September 1979): 386–404.

———. "Symbolism in Worship: A Survey III." *The Way* 15 (January 1975): 56–64.

———. Michael Downey, and Richard N. Fragomeni. *A Promise of Presence.* Washington, D.C.: Pastoral Press, 1992.

Procter-Smith, Marjorie. *Praying with our Eyes Open: Engendering Feminist Liturgical Prayer.* Nashville: Abingdon Press, 1995.

Propp, William Henry. *Exodus 1–18: A New Translation with Introduction and Commentary.* New York: Doubleday, 1999.

Quasten, Johannes. *Patrology.* Westminster, Md.: Newman Press, 1962.

Rahner, Karl. *Foundations of Christian Faith: An Introduction to the Idea of Christianity.* New York: Crossroad, 1994.

———. *Sacramentum Mundi: An Encyclopedia of Theology.* New York: Herder & Herder, 1968.

———. *Theological Investigations 2.* Translated by Kevin Smyth. Baltimore: Helicon Press, 1966.

———. *Theological Investigations 4: More Recent Writings.* Translated by Kevin Smyth. Baltimore: Helicon Press, 1966.

———. *The Church and the Sacraments.* New York: Herder & Herder, 1963.

———. "The Resurrection of the Body." Translated by Karl Heinrich Kruger. In *Theological Investigations* 2. Baltimore: Helicon, 1963, 203–16.

Ramshaw, Gail. *God Beyond Gender: Feminist Christian God-Language.* Minneapolis: Fortress Press, 1995.

Rausch, Thomas P. *Who Is Jesus? An Introduction to Christology.* Collegeville, Minn.: Liturgical Press, 2003.

Ricoeur, Paul. *The Conflict of Interpretations*. Evanston: Northwestern University Press, 1974.

Robinson, H. Wheeler. *Corporate Personality in Ancient Israel*. Philadelphia: Fortress Press, 1964.

Rowley, Harold Henry. *The Servant of the Lord and Other Essays on the Old Testament*. 2nd ed. Oxford: Blackwell, 1965.

Sanders, E. P. *Judaism: Practice and Belief, 63 BCE–66 CE*. London: SCM Press; Trinity, 1992.

Sarna, Nahum M. *Exploring Exodus: The Origins of Biblical Israel*. New York: Schocken Books, 1996.

———. *Exodus: The Traditional Hebrew Text with the New JPS Translation and Commentary*. Philadelphia: Jewish Publication Society, 1991.

Sawicki, Marianne. *Seeing the Lord: Resurrection and Early Christian Practices*. Minneapolis: Fortress Press, 1994.

Schillebeeckx, Edward. *Interim Report on the Books Jesus & Christ*. New York: Crossroad, 1981.

———. *Jesus: An Experiment in Christology*. Translated by H. Hoskins. New York: Vintage, 1981.

———. *The Eucharist*. Translated by N. D. Smith. London: Sheed & Ward, 1968.

———. *Christ the Sacrament of the Encounter with God*. London: Sheed & Ward, 1963.

———. *God, the Future of Man*. Translated by N. D. Smith. New York: Sheed & Ward, 1968.

Schlosser, Eric. *Fast Food Nation: The Dark Side of the All-American Meal*. Boston: Houghton Mifflin, 2001.

Schneiders, Sandra Marie. *The Revelatory Text: Interpreting the New Testament as Sacred Scripture.* 2nd ed. Collegeville, Minn.: Liturgical Press, 1999.

Schoonenberg, Piet J. A. M. *The Christ: A Study of the God-Man Relationship in the Whole of Creation and in Jesus Christ.* Translated by D. Couling. New York: Seabury Press, 1971.

Seasoltz, R. Kevin. "Another Look at Sacrifice." *Worship* 74/5 (September 2000): 386–41.

———. *Living Bread, Saving Cup: Readings on the Eucharist.* 2nd ed. Collegeville, Minn.: Liturgical Press, 1987.

Senn, Frank C. *A Stewardship of the Mysteries.* New York: Paulist Press, 1999.

———. *Christian Liturgy: Catholic and Evangelical.* Minneapolis: Fortress Press, 1997.

———. *New Eucharistic Prayers: An Ecumenical Study of Their Development and Structure.* New York: Paulist Press, 1987.

Signer, Michael Alan, ed. *Memory and History in Christianity and Judaism.* Notre Dame, Ind.: University of Notre Dame Press, 2001.

Spinks, Bryan D. *The Sanctus in the Eucharistic Prayer.* New York: Cambridge University Press, 1991.

Taft, Robert F. "Mass without the Consecration? The Historic Agreement on the Eucharist between the Catholic Church and the Assyrian Church of the East Promulgated 26 October 2001." *Worship* 77 (Nov. 2003): 482–509. A longer, more scholarly version of *America* 188 (May 12, 2003): 7–11.

Talley, Thomas J. "The Eucharistic Prayer of the Ancient Church according to Recent Research: Results and Reflections." *Studia Liturgica* 11 (1976): 138–58.

Teilhard de Chardin, Pierre. *The Divine Milieu: An Essay on the Interior Life*. Rev. ed. New York: Harper & Row, 1965.

Thurian, Max. *The Eucharistic Memorial*. Translated by J. G. Davies. Richmond: John Knox Press, 1960.

Tillard, J.-M.R. *Flesh of the Church, Flesh of Christ: At the Source of the Ecclesiology of Communion*. Collegeville, Minn.: Liturgical Press, 2001.

————. "L'Eucharistie et le Saint-Esprit." *NRT* 90 (1968): 361–87.

————. *The Eucharist: Pasch of God's People*. Translated by D. Wienk. New York: Alba House, 1967.

Tillich, Paul. *Perspectives on 19th and 20th Century Protestant Theology*. Edited by Carl E. Braaten. New York: Harper & Row, 1967.

————. *Dynamics of Faith*. New York: Harper, 1956.

————. *The New Being*. New York: Scribner's, 1955.

————. *Systematic Theology*. 3 vols. Chicago: University of Chicago Press, 1951–63.

Tupper, E. Frank. *The Theology of Wolfhart Pannenberg*. Philadelphia: Westminster Press, 1973.

Turner, Victor. "Passages, Margins, and Poverty: Religious Symbols of Communitas." *Worship* 46 (Oct. 1972): part II, in the context of the initiation process's ability to help the initiated persons see things anew. It has two sets of pages: part I: 390–412 and part II: 482–94.

van der Leeuw, Gerardus. *Sakramentales Denken; Erscheinungsformen Und Wesen Der Ausserchristlichen Und Christlichen Sakramente*. Translated by E. Schwarz. Kassel: J. Stauda, 1959.

Wainwright, Geoffrey. *Doxology: The Praise of God in Worship, Doctrine, and Life: A Systematic Theology*. New York: Oxford University Press, 1980.

————. *Eucharist and Eschatology.* London: Epworth Press, 1971.

White, James F. *Roman Catholic Worship: Trent to Today.* 2nd ed. Collegeville, Minn.: Liturgical Press, 2003.

————. *A Brief History of Christian Worship.* Nashville: Abingdon Press, 1993.

Wiesel, Elie. *Messengers of God: Biblical Portraits and Legends.* New York: Random House, 1976.

Wikenhauser, Alfred. *Pauline Mysticism: Christ in the Mystical Teaching of St. Paul.* New York: Herder & Herder, 1960.

Wilder, Amos Niven. *Theopoetic: Theology and the Religious Imagination.* Philadelphia: Fortress Press, 1976.

Wright, N. T. *Jesus and the Victory of God.* Minneapolis: Fortress Press, 1996.

Yarnold, Edward. *The Awe-Inspiring Rites of Initiation: Baptismal Homilies of the Fourth Century.* Slough, England: St. Paul Publications, 1972.

Index

Amalar of Metz, 11, 105, 173
Anglican Consultation, 132–135
The Anglican/Roman Catholic International
    Commission (ARCIC), 116–117
Apostolic Tradition, 137–138
application to Eucharist, 184–188
Aquinas, Thomas, 105–106, 131, 153,
    174–176, 180–181, 203, 216, 226
Aristotle, 175, 176
attitudes toward Eucharist, changing,
    144–163, 169–171
Augustine, 9, 10, 13, 73, 90–91, 103–104, 106,
    115, 149–150, 151, 163, 170, 172, 174,
    189, 201–204, 208, 216, 223

Baldovin, John F., 138
Baroque Period, 158–160
Barth, Karl, 79–80
believers today, 87–89
Benedict XVI, 72
Berenger of Tours, 13–14, 90–91, 154, 172, 174
blood, 45–48
Bokser, Baruch M., 41
Bouyer, Louis, 122
Bradshaw, Paul F., 135–143
bread, 29–30, 48–51
Brown, Raymond Edward, 12, 71, 92
Burkhart, John E., 29, 31, 33

Cabasilas, Nicholas, 176, 216, 226
call to service, Eucharist and, 67–73
Calvin, John, 90, 161, 172, 177
Casel, Odo, 15–16, 108, 113, 180, 227
Chauvet, Louis Marie, 100, 115, 189–193,
    198–200, 202, 209, 212–213
Chilton, Bruce, 140–141, 142
Christ, 78–84, 167–169
Christian adaptation, 196–199
Christian initiation rites, 139–143
corporate personality, traits of, 61–64
Council of Trent, 107–108, 156, 205–208
Cranmer, Thomas, 161, 229

Daly, Robert J., 141, 207, 210
de Jong, Johannes Petrus, 8
de Lubac, Henri, 150, 170
disciples, 84–86
Durkheim, Émile, 31–32

eating and drinking, 30–31
ecumenical reflections, 229–231
Eliade, Mircea, 2
Enlightenment, 158–160
Epiclesis, 225–228
Eucharist (celebration of service), 58–73
Eucharist, origins of, 144–151
Eucharist, Resurrection and, 74–98, 167–169
Eucharist as memorial, 99–117
Eucharist as presence, 164–193
Eucharist as sacrifice, 194–213
Eucharist as symbolic reality, 1–25, 165–167
Eucharistic prayers, 109–111
Eucharistic rites, evolution of, 139–143
Evdokimov, Paul, 224, 226

feasts, historicizing, 41–44
Fink, Peter, 3–4, 6
Fischer, Balthasar, 5, 127
food and drink in the Bible, 26–29

Girard, Renè, 199
Giraudo, Cesare, 107, 109–110, 112, 114,
    125–126
Guardini, Romano, 2, 15

Hall, Jerome M., 112
historical reflections, 214–219
Hoffman, Lawrence A., 48–49, 51, 53, 55
Holy Spirit and Epiclesis, 225–228
Holy Spirit and Eucharist, 222–225
Holy Spirit and saving history, 220–222
Holy Spirit and the believing assembly,
    112–114
humanism, 75–76
human meals, 31–34

Jones, Paul H., 172, 189
Jung, C. G., 2
Jungmann, Josef A., 151, 155, 170

Kasper, Walter, 65
Kavanagh, Aidan, 6, 132–133
Kilmartin, Edward J., 99, 103–106, 108,
    109–117, 210

La Maison Dieu, 127–131
Lathrop, Gordon, 194–195, 211

Ledogar, Robert J., 122
Lèon-Dufour, Xavier, 61, 82, 168
Ligier, Louis, 123, 128
liturgical movement, 160–163
Luther, Martin, 132, 161, 177, 203

Macquarrie, John, 14, 16, 176, 181, 204
Marion, Jean-Luc, 212
Marxsen, Willi, 171
Mazza, Enrico, 129–130
McCormick, Patrick T., 58
McGowan, Andrew Brian, 137–138, 141–142
meal, phenomenology of, 26–36
meal in the Old Testament, 37–57
memorial, Eucharist as, 99–117
Meyer, Hans Bernard, 114
Middle Ages, 151–155
Moltmann, Jürgen, 75
Mysteriengegenwart debate, 108

New Testament basis, 64–67
Nicene writings, pre, 101–102
Nicene writings, post, 201–204
ninth-century debate, 104–105, 173–177
Nissiotis, Nikos, 222

Old Testament, meal in, 38–57
Old Testament background, 59–60
origins of Eucharist, 144–151

Paschasius Radbertus, 11–13, 104–105, 173–174
Passover as memorial, 51–57
Passover context, 100–101
Passover meal, 40–51
pastoral reflections, 228–229
Patristic writings, later, 102–104
personalist approach, 182–184
Power, David Noel, 2, 5, 11, 101, 198, 209
presence, Eucharist as, 164–193

Rahner, Karl, 16–21, 82, 96, 111, 165–166, 168, 171, 181, 188
Ratramnus, 12–13, 90–91, 104–105, 172, 173–174
reactions and qualifications, 188–193
reflections, 214–231
Reformation, 177–181, 205–208
Renaissance, 156–157
Resurrection, Eucharist and, 74–98, 167–169
Ricoeur, Paul, 2, 23–25, 27, 37
ritual meals, 34–36

Robinson, H. Wheeler, 61–63
roots, searching for, 118–143

sacrifice, Eucharist as, 194–213
sacrificial terminology, 199–201
Sarna, Nahum M., 37–38
Schillebeeckx, Edward, 16, 20, 65, 71, 164, 172, 177–181, 186–188, 211–212
Seasoltz, R. Kevin, 211–212
Senn, Frank C., 157, 161, 207–209, 211
Servant Songs, 60–61
Spinks, Bryan D., 126–127, 129
spiritualization of sacrifice, 195–196
Studia Liturgica, 122–124
symbol, nature of, 17–23
symbol, Passover as memorial in, 51–57
symbol, understanding, 6–16
symbolic process, 3–6
symbolic reality, Eucharist as, 1–25, 165–167
symbols, creative approach to, 23–25
symbols, importance of, 2–3

Taft, Robert F., 217, 219
Talley, Thomas J., 118–135
Teilhard de Chardin, Pierre, 75–77, 82, 96, 168
theological issues, 108–117
theological reflections, 219–228
Thurian, Max, 99
Tillard, J.-M. R., 222–224
Tillich, Paul, 2, 16, 17, 21–22, 75, 181
transubstantiation, 181–182
Trinitarian Theology, 111–112

van der Leeuw, Gerardus, 15–16, 30–31, 35, 180
Vatican II, 156
von Balthasar, Hans Urs, 112

Wainwright, Geoffrey, 53, 133 134
Wesley, John, 133–134, 161
Wilder, Amos Niven, 4
wine, 29–30
word, Passover as memorial in, 51–57
Worship, 124–127
Wright, N. T., 65
Wright, Robert, 135
writings, later Patristic, 102–104
writings, pre-Nicene, 101–102
writings, post-Nicene, 201–204

Zwingli, Ulrich, 14, 177, 180